PENNSYLVANIA LIVES

RICHARD RUSH

PENNSYLVANIA LIVES
(Volumes previously published)

JOHN WHITE GEARY
Soldier-Statesman
1819–1873
By
Harry Marlin Tinkcom

JOHN AND WILLIAM BARTRAM
Botanists and Explorers
1699–1777   1739–1823
By
Ernest Earnest

JOHN ALFRED BRASHEAR
Scientist and Humanitarian
1840–1920
By
Harriet A. Gaul and Ruby Eiseman

JAMES BURD
Frontier Defender
1726–1793
By
Lily Lee Nixon

JOHANN CONRAD BEISSEL
Mystic and Martinet
1690–1768
By
Walter C. Klein

RICHARD RUSH

RICHARD RUSH

Republican Diplomat

1780–1859

By

J. H. POWELL

UNIVERSITY OF PENNSYLVANIA PRESS

PHILADELPHIA

1942

Copyright 1942
UNIVERSITY OF PENNSYLVANIA PRESS
Manufactured in the United States of America

LONDON
HUMPHREY MILFORD
OXFORD UNIVERSITY PRESS

FOREWORD

THE LIFE of Richard Rush spanned the fateful years which began on the eve of Yorktown and ended on the eve of Manassas. His boyhood days were spent in the Philadelphia that was the national capital, its turbulent politics swirling about the pure granite of Washington's character, and its colorful social life revolving around the Republican Court presided over by Anne Bingham. He began life when the Fathers of the Republic were forging, with the hammer blows of their strong intellects and stout hearts, the crumbling fragments of the American union into a cohesive, indivisible band of steel. He saw them at his father's table and in the streets, and if he heard their discussions, or read the vituperative pieces in Benny Bache's *Aurora* accusing Washington of everything from defaulting on his debts to political immorality, he must have been aware of the planting of the bitter seeds of political discord whose fruition came at the close of his life to challenge the nation's integrity.

He saw, as a young man entering politics, the ideas and ideals of the American Revolution spend some of their momentum in the early decades of the nineteenth century. He witnessed the emergence of new faces, new forces, and new political currents. Though by inheritance and choice inescapably wedded to patrician concepts of taste and intellect, he linked himself incongruously to John Binns, the Irish-born spokesman for the new democracy, and for a quarter of a century he was the most intimate friend of this herald of the Jacksonian revolt. Yet, at the age of thirty-eight, when he stood as his country's representative before the aged Queen Charlotte, he looked with awed respect upon the pomp and pageantry of the British monarchy, and viewed with genuine appreciation those evidences of English aristocratic "hospitalities that can neither pass from memory, nor grow cold upon the heart."

An ardent believer in the democratic ideal, he could never breathe freely in that political atmosphere which in his own country nurtured the theory of government by an *elite* of wealth and power. An equally ardent believer in genteel standards of learning and manners, he could never bring himself to risk his integrity in yielding to the necessities which an appeal to the mass of the electorate impose.

He was not, therefore, a political leader seeking the approval of the people but a holder of offices granted to him by other leaders because of his virtue, talent, and sense of public duty. In personal character an aristocrat, in political belief a democrat, he was in his own person a symbol of the great contradictions in political thought which stirred the nation during the span of his long and useful life.

It is this man of charm, integrity, and learning that Dr. Powell has portrayed. He has done this with a happy combination of sound historical scholarship and competent writing. He might have given us a dull factual account, for example, of the office of the Comptroller of the Treasury and Rush as its incumbent; instead he has given us a portrait of a gracious but honest public official hard at work, and the background of the picture is a penetrating chapter on the history of public administration. He has presented more of the story of Richard Rush than anyone else, although Dr. Powell would be the first to urge that there is much more of that record that still needs to be explored. Nevertheless, the story given here commands both our pride and our respect.

JULIAN P. BOYD

Princeton University
September 24, 1942

CONTENTS

RICHARD RUSH — *Frontispiece*
  From a portrait painted in London, 1820, aetat 40.

Chapter		Page
FOREWORD		v
By Julian P. Boyd		
I	PHILADELPHIA LAWYER	1
II	THE NATIONAL GOVERNMENT IN CRISIS	12
III	THE HEAV'N RESCUED LAND	47
IV	A REPUBLICAN ABROAD	82
V	AMERCIA AND ENGLAND	104
VI	THE OLD WORLD AND THE NEW	130
VII	NATIONAL PLANNING	179
VIII	PRIVATE CALLING AND PUBLIC DUTIES	226
IX	REPUBLICANISM AND NATIONALISM	244
X	LAST YEARS	272
BIBLIOGRAPHICAL NOTE		281
INDEX		285

I

PHILADELPHIA LAWYER

THERE is one moment in the public career of Richard Rush well known to everyone who has read even casually in American history: the moment on an August morning in 1823 when George Canning, Foreign Secretary of Great Britain, proposed to Rush as Minister of the United States that the two countries unite in a joint declaration against European intervention in the Spanish American revolutions. From the train of events that began on that morning emerged the Monroe Doctrine, corner stone of the separate national policy which the United States so long presented to the Old World. Rush's name is inseparably associated with its beginnings.

His name is also associated with another document equally honored in our relations with other nations. This is the Rush-Bagot Convention, which established between the United States and Canada the longest unfortified boundary in the history of western civilization. It put an end to a conflict over a century old, and laid a foundation on which has been built the fellowship of two peoples living next to each other in peace.

That this Convention should bear Rush's name was largely accident, as it was also largely accident that he was the one to receive Canning's overtures. In both cases the office rather than the man determined the event. But it is appropriate that he should thus be remembered in two of the early incidents of Anglo-American friendship, for to cementing that friendship his career was particularly devoted. His life began in the midst of the Revolutionary War; he participated in the second war against the British Crown; but afterwards he labored for thirty years in behalf of that enduring peace which has lasted since 1815, and which represents so much better than the preceding half-century of conflict those "deep underlying unities which stir and at decisive moments rule English-speaking peoples throughout the world" that a successor in the seat of Chatham, Pitt, and Canning has eloquently proclaimed.

Except for these two episodes Rush's history is not well known, yet few have so richly merited thoughtful attention. He was an able man of many parts, who devoted most of his life to a variety of important and difficult public services, in which he achieved a considerable measure of success. His was a long career. Admitted to the bar the year Jefferson was elected to the presidency, he died just a year before Lincoln was nominated at Chicago. His first public office came to him in Madison's first administration; he retired four decades later when General Taylor was inaugurated. He began, that is, when American traditions of government were still the traditions of his father, of Washington, John Adams, and Alexander Hamilton; he lived through Jeffersonian democracy, beyond the Jacksonian era, through the stresses of Kansas-Nebraska and Dred Scott to the very eve of Secession. Like every other public man of his generation his opinions changed, his convictions faltered and sometimes forsook him, for it was an age of momentous developments, this age of transition from sail to steam, from carriage to canal to railroad, in which new occasions taught new duties, and the fixed stars of the fathers proved apt to fail the sons in moments of new and strange challenge. Change was necessary in his generation. Those like John Randolph who remained constant in dogma were the ones who ultimately found their ancient good uncouth.

Long in duration, his career was likewise broad in scope. In 1811 he served as Attorney-General of Pennsylvania; then Madison appointed him Comptroller of the national Treasury. In 1814 he was made Attorney-General of the United States, in which capacity he edited the first authentic collection of the federal statutes, and shared the President's misfortunes during the British sack of the capital. After acting as Secretary of State in 1817, when he completed the Convention with Bagot, he was sent abroad as Minister to England by Monroe. There he remained eight years, negotiating the Commercial Convention of

1818, and carrying on the conversations intended for a treaty in 1824 which failed of their purposes. He returned to America in 1825 to be Adams' Secretary of the Treasury, in which post he became one of the leading spokesmen of the "American System." Candidate for Vice-President in 1828, he was defeated along with Adams, and retired for a while to private life. But his retirement was filled with public services. In 1829 he went abroad in the service of the cities of Alexandria and Georgetown to negotiate a loan for building a canal between the Chesapeake Bay and the Ohio River; in 1835 he was a commissioner to settle a boundary controversy between Ohio and Michigan; in 1836 Jackson sent him to England to secure the estate of James Smithson, which he brought back as the nucleus of the Smithsonian Institution. In 1847, when he was in his sixty-seventh year, Polk appointed him Minister to France, where he witnessed the Revolution of 1848 at close quarters, and participated in the planning of the elaborate but short-lived constitution of the Second Republic. "The life of Richard Rush," said an intimate friend of many years, "must be nearly the history of his country for half a century. . ."

In addition to this remarkable record of diverse public employments, Rush was a prolific writer. His best-known works are the journals of his English mission, published at various times as *Memoranda of a Residence at the Court of London*, and his account of the revolution in France. But in addition to these he wrote literally scores of articles of varying length and importance, only a few of which have been collected. Most of them were ephemeral pieces on political issues of the day, signed with pen names. They are hard to identify, but a bibliographical listing of them (now in progress) will reveal him to have been one of the most fecund pamphleteers and political commentators of the middle period of American history.

It is significant that not one of the positions Rush held was an elective office. Only once, in 1828, did he ever appear as a candidate before the voters; then it was not at his own wish, and he took no personal part in the campaign. His was not the sort of career that depended upon the hustings, with its showmanship, its electioneering, its popularization of issues for mass consumption. It depended rather upon the patronage and confidence of others in superior political position. Rush was never the popular champion of a cause, his name never became the symbol of a point of view. He was at various times Snyder's man, Gallatin's man, Madison's man, Monroe's man, Adams' man; his later distinctions were the gifts of Jackson or Polk. He had a certain independence of mind, and a gift for original expression; but he was always seen by the public as one of a group, of which he was never the leader.

The story of his public career, therefore, involves the story of many other men and their work. Often it describes the details of carrying to fruition policies others had conceived; sometimes it deals with fragments of questions, like the Fisheries dispute and South American independence, which had begun long before and were to continue long after Rush's connection with them. To a certain extent this helps explain the apparent inconsistencies in his career, for though it is not easy to reconcile the Republican of 1810 with the protectionist of 1828 and the Democrat of 1844, when the nature of Rush's services is considered, it becomes easier to accept the alterations in opinions that he seemed sometimes too ready to display.

Among his distinguished associates he moved with a graciousness and a poise that won their respect and frequently their affection. He was a companionable, friendly man, generally serious, even grave in his manner, but possessed of a gentle wit and a fund of anecdote that rendered his conversation, by all accounts, delightful. His interests were broad—as befitting a man of letters of his generation he knew his Latin and his French, he was at home in the sciences, and though like most Americans he knew little about painting, he was versed in architecture. I cannot find that he ever wrote any poetry; this alone prevents the obvious comparison with the extensive tastes of John Quincy Adams. But Rush's personal charm, to which his contemporaries bear copious witness (and few were the people who called Adams charming), communicated itself to his writing. In formal exposition he was direct, even somewhat abrupt, and meticulous in diction; but in personal letters he was merry and free, revealing the boundless curiosity, the capacity for enjoyment of any human problem, which was his most characteristic as it was his most endearing trait.

Thus the public career of Richard Rush does not offer original or striking interpretations of the American generations he served devotedly and usefully, nor does it bring to light little-known currents of the movement of ideas in the growing country; but it does present the picture of one who participated in exciting events near to the leaders of men and of thought, who reflected the intellectual concerns of a lively people in a fertile age, the picture of an earnest, hard-working, thoughtful person, whose gratification it was to be known above all else as a pleasant gentleman.

One time in Washington while looking through the archives of the Department of State, Rush came across the Declaration of Independence. As he read the familiar words in the clear, precise hand of the engrossed copy and let his eye wander over the signatures at the bottom, a curious thought struck him. There, second of the Pennsylvania delegation, was his father's bold "Benjamin Rush"; above it leading the New Jersey subscribers was his grandfather's "Richd. Stockton." Of all the citizens of the American republic only he and his brothers could boast the unique distinction of having both father and grandfather among the signers of the immortal document.

Benjamin Rush and Julia Stockton had thirteen children, of whom Richard was the third. He was born in Philadelphia on August 29, 1780, during his father's thirty-fourth year. His older brother, John, was a lieutenant in the Navy, but following an injury became a most tragic invalid; a sister, Anne, came next, then Richard; then his younger brother James, destined to even greater success in medical practice than his father had enjoyed, and closest to Richard of all his numerous family. The father and mother exerted an important influence upon the children, for they were remarkable people. Dr. Benjamin Rush was the first considerable figure in medical science that America produced. His lectures to his students every year were among his principal engagements, his labors during the plagues that visited Philadelphia personally heroic, his voluminous medical writings, particularly those on mental disorders, valuable pioneer work. Even more famous were his humanitarian activities, his temperance tracts, his educational establishments, and his participation in the revolutionary movement in Pennsylvania. Richard revered his father; he conceived also a great fondness for intercourse with those of his father's generation like Jefferson and John Adams who survived him, and whose homes, or whose correspondence, were opened to him because of his father's name.

Stocktons and Rushes inevitably went to the College of New Jersey at Princeton. Richard was the third generation when, after academy preparation, he entered the College in 1794. While there he lived with his maternal grandmother, widow of Richard Stockton, an accomplished female with a literary reputation based largely upon her "patriotic stanzas" beginning "Welcome, mighty chief, once more!" sung by young ladies of Trenton as they strewed flowers before General Washington in his progression through the town in 1789. At the College Richard made no particular mark for brilliance, but he did win prominence in debating clubs; when he was graduated in 1797 he was the youngest in a class of thirty-three.

He returned to Philadelphia, and began the study of law in the office of William Lewis, a prominent city attorney. After three years he was admitted to the bar in 1800, and opened an office of his own. He had a desire, however, to see something of the world before he settled down so his father recommended him to Madison, the Secretary of State, as a secretary to some minister going abroad. Nothing came of this attempt; instead Rush began a period of six years' diligent study of literature, history, oratory, government, and law. "At about 25," he wrote later, "I read the whole of Johnson's writings from beginning to end *twice* with a constant and close attention to the structure of his periods, his syntax, his words, determining that he should be my model. But I soon gave him up, for although I admire his style, and think it perfect in its kind, I found it was not the style for a man of affairs." He was willing to imitate Dr. Johnson, however. In the Philadelphia *Portfolio* of 1803–4 appeared two small essays, the first things Rush published, clearly little more than stylistic exercises. The first, "Value of Early Efforts at Excellence," urged the youth who desired fame to apply himself assiduously, read his Johnson and his Plutarch; the second, "Labour Necessary to Eminence," recounted a number of anecdotes from the *Lives of the Poets* to encourage conscientious labor. He was apparently contemplating a career of literary endeavor, but it was interrupted by mundane things.

Most of Rush's early contacts were with Federalists, even though his father's influence pulled him in the opposite direction; but when he began to emerge as a public figure he moved toward the radical wing of the Republican party. The first occasion on which he appeared prominently was a mass meeting in the State House Yard in 1807 held to protest the *Leopard's* attack on the *Chesapeake*, at which he delivered a speech reflecting the popular indignation against England. In 1807 John Binns, English-born publisher, rival of Duane and manager of Snyder's campaign for governor, moved to Philadelphia from Northumberland County and established in the city his *Democratic Press*, the organ for the next half-century of the Philadelphia Democratic party. Binns was to be Rush's most intimate friend for twenty-five years. Their acquaintance began during the election of 1808, when Rush took to Binns a little piece on the "Character of Mr. Madison," signed with a whimsical pun, "Curtius." It was the first of many political tracts he was to furnish Binns.

State-wide notoriety came at the end of that year, in a court of law. The Governor, venerable Thomas McKean, had sturdily resisted the attack on the judiciary the radical Republicans had been making for six years. As part of the complicated political story he was bitterly castigated by William Duane in his *Aurora*, authoritative publication of the mercantile wing of the city party. McKean in return sued Duane for libel, and Rush was chosen counsel for the defense. He made an eloquent plea for Duane, speaking nearly four hours to a great crowd. When he finished, "one of the oldest Democrats who heard it, embraced him . . . and took him up in his arms, while loud plaudits were heard throughout the court-room." He won an acquittal, but as a result of his speech had to answer a challenge from McKean's son for supposed reflections upon his father's integrity. Intermediaries were appointed and letters exchanged, but Rush successfully explained away the offensive remarks.

This case identified him with the popular party in Pennsylvania, increased his law practice, and brought him many preferments. He was made solicitor to the Guardians of the Poor, and to the Board of Health; he became a member of the Academy of the Fine Arts, and he was asked by the Duane faction of the party to run for Congress. This he refused, declaring he was too busy at his law business. In 1809 he turned out a sixty-six page tract on the question of the judiciary, *Thoughts on the Administration of Justice*.

In the fall of that year Rush was married to Catherine Elizabeth Murray, daughter of James Murray of Annapolis, relative of the brilliant Federalist diplomat William Vans Murray, whose untimely death shortly after he unscrambled our XYZ Affair with France had cut short a remarkable career. Rush was exceedingly fortunate in his wife. She was a beautiful woman, intelligent and lively. Between them existed a tender relationship which was a never-failing inspiration to Richard. His letters to her when they were separated are affectionate and gay; they reveal him at his best.

The young couple moved into a little house next door to Dr. Rush's home. The father thought Catherine "a most charming Woman"; Julia Stockton Rush found her "all that we expected her to be, not only an accomplished and captivating woman, but one possessing all the sterling qualities of the heart, we are as one family . . . and the most delightful intercourse exists between us."

"I began the world, in good earnest," Rush remarked once, "when I married."

Fame does not always bring prosperity, regrettably; Dr. Rush's warm heart so taxed his resources that he was always spending more than his income. Had it not been for his annual salary of $1,200 as Treasurer of the Mint, a position to which President Adams had appointed him in 1797, there were times when he would have been nearly destitute. He was happy indeed, therefore, to be able to write in 1810 that "Richard's business is now equal he tells me to 4000 Dollars a year. His industry, and his obliging manners have contributed no less than his talents to his rapid establishment in his profession." But the father saw only the externals of the son's situation. He was not aware of the expenses which were eating up the whole of Richard's income and running him into debt. Catherine had her first child, a son whom they named Benjamin, early in 1811; soon they would have to move to a larger establishment. It was some relief when, in February 1811, Governor Snyder appointed Rush Attorney-General of the state, an office in which, with salary and perquisites, he could make more than a hundred dollars a month to add to his private income.

Snyder's election in 1808 had been the victory of the left wing of the party over Duane and Michael Leib on the one hand, and McKean on the other. Since then Pennsylvania had been sharing in the increasing excitement of our strained relations with Britain. Snyder was the first frontier governor the state had had; he represented the expansionist sentiment of the West with its Indian problem, its lust for Canada, its animus against England. His 1811 campaign for reëlection was beginning; it was a wise move to find an Attorney-General from Philadelphia, where Duane and Leib were strongest. For Rush it meant committing himself to an administration his father regarded as dangerously radical, one which was opposed by the "best people" of the city. But Binns, Charles Ingersoll,

George Bryan, Jr., and Rush had become fast friends. They looked upon Snyder as the leader of a new, attractive movement in politics, a movement to which they took the enthusiasm and the fervor of youth.

"This new situation has opened to me a field of interesting and arduous duty," Rush wrote his father's friend John Adams, "which I meet at present with unfeigned distrust." He was plunged into the middle of a session of court, which taxed all his energy and consumed his time. "Your Office," Adams advised him, "is one of the most necessary and important in Society. A public Accusor is the Guardian of the Morals as well as the Property Characters and Lives of the People . . ." Rush addressed his new tasks conscientiously. He labored so assiduously during the spring and summer that by fall he had cleared the docket of all arrears of business, in spite of the chaotic conditions of the Pennsylvania courts. His prosecutions covered a great variety of matters, which necessitated study far into the night. His health was undermined, his hair became prematurely gray.

But in spite of his energetic application, he seemed to be losing ground financially. He had begun married life six hundred dollars in debt, for the "low" type of business young lawyers had to depend upon had not been remunerative; he had borrowed an additional thousand to furnish his house. By "hard work, good saving, and little spending" he had paid off his debts the first year. But in the second, with his family expenses increasing, even the salary of his office had not added enough to keep his bills paid. While to outward appearances his establishment was "comfortable, even splendid and luxurious," it was built, as he remarked, upon a pyramid of credit and debt. As long as he remained in his native city all he could see ahead was a mounting burden, and the city bar, dominated as it was by a few older, well-established members who got all of the large fees, offered slight prospect of ever being able to meet his obligations by the returns he could earn as a Philadelphia lawyer.

Rush was profoundly discouraged in the autumn of 1811. He cast about to see what opportunities existed elsewhere, for even a reduction of income would be profitable if he could live where it was not necessary to maintain such expensive state. All he asked of life, so he later explained to his father, was a situation in which he could see the results of his own hard work leading to respectable comfort and ease for his family.

It was at this moment, in November 1811, when his private career seemed to have landed him in a blind alley, that President Madison offered him the position of Comptroller of the United States Treasury.

II

THE NATIONAL GOVERNMENT IN CRISIS

BEHIND the appointment of Rush as Comptroller lay a story of high politics and intrigue, a story which we must outline briefly, for it determined the conditions of his work in Washington, the scope of his office, his relations with his superiors; and it prescribed to a certain extent the channels in which his opinions should run.

The Republican party in the nation had separated by 1810 into two factions, one led by Albert Gallatin, Secretary of the Treasury, the other by a group of lesser men among whom John Randolph, William Branch Giles, Michael Leib, Senator Samuel Smith of Maryland and his unlucky brother, Robert Smith, the Secretary of State, were prominent. As Secretary of the Navy Robert Smith had sat in Jefferson's cabinet for eight years, a constant source of irritation to both Madison and Gallatin. On becoming President in 1809, Madison was anxious to elevate Gallatin to the State Department, but the Giles-Smith party in the Senate so vigorously opposed this "foreigner" that the only way to prevent a party schism seemed to be to give Smith the State portfolio, retaining Gallatin at the Treasury. Madison reluctantly took this course, sacrificing competency and his own judgment for the appearance of harmony.

The approach of war, however, and the issues of 1810–11 forced the Smith faction into an untenable position. The Erskine agreement, the dismissal of the British Minister Jackson, the building of a war policy by the President quite apart from the Secretary of State's vague and ineffectual efforts for peace, all conspired to discredit Robert Smith on the one hand, while on the other the administration by the spring of 1811 had gained strength with the people. Napoleon's revocation of the Berlin-Milan decrees, the non-intercourse act against England in March, and the severing of diplomatic relations placed Madison and his

Secretary of State in undisguised and impossible antagonism. By March the President had at last abandoned his indecisive policy. He no longer needed to balance one faction against another, but depending on the popularity of the war among diverse groups in the country, particularly in that same West that opposed the Smith faction on domestic issues, he could afford to reorganize his cabinet, taking to himself the leadership of the government.

Yet anti-war sentiment was playing into the hands of the Federalist opposition, a good reason for trying to prevent Randolph, Giles, and Smith from deserting their party entirely. Therefore, when Secretary Robert Smith called at the mansion one day in March, Madison took occasion to ask him to resign his office, holding out the promise of the mission to Russia as a sort of booby-prize which he hoped might prevent an open break in party harmony. Smith asked for a place on the Supreme Court instead. He said he had long considered retiring from the State Department and had looked toward the vacancy on the Court as a proper situation. This line of talk Madison scotched at once, remarking that it would not be a proper appointment because Smith had been "too long out of the practice & study of the law, and . . . the Senate would probably be hard to please in such a case." Smith could take the St. Petersburg post or he would get nothing.

The Secretary refused the offer. It had, he said, "the appearance of a mere expedient to get rid of him." Instead he elected to retire and take his case to the people. Madison immediately commissioned Governor Monroe as his successor. Thus was a person who had constantly hoped for peace and made some attempts, however commonplace in conception and lame in execution, toward that end, replaced by a leading advocate of a firm and independent policy even if it led to war.

Smith's appeal to the people in pamphlets and newspapers in June and July was so much of a dud that Madison felt only the slightest annoyance. The power of the Maryland faction was revealed to be actually inconsiderable, its leadership inept, its effectiveness slight, while the appointment of Monroe strengthened the cabinet, made it more harmonious, more efficient, and (Monroe being what he was) more lively.

In June 1811, Justice Samuel Chase died, leaving another vacancy on the Supreme Court. A Marylander Chase had been, and if Madison could find a Marylander to succeed him it might restore some equanimity in the party—might indeed appease the Smith faction at no particular cost to the President. There were three leading candidates: Caesar Augustus Rodney of Delaware, the Attorney-General; John T. Mason of Maryland; and Gabriel Duval, a sixty-year old Marylander, former Chief Justice of that state, who had been serving inconspicuously since 1802 as Comptroller of the Treasury, and had, it will be noted, been even longer than Robert Smith "out of the practice of law." Late in the fall the President sent Duval's name to the Senate. He was immediately confirmed, and took his place on the bench where he was to sit for the next twenty-four years.

The first result of Duval's appointment was the resignation of Attorney-General Rodney, who interpreted the President's passing him over in favor of a lesser official in the government as a slight. This gave Madison the opportunity to bring into the cabinet William Pinkney, just returned from his mission in London, an even more vigorous advocate of independent action than Monroe. His appointment increased still further the number of Madison's supporters (and supporters of war) in the administration. As a matter of fact Rodney's resentment was probably not justified. Likely the selection of Duval was not an attempt to maneuver his retirement, but rather to kill two smaller birds with one little stone: to conciliate the Marylanders by this patronage, and to get rid of the last member of that machine remaining in the executive family.

Duval had been associated with the Smiths in a way particularly annoying to Gallatin. During the course of the factional strife in 1810, Gallatin had disseminated rumors in places where they would do the most good that while Secretary of the Navy under Jefferson, Robert Smith had used his office to enrich the coffers of the mercantile house of his family, S. Smith and Buchanan of Baltimore. A Congressional committee called upon Gallatin to substantiate his charges, and the Smiths wrote to Comptroller Duval asking him to declare whether their transactions had been dishonest or in any way questionable. Duval completely exonerated the Smith firm and Robert Smith's official conduct. "I never had any idea that there was anything in the whole transaction," he wrote, "that in any way impeached the integrity of your character, or that of your house. The more the subject is examined, the more satisfactorily it appears that there is no ground for such an imputation." Thus did the Comptroller dismiss the charges his superior had made against his patrons and fellow Baltimoreans. Gallatin had to accept these findings in his report published in March 1811, when he made a sort of backhanded retraction of his accusations, but he and the President had the upper hand on the war issue by this time, and his retraction was followed closely by Smith's dismissal.

It was important to Gallatin to get Duval out. The positions of Secretary and Comptroller of the Treasury, though greatly unequal in political magnitude, were complementary in their functions. No strong differences could subsist between the two officials if the department were to proceed smoothly, yet his Comptroller had differed with Gallatin on a matter that involved both the department's and his own integrity. These circumstances doubtless helped persuade the President that the ends of efficient administration and political expediency would be served if the mediocre talents and moderate intellect of Gabriel Duval were transferred to the Supreme Court where they would no longer impede or chagrin the Treasury Department, but could loose themselves on the law of the land, a far more tolerant victim.

The Comptrollership vacated by these events provided another opportunity for Madison to consolidate his strength. Whoever was chosen would perforce be an administration supporter, one who could work in harmony with Gallatin, and one whose appointment would have political significance. The party in Pennsylvania was an obvious candidate for some patronage, for the fairly even division of sentiment on the war there gave some hope of winning over the state before a crisis was precipitated. The victory of Snyder in 1811 had been a triumph for the national administration, a defeat for Leib and Duane. But why, of all the Quaker-State Republicans, was Richard Rush chosen? The records do not reveal how the strings were pulled. Possibly John Binns had something to do with it, doubtless the name of Dr. Rush, long associated with Jacobinical principles, drew attention. Gallatin himself was intimately acquainted with Dr. Rush, and he remarked long afterwards that he had "discovered" the son Richard and placed him in his national position. However his name was settled upon, Madison signed the commission of office on November 22, 1811. Rush hesitated only a short time. After a visit to Washington, talks with Madison, Gallatin, Monroe, and others, he consulted with his family and concluded to accept.

Thus Rush went to Washington at a time when Madison was remaking his administration, asserting himself for the first time since his inauguration. Two years of factionalism had reduced the government almost to ineffectualness; now at last it was being restored. Those who favored accommodation of American policy to British and French demands were replaced by others who were willing to steer a more aggressive course—not the most radical enthusiasts, to be sure; the young spirits of the new America that was emerging—Clay, Lowndes, Harper, Calhoun, Grundy, Porter, Sevier—were not yet at the council table. But Monroe and Pinkney were much more amenable to their persuasions than their predecessors had been.

The circumstances of Rush's appointment predetermined that he should mirror the opinions neither of the anti-war Republicans nor the young war-hawks, but of that group that stood between them, hoping for peace but arming for defense. Already when he arrived it was too late to resist the drift into open conflict.

On December 30, 1811, having resigned his office of state Attorney-General and closed his house next to his father's, he removed to Washington to begin nearly twenty uninterrupted years of highly diversified and important public service.

He was thirty-one years old.

I

Dr. Benjamin Rush was heartily opposed to Richard's move. He scorned "the humble office" of Comptroller which could not compare, he thought, with "the respectable and professional office" of Attorney-General of Pennsylvania. Any bank clerk would make an adequate Comptroller. Rush's literary and legal talents would be frustrated. Moreover, Washington was a sickly and unwholesome town in which to live, the salary was insufficient, the prospects slight compared with those offered in the Pennsylvania bar. He pleaded with his son not to accept, accusing him of unkindness, rashness, and folly when he did.

This attitude Richard combated as best he could. He viewed his new position as a bettering of his condition, for it offered a perfect solution of his financial difficulties, but his father's displeasure was hard to bear, and added to his nostalgia on leaving Philadelphia. "I feel, indeed, great and increasing regret at giving up my local residence in the state to which I have so many motives to be attached," he wrote George Bryan; "where, professionally and personally, I have received so large a share of kindness, where I had hoped I was cultivating the acquaintance and the friendship of estimable men, not to be parted at the very beginning of life, but to the pleasure of a more intimate and permanent intercourse with whom I had looked forward. So it is however that I am to leave them, but, I trust, not forget them. Nature must cease to operate in me before I can cease to regard Pennsylvania as my home, and her welfare and honor as my first publick wish."

His new home was hardly welcoming in the aspect it wore. "To a Bostonian, or a Philadelphian," he observed to John Adams, "Washington appears like, what it really is, a meager village; a place with a few bad houses, extensive swamps, hanging on the skirts of a too thinly peopled, weak and barren country." It was a damp, muddy little city with wonderful ambitions. The best example of municipal planning the world had seen since the construction of Philadelphia more than a century earlier, Major L'Enfant's design was proudly engraved by the government "on the scale of a hundred poles to an inch" and widely distributed; but for many years it was to remain only a joke or an aspiration, Washingtonians an easy prey to the jibes of Tom Moore, who sang

> This embryo capital, where Fancy sees
>   Squares in morasses, obelisks in trees;
> Which second-sighted seers ev'n now, adorn
>   With shrines unbuilt and heroes yet unborn.

The courage of the planners in following the original designs for the city would eventually produce a thing of wonder and rare appeal among the capitals of the world, but by 1812 all it had produced was a jumble in the forest. The inaccessibility of one office building to another had evoked the barbed witticism of the Portuguese Minister: it was a "city of magnificent distances." Someone else called Georgetown a city of houses without streets, Washington a city of streets without houses. Rush found some pleasure in this expansiveness. One February afternoon after he got settled in his new quarters he sloshed through three miles of capital mud to dine with two aunts who lived in the District. He spent the night, and had "a fine walk of three miles home" in the morning air, an exercise he appeared to enjoy. Sometimes, however, he shared in the general annoyance. The pressure of business, he wrote a friend in Philadelphia, prevented his going the two miles to the Patent Office on a political errand.

Lodgings were hard to find. Eventually he bought a house, but when he first moved into a rented building it took so long to get furniture from Philadelphia and living conditions in Washington were so unsettled that Catherine and little Ben stayed with her parents in Maryland. Rush missed them dreadfully. He filled his letters to Philadelphia with news of them. "I heard from her today," he told his mother. "She tells me that Ben can say *Mamma,* and cries *chick chick* when he sees the fowls." He dined out a great deal either with his aunts or some one almost sure to live equally far away, a practice which (at least until Catherine arrived to take care of him) did his health no good. Rheumatism and fever, contracted while trudging back and forth to his engagements in the winter dampness, were constant vexations during the first few months. He described to his father the medical details of his ills, and resolved to wear heavier "dresses" and drink no more wine when he went out to dinner. Gradually he learned, as his contemporaries all had to learn, the fine art of living healthily in the mire and cold or heat and dust of the "great Serbonian Bog" around which the nation's capital was sketchily deployed.

Every carpenter and mason in the little city was busy on the new buildings, public and private. Jefferson had characteristically concerned himself with the city's development; his encouragement had seen the Capitol completed according to plans. It now stood a magnificent "palace in the wilderness" on a hill eighty-five feet above the river, its dome a hundred and fifty feet high. The President's house, though scoffed at by Europeans, was admired by Americans; a hospital had been finished, so had the jail. Latest addition to the government buildings was the Patent Office, a Greek temple erected originally by one Blodgett for a public hotel, purchased in 1810 as a "depository for the ingenuity of the American Nation," presided over by the testy and picturesque Dr. William Thornton, "a character *per se:* learned, classic, facetious, etc. etc. etc.," a particular friend of the Rushes.

The plan of the city provided for the geographical separation of the three branches of the government in three different regions, as though to give reality in marble and mortar to Montesquieu's political metaphysics. Thus young Joseph Story and old Gabriel Duval, though their court was sitting in the Capitol building, lived with the rest of the justices at Judiciary Square about midway between the President's house and the

Capitol, while the cabinet offices and most of the administrative officials' residences were grouped around the executive mansion. Here in the Treasury building, nearest the executive residence of all the offices, Rush had his quarters.

The office of Comptroller made excessive demands on Rush's time, and was confining in its routine. It was, he wrote Binns, "one of those offices easily enough gone through when each day's business, as it arises, is regularly done. But when any accumulation takes place it is liable to become oppressive." To his father he declared he was "far from lolling at ease"; his position was, "unquestionably, and so agreed on all hands, the most laborious post under the government." Much of his time was consumed by correspondence, for a part of his duty was to correlate the activities of the Treasury officials all over the country. The department consisted of six offices, those of the Secretary, the Comptroller, the Auditor, the Commissioner of Revenue, the Treasurer, and the Register. Each office depended on the Comptroller for the warrants necessary before they could discharge their obligations, and for the communications with agents of the department in other regions, whether collectors, assessors, or enforcement officers. In addition he had to countersign all warrants drawn by the Secretary, enforce the tax laws, prosecute suits for the department; he was the officer who determined the policy of the department on technical matters of financial administration, how accounts were to be kept, how settled, how monies were to be collected, and how disbursed.

This office, therefore (which was long ago abolished, and must not be confused with the present-day Comptroller General of the General Accounting Office), was first of all a check set up against the Secretary to insure the orderly routine of the department against political interruption; second and equally important it was a legal office, its occupant not only a prosecutor but also a quasi-judicial interpreter of the law, whose rulings had the uncertain but highly important status of administrative decisions. "They make me the law-officer of the whole treasury department, and have set me already, though I should not tell this abroad, to drawing bills for congress," Rush told his father in June.

Such an official might have become almost equal in importance with the Secretary, particularly in the earliest days of the national government when it had not yet become clear that the Secretary was to be a political official rotating with administrations. But the sequence of strong secretaries and negligible comptrollers had routed the real policy-making decisions to the former, and under W. H. Crawford in Monroe's first term the reorganization of the department, the appointment of another comptroller and four additional auditors, and the delegation of the final adjustment of routine duties and functions to the executive regulation of the President and the Secretary, stripped the Comptroller of prestige and removed from his jurisdiction an area in which his discretionary powers might alter the whole conduct of the department.

Rush's duties, both because of the way the administrative organization of the department was developing and because of his willingness to follow Gallatin's lead, did not include shaping policies of importance. The routines had been established for more than a decade. He had only to conform to them. But the experience he gained in his two years at the Treasury was immensely varied. His own official reports dealt with the Mint and its annual transactions (which consisted until Benjamin Rush's death in 1813 largely of reviewing his father's works as Treasurer of the Mint), the unsettled accounts of the government each year, and the financial statements of various kinds that his predecessor Duval had made as a separate report to Congress, but which during Rush's incumbency and thereafter were incorporated with Secretary Gallatin's report.

In addition he dealt with a large number of details of administration in his correspondence. The United States of America in 1812 was a government operating on an annual budget of about twenty million dollars. Rush supervised the collecting and spending of that money by federal agents in every state. He studied the affairs of the agent of the United States to the "Six nations of Indians," and the collectors of revenue at ports of entry, the Navy and War Department accountants, the commissioners of loans in the various states, the banks of deposit, the state banking officials, the Mint, and the Treasury houses in Philadelphia. He was constantly surrounded with a press of duties which made it always "hard work to squeeze out a letter."

There were also duties that depended upon immediate issues of war-time politics. A circular had to be prepared for collectors giving the form of a bond under which goods could be transported in coastwise traffic in spite of the non-intercourse acts, another on the funding of the six percent stocks of the government; these and a hundred other matters revealed the impact of the new policies on administrative machinery.

By far the most serious problems Rush had as Comptroller during the years 1812-13 were connected with the loans authorized to defer anticipated war expenses. These loans were the center of Gallatin's financial system. Believing that war would reduce the profits of merchants and shippers, impoverish farmers, and generally upset the economic processes of the country, he had proposed as early as 1808 that war costs be borne by government loans rather than by taxes which would only serve to aggravate hardships and losses. This policy he adhered to until Congress over considerable opposition acted on his recommendation in March 1811, authorizing a loan of five million dollars. But a few days earlier the deciding vote of Vice-President Clinton in the Senate had ended the career of the United States Bank, in spite of a strong recommendation in its favor by Gallatin; thereby a source of funds and credit with which the loans could be supplemented was removed. Disappointed and discouraged by this action, one more maneuver of his Senatorial opponents, Gallatin handed his resignation to the President. Madison refused to accept it. The "purge" of the administration during the summer and fall strengthened and reassured the Secretary. He felt himself strong enough in December to urge Congress to levy new internal revenue taxes, a reversal of his position which he intimated had been rendered necessary by the abolition of the Bank. Even some of Gallatin's warmest supporters were unable to accept his proposals for taxes. Rush was puzzled. Plunged into his association with the Secretary in the middle of this change of policy, he had not yet learned enough about his chief to understand fully what the issues were. He continued to look upon the loans Congress granted in resistance to Gallatin's proposals for taxes as victories for the Secretary, and seems for some months not to have grasped the full significance of what was going on.

Congress could not be persuaded to accept Gallatin's proposal for new taxes, but rather adhered to that point of view for which he had earlier contended and in March 1812 authorized another loan, this time of eleven million, to be obtained like the one the year before partly from holders of government six percent stocks then falling due. Rush issued a careful circular with meticulous directions to commissioners of loans as to how this was to be done. All through the spring he continued to work not only in routine ways but with his political connections also for the success of the loan. On the first of May subscriptions were opened in every part of the country, advertisements were published, and newspapers editorialized vigorously both for and against. Few Americans could have remained unaware that their government was going to try to finance a war without taxation. The conditions of the loan were easy and convenient. Any person could subscribe a hundred dollars, paying twelve and a half down and the same amount once a month for seven months. He received six percent interest on certificates that matured in twelve years.

May first found Comptroller Rush excited and apprehensive. Things seemed to be going all right in Washington: the loan was subscribed "wonderfully, for so small a place," and Congressional leaders appeared firm in their determination to carry it through. But in the cities, especially in Philadelphia, there was vociferous outcry against subscribing to a war which had not yet begun, and which the commercial interests were determined still to prevent. Rush could not understand why: "This is extraordinary considering what has been done, and what is doing." He advised his father not to believe the city journalists who were predicting failure for the loan. "If it will affect, in any shape, any of your pecuniary plans or objects, I beg you, sir, to regard what I here write in preference to what I see in most of the Philadelphia papers. It will be your safest course."

By the sixteenth of the month the results of the campaign had been computed. Of the eleven million authorized, six million had been subscribed, one-third by individuals, two-thirds by banks. Federalists in the cities were making every possible advantage out of this apparent failure; in all New England not a million dollars had been raised, results in the South were meager; it seemed a triumph for those who had cried, "No commerce— no loan!" "Let those who want war pay for it."

Rush was deeply agitated by the opposition. He sought every way of proving the defeat a victory. Six millions, he acknowledged, was not eleven, but still it was more than any previous administration had been able to raise: in 1796 a six percent loan of five millions had raised only eighty thousand dollars, even though the Bank of the United States acted as agent, and General Washington was President. Gallatin had told him many times that he did not expect more than half the eleven million dollars to be raised, and would be satisfied with that on the first try. The Comptroller could think up these and many more justifications, but none of them was really adequate. In the midst of his protestations of satisfaction he was deeply worried.

There was good reason for his concern. Gallatin's financial program was losing ground in Congress. The salt tax, the volunteer corps bill, the navy bill, other measures to provide adequate war preparation either had been defeated or had drawn still sharper the line between those who did and those who did not favor the imminent declaration. On April fourteenth Clay's embargo had begun to operate, offending all mercantile interests, and most of New England. Immediately it was followed by the election in Massachusetts, a severe test because of Federalist strength, which resulted in Gerry's defeat by sixteen hundred votes out of the amazing total of 104,000, a serious blow to the administration and the war leaders. New York elections the same month showed Federalist gains likewise. In all parts of the country the issue of peace or war appeared to be dividing the people according to their economic position, their geographical location, their aspirations toward Canada and Florida. Political loyalty counted for very little.

In the face of these adversities it is not surprising that Rush, like so many others of his party, was uneasy. The administration, he told his father, was resentful of the misrepresentations employed to defeat the campaign in the cities, a state of mind likely to give "higher and quicker tone" to contemplated steps toward a declaration against Britain. The army enlistments were filling up rapidly, the "machine of power" was getting into motion, "the cities . . . are one half, or more than one half, English; but the country at large is ripe for the crisis." As yet there had been no commissioner of loans appointed in Philadelphia, but one would soon be chosen. Should he come from the Snyder-Binns faction, or should he be one of the opposition, appointed to conciliate and appease? Rush was determined on this point. "Conciliation was tried in the distribution of the military commissions, and what has been the result? It makes enemies of democrats without turning federalists into friends." Conciliation would have to give way to a direct trial of strength, in which victory would go to that side which could "lift up the most arms." The government, he wrote in confidence, had information of the most disloyal attempts to defeat the loan in some of the cities. Sentiment was growing, that to preserve itself the national sovereign would have to use its power to "stop unfair opposition," even by force of arms. Whether the Comptroller shared these malevolent designs and hysterical opinions, he did not tell his father, but certainly by the end of May he was prepared for any eventuality.

It is clear from his letters of this spring that Rush relied on Democratic members of Congress or on Madison, Gallatin, and others of the administration for his opinions. He tended to think of the opposition as factional discontent, except for New England Federalism; he regarded it as that "unfair" type of political machination which could be suppressed even in a democracy as he conceived it without damage to the spirit of free institutions. He failed to perceive that the dazed, divided condition of the party in Congress was but a poor mirror to an excited country divided against itself. The loan he regarded, probably with good reason, as a referendum on war. It seemed a proper prelude to a declaration. When Madison's message came, he expected unfavorable reaction from the cities and the merchants, but nothing quite so vigorous and searching as the eighteen-day debate in both Senate and House. Like Madison himself, Rush had to recast his political net. For him it meant learning to think of national problems in a national way, no longer in Pennsylvania terms alone. This was the lesson the summer of 1812 was to force upon him.

Because Rush was a genial companion, a good listener, an accomplished talker, and because he was so closely associated with Snyder, Binns, and the Pennsylvania Republicans, he was an agreeable and informative companion for the party leaders in Washington. They quickly discovered how trenchant his pen could be in articles on political questions for the *National Intelligencer* in Washington or the *Democratic Press* in Philadelphia—articles under one classical pen name or another which Rush began to write the first month he was in Washington, and was to continue all through the war. They also soon began to have him in to dine. His importance in the administration quickly outdistanced the political importance of the Comptroller's office.

Rush got a real thrill out of living among the great. He was exhilarated by his experiences, and wrote his happiness into his letters. "I think yesterday was the most agreeable one I have had since I came to Washington," he told Binns in February 1812. "The President, whose near neighbour I have the good fortune to be, a great point here—did me the honor to send to me in the morning to take a family dinner. I went." The company was small, only Secretary Monroe and General Dearborn; Speaker Clay dropped in later. Conversation turned on the war issues: on impressment the President proved "up to the very best of us in Philadelphia."

By far the most stimulating friendship the Comptroller was making was with his superior, Secretary Gallatin. This quiet, courtly gentleman from another land, erect, firm, reserved, presented to the world a picture of the aristocrat deserting his high birth and easy position to live close to the soil among people of the country, rigid and austere in his republicanism. A man of two worlds, experienced in the shortcomings of democracy yet not cynical or faithless, he was the perfect exemplification of his ideals. The forces physical and historical which produced an Albert Gallatin were far more subtle and complex than Richard Rush had ever known, for all the roughness, the crudity, of the primitive Youghiogheny country in the Pennsylvania mountains had not erased those ancient inheritances from the Calvinist commune of Geneva which lived in Gallatin's soul; but the externals of his character Rush could appreciate, and he found them attractive. His foreign accent gave a piquant flavor to his simple, direct manner; his long record of successful administration of the Treasury, his great prestige in the government, the bitter animus against him in Washington among men whose political opinions were compounded of gossip and envy, set him apart as a personage even in a capital that thronged with colorful and picturesque individuals. The intellectual refinement of his political thinking Rush found compelling. Emotional excesses like John Randolph's, truculence and strong opinion in a narrow frame of reference like Monroe's, or in a very different way Henry Clay's single-mindedness in 1812, impatience, flamboyance and stubbornness like Pinkney's, did not evoke any response in Rush, seeking as he was his niche in the government and his circle of friends. Neither did the indecision of Madison, nor the careful weighing of issues, the independence of mind, the unwillingness to be of any party or any faction, of Joseph Story, for these did not afford sufficient guides to action. Gallatin was the perfect cicerone. He was resolute but wise, and never failed to see the full picture of a national issue. He could anticipate objections and opposition, he could furnish answers in terms of his theories of government. He was as near a philosopher as American politics could offer; something of Jefferson's mantle was about him, and to Rush he gave much the same satisfaction that came from correspondence with President Adams. Finally, of course, Gallatin had shared in the Democratic party's revolution in Pennsylvania in 1808—shared vicariously, to be sure, but he was a part of it nevertheless. Like most Pennsylvanians, Rush considered him their state's leading delegate in Washington.

The Secretary began using Rush's political connections at once. The loan of ten million dollars was necessary; it would be "extremely useful" if the Pennsylvania legislature would consent to a subscription by state banks to the government. Could Rush suggest the proper person to whom to apply? Would the Comptroller call upon the Secretary to discuss some appointments in which Pennsylvania had an interest? Whom did Rush recommend for commissioner in Philadelphia? Who would be the most pleasing to our friends in that state?

Personally their relations were affable, but intimacy came slowly. Gallatin was not a man that one came very close to, and Rush became really intimate only when he went to London, Gallatin to Paris. But by the end of February he was sufficiently well acquainted to begin soliciting positions for various friends (and relatives) in Pennsylvania. He was pleased with the political opinions he discovered in his chief: "From all I can see of the head of our Treasury," he told Binns, "he is ardent, firm, thorough-going on all points. His powers of business and capacity to keep the Treasury going during a war would be prodigious. His attachment to banks is, indeed, *invincible*, but touching all other things it seems to me no man is more orthodox."

Already in January preparations were being made for the 1812 election. New York Democrats were split on the issue of the Bank, the renomination of the Vice-President, George

Clinton, was in doubt. Rush saw a chance for his own state here. He mentioned to Binns the possibility of finding a running mate for Madison among the Pennsylvania Democrats. Everything he could do to strengthen the position of his party in his state he made during the winter and spring his first concern, whether it was striving for unity in the Congressional delegation on the problem of the new taxes, or weaving through the delicate and difficult task of dispensing patronage in the appointment of revenue collectors, loan commissioners, army and navy officers, and postmasters, or keeping Binns up to date on dispatches from the southern states. His political ambitions, his opinions, and his emotions were still largely centered in Pennsylvania.

In mid-February Virginia nominated electors for Madison and Clinton. Rush urged Binns that Pennsylvania follow suit at once; he was delighted when early in March the Democrats meeting at Lancaster did so. The congressional caucus, however, was delayed, for the war party hoped to secure a decisive commitment from Madison before renominating him. Probably in response to pressure like this, Madison acceded with some reluctance to the embargo bill in April, a bill which Congress made much stronger by lengthening the term. Of course this alienated the mercantile interests; it helped the Federalists to their victory in Massachusetts, and precipitated a political crisis in late April and May.

Few moments of crisis in American history are so confused, so involved, so difficult to describe as this one, for except the war party in Congress no two persons were of the same mind. On the one hand a bill passed providing for retaliation against impressment, entirely unnecessary if war was to be waged; and the Smith faction in the Senate defeated a reorganization of the inadequate, underpaid War Department. On the other hand administration supporters, apparently blind to the implications of the embargo bill, were favoring an adjournment for a month or more, and nearly carried it. Many, indeed, did go home to participate in state caucuses with the understanding that no declaration would be made during May. As a result, in spite of the failure of the loan, which we have seen, nothing was done about new taxes and revenue bills. The House leaders preferred to delay them until after a declaration. Then came the question, How should this declaration be made? Madison himself was willing to sign a congressional bill declaring war; but Clay and his followers wanted no appearance of a war forced on the President. There must be a message from the palace, or they could not support Madison for renomination. In the midst of this fast-moving conflict of wills, the Vice-President suddenly died.

All the issues of the national crisis seemed to crystallize in these few weeks. Rush, between the loan and the political tangle, found his office feverishly busy; when he went home at night he found his household distraught over a prolonged pregnancy Catherine was suffering. The complications of his private and public life were multiplying more rapidly than he knew how to deal with them. In the matter of George Clinton's successor, he urged Simon Snyder as the strongest and best candidate, but acknowledged the advisibility of having a New England man at this particular time. Pennsylvania was "safe" enough to defer to New England.

The "safe" Republicanism of the Quaker State was only relative, however. When the Commissionership of Loans in Philadelphia was vacant, Rush had secured appointment of a saintly but indigent man, Dr. William White, preacher and social worker of the Northern Liberties who had been in turn instrumental in securing Rush's appointment as Pennsylvania Attorney-General in 1809. The choice, when it was made at the end of May, was bitterly attacked in Philadelphia, and oddly enough one of the persons most upset was Dr. Benjamin Rush. He considered White of no consequence, unknown and hardly respected in the city.

But the Comptroller sturdily defended his selection. White, he told his father, represented the same interests that had given Governor Snyder a thirty thousand majority, and would give Madison the same. There were, as he saw it, six sets of politicians or parties in Pennsylvania, ranging from the Anglo-Federalists through the Federalists, the McKean party, "The Duane or Leib party not only quite distinct from, but bitterly hating, the McKean," those who were of no party at all, and lastly the "great state democratick party, or Snyder party, as it is sometimes called." The last was small in the city, but great in the state as a whole.

Your intercourse, Sir, is almost entirely, if not quite, with the five first, and I have no doubt that, with them, the appointment of parson White is unpopular, perhaps odious; for among other general reasons there is this particular one—that I know the four first each had a candidate of there [sic] own whom they were pushing with all their credit and zeal. Hinc illa lacrymae [sic]!

He advised his father to go out in the state, even into the Northern Liberties, to discover the true opinion of the common people, scarcely represented by the clubs, the society, and the intellect of the city. Thus was he still the disciple of Simon Snyder. His father, who needed no lesson in politics, was the further bemused because he himself had been urging the appointment of Timothy Matlack, a destitute relative by marriage.

Congress in the meantime was following up Madison's agreement to give a war message by renominating him in caucus, selecting Gerry for Vice-President after Langdon had refused. Then on the first of June, having consulted with Jefferson, and after a defeat of Randolph in the House, with most of the absent members returned, the President sent his confidential message recommending war to both the Houses.

Once the die was cast Rush, like many others in the capital, was relieved. The uncertainty had taxed men's patience and destroyed their ease; the declaration called for the utmost firmness and resolution, but it was at least a stand taken. Not for some time did the reaction throughout the nation make itself felt. When Rush learned of the bitterness in Philadelphia, he was thoroughly angry. The charge that Madison and Clay had thrown America's lot in with Napoleon made him smart, but most distressing of all was a timorous letter from his father. Old John Adams had written Dr. Rush that the unpopular measures of the government, castigated as they were in Massachusetts (and in Philadelphia) would surely bring doom upon all the administration at the election; his own son, John Quincy, at St. Petersburg, and Dr. Rush's son the Comptroller would certainly be turned out.

The doctor sent the letter on, with a strong plea to his son to resign his present position and return home. There, with the support of the Democratic party in the state and his thousands of friends in Philadelphia he could certainly win an important position in the state election. He owed it to himself and his family to do this, for if he did not he would find himself without income next March.

Rush was deeply hurt to feel a gulf widening between himself and his father, but he refused to have his bubble pricked like that. He replied by asking if it were not impossible to ruin a man "who feels that he is willing and able to go through any kind of honest, hard work in his line twelve hours every day in the year while his health lasts, and who, with his wife to join him, can live upon bacon and greens and potatoes and drink nothing but water every day in the week?" His situation in Washington was, he explained, wonderfully improved over that he had known in Philadelphia. He received nearly four thousand dollars a year, spent only two. A position such as his would probably not be disturbed by a change in the administration anyway, so he could look forward to an indefinite future. And then, even if he were to be turned out in March, he could make just as good a living after that much more experience as he could if he quit now. Regarding a state political job, why should his "thousands of friends" wish to send him up in the state political balloon instead of that of the United States? "Philadelphia I like; to Pennsylvania I belong and trust always shall. But Philadelphia as I had it, and as, unless through a train of improbabilities, I should always have had it, I do not crave again; and, let come what will, have steadily thought the decision right that took me away."

Furthermore, he had faith in the enterprise of the government, for he was in a position to see that which Dr. Rush and Mr. Adams could not, namely, the great popularity of the war in other sections besides New England and the Quaker City. He was deeply impressed with Clay, Cheves, Calhoun, and Lowndes, and with the other statesmen from the South and from that "empire of freedom and anti-Britonism," the West. They impressed him as "incomparably superior to the 'bedollared' commercial delegates of the East; their risk was greater, their sacrifices more extensive, yet they supported the war. "But some of the Yankees seem to think there is nothing but their codfish and skippers to suffer!"

Dr. Rush was not alone, apparently, in his forebodings. The Congress, instead of immediately accepting and endorsing the war message, debated it for nearly three weeks behind closed doors. Rush kept insisting that he expected the declaration momentarily, but Federalists were already declaring that even if the measure passed England would not fight us, and there would be no war. By the middle of June the Comptroller, who was diligently laboring long hours every day at his office, writing far into the night careful letters to his father and his political connections in Pennsylvania, and suffering torments of anxiety for his wife, whose confinement was due, found himself on tenterhooks all the time; the suspense was almost more than he could bear.

But on the eighteenth he was able to send off a note in haste to the Doctor: war was this day declared against England. Madison's state paper was "of irresistable argument and impressive solemn dignity. The God of nations and of battles will, I hope, be upon our side."

The next day Catherine was delivered of a stillborn son.

II

When Rush intimated to his father that the position of Comptroller was so important to good administration and so unimportant politically that even a change of the party in power would probably not displace him, he was talking nonsense and he knew it. His career was far different from his predecessor's in the same office. He was becoming politically a key man in the party, and consequently was by June popularly identified with the President and his advisers. It would have been impossible for him to pose as neutral or non-partisan.

If he had not already made it publicly clear what his position was, all doubts were soon removed, for he, surprisingly enough, was chosen as the official spokesman of the government on the war. While the debate was proceeding in Congress on the declaration, the committee for the Fourth of July celebration had to arrange for the annual oration in the House chamber. The choice involved some political considerations. There was no need to pick a man from the South or West to defend the war, and New England seemed impossible; a Pennsylvanian would fill the bill as a Northerner, a representative from a loyal state in which nevertheless pro-English sentiment was strong, and possibly as one with some influence among the commercial interests in Philadelphia who were opposing the war. Gallatin was not available, the Congressional delegation contained no one of any particular note. Probably at the suggestion of the President the committee called on Rush and asked him to make the speech.

It came as a complete surprise to the Comptroller. He suggested that some venerable revolutionary statesman ought to be asked, but the committee was so pressing and so flattering that he agreed to do it. The occasion was to be "peculiar and novel," he wrote his father. "It will be before the government, and at the commencement of a war, the first in which we have ever been engaged, and the first, which is a remarkable fact, ever waged by a genuine democratick, representative government since the days of the antients."

He begged his father for help. He especially desired some "ornament," some anecdotes or reminiscences to garnish the oration. He did not mean, he wrote, to mount a pair of stilts; rather he intended to be argumentative, persuasive, and, he hoped, convincing. He would not refer to Warren, Montgomery, or Mercer or Washington or the Declaration of Independence. "The same sermon preached every day for a month would tire however good, and we have now had more than a month of 4ths of July, on every one of which orations have been mouthed out from the same text." Dr. Rush responded with lively, amusing letters, filled with suggestions and anecdotes. Many of his phrases, several of his stories, Rush wrote into the draft of his speech.

He was excessively apprehensive of the occasion. For two weeks he devoted himself to composition; by the end of June it was finished, but it proved three times as long as he could impose on the audience. He cut and cut; his father was drawn upon to help decide what should stay in and what go out. When he rose on the dais of the House chamber, before the government, the diplomatic corps, and Washington society, his manuscript was so interlined, erased, and scratched that he could hardly make it out.

But he got through the speech very well, scoring a great success. Taking a reasonable tone, he argued carefully and moderately for the government's position. As an oration it conformed to all the classical rules of rhetoric expounded in John Quincy Adams' Harvard lectures of 1810. It was clear, concise, and eloquent enough, with few flourishes. Its simplicity cost him great labor. "I have been full ten years endeavouring to acquire such a stile, and have yet much more to learn before I shall be satisfied. That which I possess is the result of a pretty close study of almost all the classics in our language, in regular succession, from Queen Elizabeth's time to the present—prose writers, historians, poets," he wrote his father.

War was admittedly bestial and brutal, he began, but it was not the greatest evil. "Long submission to injustice is worse. Peace, a long peace, a peace purchased by mean and inglorious sacrifices, is worse, far worse." For thirty years America had remained at peace, enduring spoliations and encroachments on her essential rights without violent resistance. The country had been prosperous, but its prosperity had been constantly endangered by British and French depredations. Now the decision to assert every means of honorable defense ought to destroy party spirit and challenge the patriotism of every citizen.

The choice to make war on Britain rather than on France, or on both at once, he laid to the common inheritance of America and England which created animosities peculiar to these two countries. By oppression, neglect, and attack, by exercise of unjust powers and by insults Britain had broken the ties that bound her colonies to her; now again she was revealing the weaknesses in her national character—harshness, arrogance, ferocity, a "self-assumed superiority," a ghastly criminal law, army whippings, vice in her upper classes, "the overweening distinctions shown to opulence and birth, so destructive of a sound moral sentiment in the nation, so baffling to virtue." Against these the Americans were opposing a sturdy democratic spirit.

The central issue, the real cause of England's jealousies, was her supremacy on the sea. It was her naval pride that had led to the gruesome story of impressment, the evil which overshadowed all others as the cause of war. This "plunder in the flesh and blood of freemen, of which she has afforded the first example, in all time, to the eyes of an insulted world," this unpardonable inhumanity that forced every American to prove he was an American, this "flagitious crime," had for five and twenty years caused American citizenship to be "the signal for insult, and the passport to captivity." Against it America was waging a defensive war. For impressment was invasion, not of our shores, to be sure, but of our persons, property, rights, character, sovereignty, and justice.

It is an imperfect view of this question which takes as a defensive war only that which is entered upon when the assailant is bursting through your doors and levelling the musket at the bosoms of your women and children. Think how a nation may be abridged, may be dismantled of its rights, may be cut down in its liberties, this side of an open attack.

War against Britain would free us from the unhealthy dominion in cultural, historical, financial, social, and economic things she exercised over America. It might throw us farther off to a safer position from "so contaminating an intimacy" as that we had with England. "From no other nation are we in danger in the same way; for, with no other nation have we the same affinities, but, on the contrary, numerous points of repulsion that interpose as our guard." Delivered by war from this state of unnatural affection, America could mount to a permanent position of rivalry with the "mother-country" that would stimulate the creative energy of our people.

The thrill Rush got from his performance was sustained for many weeks, his excitement kept at a high pitch by the success the published copy of his speech was having. There were demands for it everywhere. It was reprinted in Republican papers in every state, and congressmen asked for hundreds of copies for free distribution. Rush was "more flattered than I dare tell, and certainly more than I deserve," in spite of the fact that he learned the delivery of it had driven Randolph out of the Capitol building, and Senator Lloyd had called it "a stupendous and daring attack on good principles." He was indifferent to such opposition. "When I write another pamphlet," he observed, "*or make another speech*, I must try to repay them."

His father was pleasant in his approbation; equally gratifying was a long letter from John Adams. "Your Oration was first read to me," he wrote, "by the oldest Colonel in the continental Army now living; who has commanded Wilkinson and Brooks, whose blood flowed in the revolutionary War, and whose crippled Limb, tho not lost may be compared to Uncle Toby's. The Veteran exclaimed 'This young Gentleman, makes my old blood fly through my Veins as it did when I was young.' The Oddity of the Circumstance induces me to note it." He assured Rush the piece was "worthy of the orator and his Father; worthy of the Sacred Temple in which it was pronounced, worthy of the August Audience assembled to hear it; and worthy of the great Cause in which We are engaged."

The Fourth of July speech committed Rush to an endorsement of the war policies, and once in so public a way his opinions had been given he could not act a milder or an equivocal part. Nor did he wish to. "I may be in error," he wrote his father; "but at the commencement of a new and great crisis to my country I have promulgated under my name principles which I believe to be correct, and design to pursue a conduct to correspond with them. By these principles & by this conduct it is my intention to stand or fall, as so old a man as Mr Adams has said—happy if the former, prepared I trust if the latter." Adams indeed gave him inspiration. It was a welcome balance to Dr. Rush's misgivings to hear from the old sage of Quincy: ". . . a more necessary War, was never undertaken. It is necessary against England; necessary to convince France, that We are something; and above all necessary to convince ourselves, that We are not, Nothing."

Every aspect of his environment in Washington confirmed his resolution. After the adjournment of Congress, with the city nearly empty except for the administrative personnel, he grew close to his colleagues in the companionship of a common effort. Some of his letters of the late summer are among the most colorful of his whole career. In one he described official Washington to his father:

> Since the bustle of Congress has passed over I visit the President very frequently in the evenings, where, whether he is alone, or whether like myself, his secretaries or neighbours have strolled in to his tea table I pass the time delightfully and with, I trust, as much advantage as pleasure. He is a most enlightened man upon all subjects, and as regards the whole of our politicks and history, astonishingly prompt, accurate and profound, a great civilian, a great diplomatist, a great statesman, and as, I believe, a more pure and virtuous man—in his parlour not to be surpassed in whatever is kind-hearted, hospitable, and amiable.

The cabinet members were of uneven quality:

> Mr Munroe is also fine company, improved no doubt by travel. Having for fifteen or twenty years past divided his time be-

tween the courts of London, Paris, and Madrid he unites the ease of the courtier to the honesty of an old Roman. Eustis [the incompetent Secretary of War] is well enough—far better in a parlour than *another place I could name.* Hamilton [Secretary of the Navy] so, so. Gallatin, though away at this moment, a prodigy of genius and quickness in every thing. Pinkney, who is occasionally of the circle, very dashing, well informed and ambitious.

It was a lively, spirited group:

To these add a few agreeable men of the place who have nothing to do but visit, some more, others less, enlightened, like men every where—with a constant succession of strangers, and you have the summer society of Washington. The President is cheerful, tranquil and firm; seeming to have a sturdy and consoling conviction, that let things end as they may he has done his duty, has done what the just rights of his country demand and what posterity will approve.

In his established conviction of the justice of the government's course Rush could not condone the vigorous opposition to the war that permeated the whole country north of the Potomac. Much of it he attributed to the selfish commercialism of the people. "At present we have lost our sensibility to national justice and honor," he complained, "and provided we can have banks and lotteries and discount notes at 2 per cent a month, and get 10 dollars a barrel for flour and call ourselves the disciples of Washington, we care nothing for the groans of our countrymen." When the "Friends of Peace and Commerce" of Essex, Massachusetts, passed resolutions against the war, and Republicans responded with defenses, he was struck with the "extravagance of the falsehood, violence, and folly" of the Federalists. "If therefore Massachusetts is resolved to have a civil war of it, it looks most probable that she will have it in her own bowels first; that it will be Massachusetts against Massachusetts before it can be Massachusetts against the nation." In Pennsylvania likewise the bitterness of the opposition was almost intolerable, particularly as their claims were so absurd. He heard that the city was Federalist, but he denounced this as nonsense. There were five Federalist papers to one Republican in Philadelphia, and naturally they made more noise, but if the brokers and merchants of Chestnut Street, those "Regulators of Pennsylvania," predicted an opposition victory they would prove foolishly mistaken.

Rush worked diligently throughout the summer and fall in behalf of the party in his state. He wrote a number of tracts, most of them very brief, and sent them to Binns for publication in the *Press*. "You have made the most discreet and valuable use of all I have written you lately, and I trust have done good. Do you observe how your peices [*sic*] have been copied by all the democratick papers?" he asked as the election drew near. In this work he was deeply contented, for with Binns and Charles Ingersoll he conceived himself laboring in a cause that transcended party politics and faction.

But his father's associations did not include the young Republicans of the town. His friendships were with Federalists, the commercial magnates and shipowners. One day in September, he wrote Richard, he had heard it intimated in oblique but unmistakable terms that the Comptroller of the Treasury was the author of some of "those articles" that were appearing in "Binns' paper." He trusted that the imputation had no basis in fact, that Richard was more discreet if not more intelligent than that.

The gulf between father and son had widened until it was no longer possible for Richard to try to bridge it. He returned a twenty-page letter tenderly but firmly rebuking the doctor for repeating gossip, and for having no more confidence in him than to be upset by it. He carefully avoided admitting that he had written the articles for Binns, but he defended his right to do so with barely suppressed anger. "I am *suspected*, let me repeat the word, *suspected* of writing for Binns' [paper], as if I had been caught in the very act of something decidedly criminal!" If he had written for any of the other publishers, the Federalists would have been pleased; why had he not as much right to declare for the opposition? "I *approve* of Binns," he said. He thought him more valuable to Philadelphia and the nation than all the other publishers of the city put together. Some thought Rush had written the pieces signed Lewis Cass; this he indignantly denied, defending Cass (who was indeed as literate as any of his Philadelphia readers) as an educated man of the law. "Do the citizens of Philadelphia think every democratick Colonel from the western country a boor and a bearskin?" He assured his father that any public man, as he ought to know, was bound to suffer some calumny and castigation if he remained fixed in his principles. He had escaped for many years, and indeed had begun to fear that his lack of enemies only testified to his insignificance. One ought to rejoice in such criticisms rather than fall a prey to them. "Is it not to make women of us to persuade us to live in fear of such things?"

"Foster your other children," he advised his father, and begged him to stop writing such things to him, which could only destroy his contentment and accomplish no change in his attitude, for, he said sharply, "I am on my own legs." He won his point, and he did it in a way that preserved the warm personal relations between his father and himself; he had cut an affectionate bond that had been at times confining, at times painful. It was a little personal declaration of independence.

The election, when the results were all in, proved a victory for the administration, though one very definitely sectional in character. The South and West reëlected Madison. He carried only Pennsylvania and Vermont of the states north of the Potomac. But the victory in Pennsylvania was a triumph for Rush. It vindicated the stand he had taken with his father, it returned Charles Ingersoll to the House from Philadelphia itself, and set the cap on Binns's tireless labors.

Considerably less edifying than the political victory was the progress of the country's preparation for war. John Adams' anecdote seemed the *bon mot* for America's difficulties: "Marlborough revealed to Tallard, the whole Mystery of War. 'The only difference between you and me is, We have committed an hundred faults and you have committed an hundred and one.'" America was committing blunders aplenty in 1812, most of them in choosing her military leaders. Rush replied to Adams with the story of Count Strahenburgh: "A colonel in the imperial service once told Count Strahenburgh that the emperor had made him a general. He has nominated you a general said the count, but I defy him to make you one." He was finding reason to concur with Jefferson's remark, "The Creator has not thought it proper to mark those on the forehead who are of the stuff to make good generals." Dearborn, Hull, Wilkinson, Smyth, Van Rensselaer, all, one after another, were proving dismal failures. But Madison preserved an equanimity that helped everyone in Washington. Rush wrote admiringly of him in the early summer:

He visited in person, a thing never done before, all the offices of the departments of war and the navy, stimulating every thing in a manner worthy of a little commander in chief, with his little round hat and huge cockade! He is wonderfully animated and firm inflaming the young officers about him by his remarks.

This was the first time Madison had left the walls of the executive mansion for more than four months, except to attend the funeral of the Vice-President. Overwork and the strain of the war sapped his health, so that throughout most of the fall he was continually ill, but he pushed things on as well as he could from his sickbed.

Though Mrs. Rush found the capital "as quiet, as if we were at peace with all the world," there was tremendous activity backstage, for the military appointments were becoming the subject of political and sectional rivalries. A disgraceful scene of incompetence, bungling, and stupidity was being enacted. In spite of the fact that the Republican party had been united by the war, every political string was pulled, every pressure exerted for the selection of favorite candidates. John Adams was irate over the neglect of New England; even long-time Republicans there like General Heath were being passed over, and Pennsylvanians similarly thought the state which appeared to be bearing most of the cost of the war should have its share of the leadership. Throughout the winter this spectacle of preparation and organization kept the Comptroller at his desk manipulating his political connections in behalf of the administration. It was a tiresome and tedious job. Once he relieved himself by writing a satire on factionalism and sending it to Binns for publication.

Then on April 19, 1813, following a three days' illness, news of which had not reached Washington, Dr. Benjamin Rush died. Rush hurried northward as fast as horses and boats could carry him, but he "reached his disconsolate house just as the funeral obsequies were over, and the gates of the tomb shut forever upon me." John Adams sent an affectionate tribute.

There is not another Person, out of my own Family, who can die, in whom my personal Happiness can be so deeply affected. The World would pronounce me extravagant, and no Man would apologize for me if I should say that in the Estimation of unprejudiced Philosophy, he has done more good in the World than Franklin or Washington.

In spite of their disagreements over policy, the doctor's death made a serious difference in Rush's life. He had been a wonderful correspondent, his sprightly letters filled with the rich experiences of his full and useful career. To him Rush had been able to write more candidly, more openly, than to anyone else, even Binns. He had used his weekly letters to his father as a safety valve, to discharge the excesses of enthusiasm, delight, or worry that he experienced in war-time Washington. This opportunity was gone, and though he could feel a certain independence now as living no longer in the reflected glory of his distinguished parent, he needed the sort of confidant his father had been.

John Adams made a welcome and picturesque substitute. His correspondence with Dr. Rush had kept up until the latter's last months, and had been supplemented by occasional letters to Richard in Washington. Now the Comptroller turned to the venerable patriot as a friend whose counsel would be even more in accord with his own views than the doctor's had been. For the next five or six years, frequent letters went back and forth, into which both poured their deepest convictions, their observations on passing issues, and their mutual regard. It is one of the most interesting literary remains of the period, revealing both men at their best in epistolary style and personal charm. President Madison remarked, on seeing one of Adams' letters, "opinions from such a quarter had the smack of rich and old wine." "It is no interference with my publick employments to write to you," Rush assured Adams. "I can command some portion of almost every day, and the privilege of using it in this way is most gratifying to me." On another occasion:

You have a claim, coeval with your life, to know what your country is doing, and many more and much stronger claim[s] upon it than this. To be accepted as your Washington correspondent is a source of great gratification to me. The sight of your hand, too, will serve to keep up the pleasure I so often knew from it in my lamented father's time.

Adams returned the compliment with pleasure. "Every Line from you will oblige your Friend," he wrote. "The 'Portion of time that you can command every day' affords me very pleasing hopes." One letter he closed with the remark, "In writing to you I almost forget that I am not writing to your Father."

The material they had to write about in 1813 was not pleasant, for America was suffering reverses on all fronts. Adams constantly pleaded the necessity of naval armament on both the ocean and the Great Lakes. He begged Rush to be aroused, "you and your Contemporaries," for the nation was on the brink of a precipice.

To this Rush agreed. He was in despair through the summer and fall. In a field next to his summer home at Georgetown a company of volunteers was drilling; in July he acquired a musket and joined them. He considered the situation desperate. His letters to Binns were mournful: ". . . we must continue to live on what alone has long supported us—hope." Sectional rivalries over military appointments were persisting, each defeat adding bitterness to the spirit of faction. But in September, with plans under way for a general movement of three armies against

Canada, news suddenly came of the victory of Perry on Lake Erie. First success of the inland war, it nearly made up for the disgraceful failures of Hull, Dearborn, Van Rensselaer, and Smyth the year before. "It is indeed thrice glorious, unexampled in our annals, and big, I hope, with great events to our cause and country," Rush exulted in a letter to Binns. To Adams he was equally jubilant. "I know of nobody who will take as much pleasure in [Perry's victory] as you. I know of nobody, Sir, who has so just a title to rejoice at our splendid naval trophies as you. The Navy is yours." Adams was truly excited. "Perry's Triumph, is enough to revive Mr Madison, if he was in the last Stage of a Consumption," he wrote gaily.

But the interlude of victory was short-lived, for the fall campaigns in Canada ended hardly more favorably than those of the year before. Rush was able to report a measure of success with the loan of 1813; at least it filled sufficiently to save the Treasury from bankruptcy, though it cost the government some moral scruples to manage it, for John Jacob Astor and a Philadelphia banker took most of it at a prearranged premium rate. He was also able to find satisfaction in his work in the courts. For some reason all the lawsuits of the government had been turned over to him, though they were not properly within his jurisdiction, and he had delegated all other tasks of his office to subordinates that he might give himself entirely to prosecutions. This work proved entirely congenial to him, for he was beginning to think more and more of legal problems connected with the national government. But no one in Washington that winter could withstand the discouragement that greeted the news of Wilkinson's and Hampton's retreat, undertaken apparently for trifling reasons.

Rush was as despondent as everyone else. "The season of greatest trials" was just coming on, he thought. The embargo and the new taxes, coinciding with the dismal failure of Wilkinson, turned the people's hearts against the war and the cause of freedom. On the last day of 1813 he wrote Adams: "What, Sir, should be done. The prospect looks black. It is awful. Is it still left for us to 'take courage' in the hope that 'the tide will turn'? or is not the torrent rolling too fiercely upon us to be turned back?"

Adams could offer only philosophical consolation.

Nature must have its perfect Work: the Business of the World will do itself. This Nation must be purified in the furnace of Affliction. Politicians and Warriors, at the most and at the best, are but Mid-wives to watch the throws of nature and assist a little in ushering into the World, great Events.

III

THE HEAV'N RESCUED LAND

The New Year of 1814 brought no relief from disasters and defeats. Occasional victories on the sea were briefly heartening, but they could not counteract bad news from Europe. Indeed, though America's future probably depended upon what happened to Napoleon, no one seemed to know exactly how this relationship worked. Would the Emperor's overthrow be a defeat for America, or would it not matter so long as an aggrandizing peace was avoided? Rush believed the nub of the question was England rather than Napoleon. To what heights would she rise? How would "all these great vibrations" affect us?

The news of the battle of Leipzig the previous October had brought the picture of allied armies converging on Paris. All America knew their measured march was part of our own struggle. To some, even staunch opponents of Napoleonic despotism, the hard-pressed Emperor's defense of France seemed also a defense of American republicanism, for so long as Britain's strength was busy on the continent it could not reach across the sea. "If Europe submits to the maritime Despotism of England," Adams wrote, "the whole Globe is enslaved. Napoleon's Despotism could not extend beyond Europe. Is Mankind to submit to one or the other? . . . If Russia Austria and Prussia submit to Castlereagh I shall think Mankind degraded indeed, and all Europe ready to throw Firebrands Arrows and Death at the bidding of George Prince of Wales."

Amid these uncertainties Rush was elevated to a cabinet position. Since April 1813, Gallatin had been absent from Washington. Madison had appointed him a special envoy to join John Quincy Adams and James A. Bayard in peace negotiations, holding the Treasury post open for him until his return. He had been glad enough to leave Washington for a while to allow factional acerbities of which he was the target to quiet. But the Senate not only refused to confirm his appointment; it also refused to permit William Jones, Secretary of the Navy, to administer both departments indefinitely. Though Madison resisted as best he could, on February 9, 1814, the Senate declared the Treasury vacant. Gallatin was immediately appointed Minister to England, in which post he was confirmed.

Rush had been frequently suggested for the Treasury portfolio in the months following Gallatin's absence, but he had scouted the notion. "With all your kind opinions, Sir," he had declared to Adams, "I am by far too great a tyro for its present labours and responsibilities." He wished to remain loyal in every respect to his chief; to succeed him in the place from which he had been so unceremoniously removed would be to appear to condone the treatment the Senate had meted out. Therefore when Madison offered him the choice of the Treasury or the Attorney-Generalship in February he chose the latter. Vacant through Pinkney's retirement, it offered Rush a logical extension of the heavy burden of legal prosecutions he had been carrying for more than a year anyway, it enlarged his scope, it bore nearly as large a salary as the Treasury, it implied no disaffection with Gallatin. On February 10 he entered his new office, and George Washington Campbell, though ill and physically unable to discharge the obligations of the position, became Secretary of the Treasury.

"I must congratulate you on your transmigration," wrote Adams when the Boston papers noted Rush's promotion.

The office of Attorney Gen. must be more congenial than that of Controuler. But your Entertainment, is not my object. Any Plodder, like John Steel or old Duval could cast accounts in Eagles Dollars Cents and Mills. But Laws and Gov^t and History are very different Things. Pursue the History of your own Country, and of England and of France and of all Nations in all Ages. Apply an impartial Philosophy to it all.

Rush was having very little time for philosophy, impartial or otherwise. His migration was so sudden that he had no period even for adjustment to his new work.

At the very beginning of the last month [he wrote Adams in March] my new appointment was bestowed upon me, and I was suddenly thrown into the midst of the supreme court the very day after, without the least previous acquaintance with any of its business. There I have been, day in and day out, ever since last thursday blundering on in an agony of embarrassment and ignorance, doing the business of the court and not doing it; with Mr Pinkney, the late attorney general, for the most part as my prompter, but sometimes left awkwardly to stand upon my own legs, doing every thing but wearing the fool's cap and almost that. The scene is now, thank heaven, over, and I have until next February to look about me.

He laid out a careful program of study and reading to help him in his new tasks. "I feel what an immense deal of law, history, literature, and every thing else, I must subdue before I can stand erect in this post, should I ever be able to do so," he confided to Adams. "I am at least determined to be industrious. I feel its difficulty; its great responsibility; but there is thus much of hope—that its duties while anxious, are infinitely animating." He made a visit to Philadelphia, "to lay in a stock of new law books, as I hope, by hard study, to lay in a stock of law knowledge."

His previous legal experience, indeed, scarcely qualified him for the Attorney-Generalship. His practice in Philadelphia had been, by his own description, of a "low" sort; his work at the Treasury, until the last twelve months, almost entirely prosecutions of cases associated with the revenue; his superintendence of the government suits involving only those in the lower courts. Now he was plunged into a welter of private and public law cases which were almost as new to him as they would have been to the youngest novice in the profession. Prize cases, hundreds of them new and old, courts martial, admiralty decisions, constitutional problems, suits in international law—these and a myriad other matters he was suddenly called upon to master.

Rush succeeded one of the most colorful Attorney-Generals in American history, he was followed by one of the most able.

His own career in the office was neither picturesque nor distinguished, but it was industrious, efficient, and generally satisfactory. In pleading he was not the prima donna Pinkney had been. That remarkable individual customarily covered over his really prodigious abilities with an elegant but vacuous appearance; his affectations, his posturing, his lush eloquence and elaborate dress had often attracted full galleries of Washington society, male and female, to the courtroom. They came to be entertained, they stayed in tribute to Pinkney's genius. Such melodrama was not to Rush's taste. He was having too hard a time learning his duties and discharging them adequately to indulge in any histrionic tricks. He was plain, simple, and direct in his arguments, and though he drew few crowds he gained the respect of the bench.

The Court was a place of business, of which he expressed no awe. Story he knew, and Duval; Marshall, Johnson, and the others he respected as a group though he knew them but slightly as persons. The 1814 term, sitting when he took office, was "stuffed with all sorts of complicated questions," Story declared, mostly involving prize law, violations of non-intercourse statutes, and trading with the enemy. The Court was the branch of the government that put teeth in war-time trade regulations. Public attention was focused upon its work to such an extent that, as the *National Intelligencer* noted on February 24, " . . . notwithstanding the importance and interest of the debates in the two Legislative bodies holding their sessions in the same pile of buildings, it is frequently difficult to keep a quorum in either House of Congress owing to the number of members who crowd to hear the pleadings in the Court." In the most important arguments he conducted Rush usually had the help of Pinkney; even in other cases where he appeared alone the briefs had sometimes been prepared by his predecessor while still in office, so he was not entirely unaided. In the famous case of *The Aurora* (8 Cranch 203) Samuel Dexter of Massachusetts appeared against Pinkney. It was a brilliant occasion; Rush wrote Adams that he hoped to see Mr. Dexter governor of Massachusetts. He got through the session somehow without disgracing himself, and then began a thorough preparation for the next year's term.

It was after the Court rose in March that he turned to what would be his most notable achievement as Attorney-General, the editing of the *Laws of the United States*. This project had been under consideration for some time, but no one had taken the trouble to push it through. Justice Story was much interested in it, but so much bemused had the Court been by lack of a quorum for one whole session (1813), Senate quarrels over ratifications, Madison's political appointees and other distractions, that there had been no opportunity to plan the work. Attorney-General Rodney had thought some about it, and had even gone so far as to draw up some proposals, but Pinkney had let it rest. In Rush, however, Story found a companion spirit. The Justice saw a convenience to the legal profession; Rush saw an opportunity to express the national achievement of America in the law. It was part of his increasing consciousness of American particularism and separatism that Rush manifested in his introduction and his editorial labors. If America, as he had said in 1812, was to free herself from intellectual and cultural bondage to Britain, how better do so than by publishing the results of her own creativity in jurisprudence? It would be a code of laws that would testify to our independence of mind, and by its contrast with the cruel criminal codes of England and European nations would display the moral superiority of the New World.

Story and Rush corresponded throughout the summer of 1814, discussing various points, Story giving help and advice in editorial problems. Every statute, repealed or not, every private law, every public law, and every public treaty was included; all decisions, all commentaries were omitted. Rush printed a brochure, which was approved by the government, and finally late in the summer two publishers, Bioren and Duane in Philadelphia, Weightman in Washington, brought out at fifteen dollars a set the five-volume edition of the *Laws of the United States*. It appeared on the market at a moment when the country's stocks were very low indeed, but it was an infallible harbinger of the national spirit which was about to sweep over the nation.

Meanwhile Rush was doing what he could to oppose the anti-war activities of New England. He sent Binns a piece he had written for the Boston *Patriot* on the law of treason and intercourse with the enemy. "The New England lawyers have taken up a notion that it is perfectly innocent in our citizens to visit the British ships of war off the coast at their pleasure; but I confess I can subscribe as little to their learning as their patriotism on this point." Story complimented the piece, and Binns republished it.

In Philadelphia there was one person ready to do something effective to coalesce national sentiment against factional opposition. Mathew Carey, Irish-born publisher, nationalist, and inveterate organizer, began soliciting Rush's support for some of his imaginative and fruitful schemes. Rush encouraged him in the formation of societies and clubs for the promotion of American manufactures. He read his pamphlets, among them the popular *Olive Branch*, with appreciation and approval. The work Carey was thus beginning was to be of great importance to Rush ten years later, and was to be one of the focal points of the nationalistic plans soon to be known as the "American System."

In June, when news of Napoleon's abdication reached America, together with some intimation of the plans of the allies, Rush was convinced that American democracy was threatened. "The late events of Europe have so fortified aristocracy & thrones, that it behooves us to look well to our system of republican liberty," he wrote Carey. "We know not what vital aims may be intended even at this." The cabinet was considering the question with great care. The underlying issue was, what part should America take in the reconstructed world after the peace settlement, and how could she take this part while still at war with Britain? On June 7 the department heads (with Rush, who, though not the head of a department, for there was no Justice Department as such at that time, nevertheless customarily attended cabinet sessions) determined on the opening of the campaigns for the summer, resolving to launch a still more elaborate attack on Canada. Later in the month, Madison put three questions to his advisers, which uncovered some remarkable disagreements on policy. To the first—"Shall the surrender by Great Britain of the practice of impressment, in a treaty limited to a certain period, be an ultimatum?"—all answered no but Rush; on the second, whether a treaty of peace silent on impressment should be authorized in instructions given the commissioners, Armstrong and Jones voted yes against a majority no. A compromise, proposing a treaty referring impressment and commerce to a separate negotiation, all favored but Rush, who recommended awaiting more information from Europe. Obviously there was confusion in the administration over peace plans; these could not be concluded so long as the outcome of arms remained dubious.

Not the least interesting revelation is that Rush was in this uncertain year dealing with problems he would face again in very different ways. He never ceased to be resolute on impressment, but on other matters he was acting a rôle that would embarrass him in later years if he were to remember. For example, he was destined to be in the period 1825–29 one of the leading American protectionists; yet in 1814 at his very first cabinet meeting he advocated repeal of all duties. "It was a matter of serious satisfaction to me," he informed Adams, "that at the first meeting of those officers of the different departments with whom the President consults at which I had the honor to express an opinion, it was given in favor of 'free trade' which I have ever valued no less than 'sailors rights.'"

But almost every public man of 1814 was bound to change his opinions on fundamental issues in the next ten years. Rush was only as inconsistent and as apprehensive as most others in the face of Napoleon's defeat, the release of England's armies from continental engagements, and the prospects of another long summer of accelerated conflict. Like old Mr. Adams he was being forced to rely more and more on his faith in the American spirit, in the republican character. This was the last line of defense.

At Quincy, Adams was not deeply perturbed over the consequences to America of Napoleon's defeat.

> The annual Threats of thousands and tens and twentys and thirtys and Fortys of thousands of Men, to be sent to America, have sounded in my Ears, these forty Years.
>
> My Answer is How many Tons of shipping are necessary to transport one Soldier, with his Trimmings from Europe to America? And as one is to three, What is 40,000 to a fourth Number?
>
> Here! Tory! State your sum and try your skill in the rule of Three.
>
> 1:3::40,000: And when since Noah Ark was a fleet of 120,000 Tons of shipping seen upon the deep?

Rush showed the letter to Madison, who was amused; but neither of them could view as lightly as the elder statesman the possibility of a more impressive invasion effort than Britain had yet made. It was easy enough to prove theoretically the impossibility of invasion in large numbers, but it was infinitely more difficult to believe that Americans in their lackadaisical state of mind would bestir themselves to resist the smaller numbers of troops which could effectively be landed.

Through the 1813 campaign Cockburn had harried the shores of the Chesapeake; it was confidently expected that this entrance to America's coastline would not be overlooked in 1814. Some of the cities along the bay and adjacent rivers had appealed to the government in the spring to put the region in a posture of defense; Washingtonians were frankly alarmed.

At a cabinet meeting on June 30 it was agreed to begin measures of precaution and defense. Brigadier General William H. Winder, just exchanged after nearly a month as a prisoner in Canada, was put in charge of a new military district including Washington. He set up headquarters and spent what brief time he had surveying the surrounding territory minutely and repeatedly, until he certainly knew the terrain as well as ever a general knew a prospective battlefield. After such a good start he could do little more, for the apathy of the government, jealousies, delays, and foolish vexations encompassed him about. Winder was not a superior man, but he was ordinarily competent, and did have a good plan for defense. But support and coöperation were refused him; few generals could protect a government without its help and without its support in raising troops.

The conduct of the executive branch of the government was fatuous and ineffectual. General Armstrong, Secretary of War, was a proud and sensitive man of some ability, whose misfortune it had been to bear the brunt of criticism for the failures of his generals in the north. He was the target of bitter popular resentment, and the object likewise of Monroe's jealous dislike. The President tended to stand by his War Secretary until early August, when he unaccountably wrote him a long, sharp letter practically accusing him of insubordination, and limiting very exactly the things Armstrong might do officially without the President's prior knowledge and consent. Armstrong smarted under this rebuke, unexpected if it was not unwarranted, and of the latter there is scarcely a doubt; but he returned a dignified answer and continued to discharge his functions with conscientious care, though he insisted until almost the time of the battle that the British would attack Baltimore rather than Washington. "What the devil will they do here?" he asked.

Monroe, though he held no military rank, assumed the rôle of adviser and expert on army affairs. His constant interference was probably more the product of restless enthusiasm than of ambitious scheming, but from whatever motives he officiously stuck his fingers in every pie, almost invariably upsetting the plans of responsible administrators. His ascendancy over Madison was such that the diminutive President relied upon him in most matters, sometimes when more authoritative advice would have been wiser. His bubbling energies overwhelmed his colleagues, persuading them he was a veritable virtuoso. Even when the shooting ended he was still able to conceal the fact that for the most part he had bungled.

It is not possible to lay the blame on any one person in the government for the dreadful calamities of that August, for the stupidity was general, shared by everyone in high position. Madison was personally brave, devoted, calm, and poised, but he was tragically inept at handling people in a situation that called for inspiring leadership rather than merely a good example. No one doubted his earnestness or his sincerity in the cause of the nation, but popular feeling with an unerring instinct held him responsible for the chaos and confusion that ended in debacle. Mismanagement all down the line through the civil and military departments prepared the way for a ghastly and discreditable episode in the annals of the American republic, an episode which Rush witnessed first hand, and which left an indelible impression upon his mind.

Rush's own part in the failure to defend Washington was that of a spectator. He had no responsibilities other than that of giving legal advice to the president. He was hardly in a position to control or direct any of the operations even had he essayed to; and if he appeared on the black Wednesday in a silly rôle, he was only one of a whole company of well-intentioned but ridiculously culpable officials. The most charitable estimate would exempt him from any of the responsibility, the most harsh would judge him by his companions in the administration.

He well knew the effective organization, the steadfastness, the firmness of the British army. His sister Mary was the wife of Captain Cuthbert, an English officer serving under Prevost in Canada, and had joined her husband as soon as war was declared. Her letters to the family in Philadelphia gave grim accounts of the tepid, flagging spirit of the American invaders, the contrasting vigor and resolution of the English defenders above the St. Lawrence. The British army was nothing to be trifled with, yet it required no particular insight to realize that most of the preparations around Washington were trifling.

Therefore when it was learned that Admiral Cochrane and General Robert Ross were sailing through the Capes of the Chesapeake, Rush was gravely concerned. In spite of the six-weeks period for preparation of defenses, there were none visible. The President ordered out all troops in the city, and sent requests for more militia to the governors of neighboring states. On Thursday, August 18, Monroe learned from the President that the enemy had moved up the Patuxent and was effecting a landing at Benedict, fifty miles south of Washington. He volunteered to take a troop of horse and go at once to observe the British force, "report it, with my opinion of their objects, and, should they advance on this city, to retire before them, communicating regularly their movements to the Government." Madison agreed, so Monroe set out next day with Captain Thornton and two dozen dragoons. He rode all night, reaching Benedict at ten in the morning, Saturday the twentieth. From then on he continued to watch and report the British moves until the battle at Bladensburg.

Another president might have thought of better employment for the Secretary of State than scout duty, particularly since he held no military commission and was essaying work that Captain Thornton could have done just as well. But Monroe was in his element. He was in the best position to tell the government what to do, yet not to blame if they did not do it. On his first reconnaissance of the English squadron he dispatched a dragoon to Madison with what surely must be one of the most inane field-notes in military history:

The enemy landed yesterday. . . . From a height . . . I had a view of their shipping; but being at the distance of three miles, and having no glass, we could not count them. We shall take better views in the course of the evening, and should any thing be seen, material, I will immediately advise you of it. The general idea is, that they are still debarking their troops, the number of which I have not obtained any satisfactory information of. The general idea also is, that Washington is their object, but of this I can form no opinion at this time. The best security against this attempt is an adequate preparation to repel it.

The next day, Sunday the twenty-first, he estimated their strength as the enemy barges moved farther up the river, and advised Winder to send five or six hundred men to Nottingham, to prevent debarkation. Unfortunately Winder did not follow this reasonable counsel, which might have discouraged Ross or sent him elsewhere to land. He did set out on the twenty-second with a small force, meeting the enemy already debarked and marching toward Washington, about twenty-five miles from the city, but he retired rather than engage the whole British strength with too small a detachment. Monroe sent a hasty message to the President: "Have the materials prepared to destroy the bridges. You had better remove the records."

Madison was simultaneously writing to advise the Secretary of State that the archives of the nation had been sent to "retired places." In spite of misgivings, he doubted the British were as strong as had been reported, and appeared confident of the outcome.

Winder was retreating at the same rate the British advanced. On Monday the twenty-second Commodore Barney blew up his own gunboats in the Patuxent to prevent their capture by the British naval squadron which was moving up the river. He with his sailors and marines hurried inland to join Winder's main force. On that day Ross leisurely marched without hindrance along good forest-shaded roads right around Winder's flank within plain sight of the Americans to the town of Upper Marlborough. There he camped for the night.

Winder's camp was at Old Fields, eight miles east of Washington on a road crossing the Eastern Branch of the Potomac over the Navy Yard bridge. Here on Monday evening arrived the President and the heads of the departments, including Rush. Under escort of a captain's guard they spent the night at the house of a Mr. Williams, to the rear of the camp. It was hardly a quiet rest they got, nor did the much-beset General fare well that night. Somehow Winder could never delegate tasks. In command of an army and a military district, he still did his own scouting, and was always busy performing duties he should have given over to junior subalterns. This was due partly to the inexperience of his officers, but mostly to his own temperament. Never was a commander less able to command himself and those about him than this unhappy man. ". . . after having waded through the infinite applications, consultations, and calls, necessarily arising from a body of two thousand five hundred men, not three days from their homes, without organization, or any practical knowledge of service on the part of their officers, and being obliged to listen to the officious but well intended information and advice of the crowd, who, at such a time, would be full of both," he pitifully complains, "I lay down to snatch a moment of rest."

But that night an inexperienced sentry acutely conscious of the British just five miles away gave the alarm. Before it could be denounced as false, the whole force was under arms, at three in the morning!

At sun-up after this maddening night Winder called upon the President. The troops were assembled and paraded for review by Madison and his ministers. Sixty-three years old, weakened by illness, the little President nevertheless moved through the lines all the forenoon of the twenty-third, cheering and encouraging the soldiers. He noted they were "in high spirits & make a good appearance." Winder reconnoitered, and saw the British were making no preparations to move from their camp at Marlborough; on learning this Madison and his party returned to Washington.

At about two in the afternoon, however, Ross did begin a march, pushing six miles west directly toward Winder's encampment. He reached the American outposts at five o'clock, formed his lines and prepared to give battle. But the American outposts promptly vanished! Winder after posting strong forces to the north and south—on both his flanks, that is to say—gathered up his center and retreated with great speed into the city of Washington, for reasons which he had some difficulty explaining, and other subsequently have had more difficulty accepting. It was a foolish, pointless move, designed to prevent the enemy's doing things they would have been mad to attempt, clearing the way for them to do the one thing they were obviously intending to do.

Why Winder made his "eight-mile run" was questioned at the time, for everyone in Washington certainly expected the battle to come at Bladensburg, northeast of the city on the best highway leading into it. But the General established headquarters at a house next to the Navy Yard bridge, the least effective, the most useless spot he could have chosen. He borrowed a horse—both of his were exhausted—and called at the President's palace to inform Madison of his move. Though he expected to find the heads of departments there, he was disappointed, for on his assurances that the British were not going to move that day, they had gone to their homes and by this time, presumably, to their beds. Winder returned to camp stiff, sore, and tired. Characteristically he spent the rest of the night in a hundred little jobs that he should have left to others.

About nine in the morning on Wednesday, the twenty-fourth, Richard Rush called round at Secretary Armstrong's "to ask him for his latest intelligence respecting the enemy's movements." Armstrong handed him a note he had just received from Winder, which read in part, "The news up the river is very threatening. Barney's or some other force should occupy the batteries at Greenleaf's Point and the navy-yard. I should be glad of the assistance of counsel from yourself and the Government. . . ."

This note Winder had sent by express, addressed to Armstrong, but the courier had taken it (for reasons unexplained) to the President. Madison, "not doubting the urgency of the occasion," opened and read it, and after sending it on by the express to Armstrong he at once left the mansion for Winder's headquarters by the Navy Yard bridge. Armstrong in his account makes the most of the interruption of the dispatch. The letter, he says, "was late in reaching me. It had been opened, and passed through other hands." He goes on to say that the moment he received it he hastened with Secretary Campbell to the General's headquarters. All other accounts cast doubt on this. Rush says he found Armstrong in, after the note had arrived, and he left him still at home.

From Armstrong's house Rush went to the President's, where he learned that Madison had already gone to headquarters. He followed at a gallop. When he arrived he found the President, General Winder, Commodore Barney, and several other military officers in conference. Jones, the Navy Secretary, came in almost at the same time. Monroe had previously been there, but had gone on to Bladensburg.

For an hour these individuals held a council of war, debating which way the enemy would march. Then came a courier from General Stansbury commanding the Baltimore militia at Bladensburg with information so positive even Winder could no longer doubt it, that the British were approaching that town. Accordingly the General ordered his whole force to march to Bladensburg.

As the council emerged from the brick house they had been using as headquarters, Armstrong and Campbell, the frail Secretary of the Treasury, rode up, more than an hour behind Rush. Armstrong was both offended and reserved, refusing to make any other comment on the arrangements that were explained to him than to growl truculently that, "as the battle would be between Militia and regular troops, the former would be beaten." Campbell, "who though in a very languid state of health had turned out to join us," held a private conversation with Madison, giving him a brace of dueling pistols to carry for his protection, and remarking that he was grieved to see the Secretary of War unwilling to help on this critical occasion, due to an excess of delicacy. Madison had better reasons than anyone else to understand Armstrong's reserve; but he rode up and talked with him, urging him to go to Bladensburg to help Winder with advice and assistance. If any questions of authority should arise, he added, his own intention was to proceed to the field of battle as soon as possible that he might be on hand to settle them.

As Armstrong rode off to Bladensburg, Madison bade Rush come with him to the Marine Barracks close by. Here Commodore Barney was vigorously protesting the absurd decision that he and his men should go to the already strongly defended arsenal at Greenleaf Point. It was a duty that needed only "a corporal and six men," Barney declared. Jones and Madison acceded to his earnest wishes, and Barney, thus delayed, set off with his command in the wake of Armstrong. He was independent as soon as he left the President and the Secretary of the Navy, not responsible to or in the confidence of Winder; but he and his sailors proved the only real fighters America had in the field that day.

After all these persons had been sent on their way, Madison himself with Rush at his side started out. They soon passed the body of their troops, and hurried on to find Winder, Armstrong, and Monroe, the last just then busily disarranging the placement of troops Stansbury had carefully worked out, and in other ways vexing that General sorely. As they rode Madison repeated to Rush what he had said to Armstrong, that his authority ought to be near at hand to adjust any disputes which might arise between Winder and the Secretary of War.

As they neared Bladensburg village, Armstrong and Monroe joined Rush and the President. They were all about to ride across the bridge into the town several miles in advance of their forces, when a volunteer scout who had been observing the moves of the British caught sight of them. "Mr. Madison, the enemy are now in Bladensburg!" he cried as he rode up to them. Madison "exclaimed, with surprise, 'the enemy in Bladensburg!'" He and his whole party turned their horses and began to gallop back toward the American lines.

The scout called out, "Mr. Madison, if you will stop I will show them to you; they are now in sight." But the President rode on, paying no attention. The disastrous farce of his blundering with three of his cabinet into the hands of the British vanguard was thus narrowly averted.

Rush, however, did wheel about to see the enemy. The scout

pointed them out: "There are part of the enemy stopping at that lane." It was just across the river.

Rush demurred: "That cannot be the enemy, they are not in uniform," he said.

His companion explained that it was an advance party.

At this moment the red-coats began to heave in sight, in two sections . . . and were forming in the Annapolis road. Mr. Rush, on seeing them, observed, "I am satisfied;" and turned his horse very suddenly to ride away, when his hat fell off, and he rode some distance without it, when I called out to him, "Mr. Rush, come back and take up your hat;" which he did, and then pursued his company with all speed.

When he reached the American lines at the top of a hill west of the river Rush saw the President bring Armstrong and Winder together for a hasty conference in the saddle. But Madison's horse began to rear and plunge, doubtless alarmed at the firing which had already begun. Neither the President nor the Attorney-General therefore heard the conversation between the two prima donnas of the day.

The President observed to Monroe and Armstrong, after the battle had "decidedly commenced," that they should withdraw to the rear, "where we could act according to circumstances; leaving military movements now to the military functionaries who were responsible for them. This we did, Mr. Rush soon joining us."

Of the battle itself, of the British charge led by Colonel Thornton, of its impulse, of Barney's magnificent though futile resistance to the orderly attack led by Ross, Rush saw nothing. He noted only that "It commenced in a very few minutes, and, in not many more, some of our troops began to break." He disclaimed any competence to judge of the ability the American commanders displayed, "as my attention was partly taken up in viewing, from hill to hill, the contending movements. To me it appeared plain that entire ranks of our men, in front, were dispersed by the shock of the enemy, before any order for retreat was given by the commanding general."

When, as the President put it, "it became manifest that the battle was lost; Mr. Rush accompanying me, I fell down into the road leading to the city and returned to it."

He and the Attorney-General after an hour's hard riding reached the city at three o'clock. Meeting Mrs. Madison near the Navy Yard, they all proceeded to the executive mansion. The President remained there for three hours gathering what he could, unfortunately losing Campbell's pistols from his holsters. Then, rejoined by Rush and Jones, who had visited their families, and by General John Mason, Rush's brother-in-law, he walked down the presidential grounds to the river. The party climbed in a boat and were conveyed to the Virginia shore, Mrs. Madison waiting on the Washington side until they were out of sight. As she was driven to Georgetown, the President with his attendants took a carriage to a house a few miles above Little Falls. Here, while a violent thunderstorm raging outside extinguished the distant blaze of the burning Capitol, he spent the night.

The next day Mrs. Madison made her way across the river, through a host of refugees, soldiers, and sightseers, to a little tavern in an apple orchard where she was to meet the President. The tavern was already thronged with persons so bitter against Madison that they would not admit her until late afternoon, when a storm of cyclonic proportions forced them do do so. The family of Secretary Jones joined her. The executive party did not venture out till after dark; then the six miles from their place of hiding to the inn was lengthened by the rain and wind. Arriving late at night, they were subjected to insults and indignities, which the President bore with equanimity. At midnight a courier brought word that he had been discovered; the British would soon be upon him. Hastily Madison crept out in the storm to a remote shack in the woods. The next morning he emerged, recrossed the river and proceeded with Rush and Mason to Brookville, Maryland, where Winder was reported to have camped. Jones stayed behind with his own family; Mrs. Madison returned to the city to her sister's, Mrs. Cutts. At

Brookville the party was greeted with respect and made as comfortable as possible on improvised beds in the parlor of Mrs. Bently, a Quaker lady. Winder, however, had moved toward Baltimore.

Next day word came from Washington that all was quiet, the British gone, Baltimore ready to defend itself, and civilians returning to the capital. Slowly Madison rode back, Rush and Mason beside him. Rush offered him the use of his own house, for word had been received of the burning of the mansion and the Capitol building, but Madison chose instead to set up temporary headquarters with Mrs. Cutts on F Street. Though the public offices were destroyed, including the Treasury and the building where Rush had worked, no private homes had been disturbed, and his own family were safe.

The town was a shambles, however, the government thoroughly disorganized. Most of the country felt keenly the debasement of a symbol; those who lived and worked in Washington suffered even more. The inexcusable incendiarism of Ross and Cockburn had turned a relatively unimportant diversion maneuver into the greatest catastrophe of the war.

Gallatin, in arduous negotiations at Ghent, expressed the horror the news from Washington caused.

A sudden raid and the destruction of an Arsenal and a frigate are a mere trifle, but to blow up and burn the House of Congress and the President's Palace, and the offices of the various departments, is an act of vandalism to which the Twenty Years' War in Europe, a war that extended from the Russian frontier to Paris, and from Denmark to Naples, cannot offer a parallel. . .

"Should some Walter Scott in the next century write a poem," a Federalist editor in New York scornfully chortled, "and call it *Madison, or the Battle of Bladensburg*, we would suggest the following lines for the conclusion, to be put into the mouth of his hero:

> 'Fly, Monroe, fly! run, Armstrong, run!
> Were the last words of Madison.' "

Though Republicans and expansionists were outraged by the British savagery, those who had opposed the war from the beginning were even more incensed by the government's tragic failure to defend the capital, and as always the tragic gave impulse to the comic. Campbell's dueling pistols which Madison had lost became famous symbols of all the guns that had remained silent that day, Rush's flying hat the jokesters' weapon for ridiculing the befuddlement of learned gentlemen at war. The unfortunately quaint name of Dolly Madison's sister furnished the chorus of a popular ballad, in which the gracious First Lady was represented as leaving this message for the President:

> Sister Cutts, and Cutts and I,
>   And Cutts's children three,
> Shall in the coach—and you shall ride
>   On horseback after we.

But, ridiculous or not, the government had to pull itself together. Congress assembled in the despoiled city for a special session in September, receiving the President's annual message then rather than at the regular time. Armstrong resigned, convinced that he had been betrayed by Monroe and abandoned by the President; Monroe was made Secretary of War, holding both that and the State portfolio for a few months. Jones likewise asked to be relieved, having intended to serve only during hostilities; Madison nominated Commodore Rodgers, but when Rush informed him that a naval officer could not legally serve as head of the department he selected Benjamin W. Crowninshield. Postmaster-General Granger was replaced, Campbell retired to his Nashville home to recuperate, shortly resigning to be succeeded by Alexander J. Dallas, of Philadelphia, an intimate of Rush, recently returned from Europe. Of all the cast of the Bladensburg playlet, only Monroe and the Attorney-General remained on the stage with the President.

As a by-product of the invasion Rush was caring for Colonel Thornton, second in command of the British forces, who had been seriously wounded leading the initial charge across the bridge from Bladensburg village, which the Americans had successfully withstood. A friend of Mrs. Cuthbert, he had been recommended to Rush by his sister, and for a long period while he lay bedridden the Attorney-General paid him many courtesies. He became indeed much attached to his erstwhile enemy.

The attack on Baltimore, with the death of Ross and Parker; the sturdy resistance of Fort McHenry; Plattsburg; finally New Orleans, the only unqualified success America won on land during the whole war, served to revive the government's spirits somewhat; then, as the winter passed, news of the Treaty of Ghent was received. Rush was prostrated by a serious illness during February, and could take no part in cabinet meetings or the sessions of the 1815 term of the Supreme Court. But by the middle of March he was recovering. "Daily rides and walks this fine weather, with fish, oysters, and other good things in moderation, are fast giving me my normal strength." As the "first small effort of industry" of his convalescence he wrote "some loose reflections" for Binns on the war, published of course under a pseudonym. In the summer he visited Philadelphia, leaving his family there for the hot weather while he returned to Washington. Work of reconstruction he found proceeding very slowly. "If you wish a retreat to the country for a few days," he wrote his brother James, "I invite you to jump into the steam-boat, and come down to Washington. As you are fond of architecture, you will still be in time to see very superb ruins. I am quite alone, but can give you batchelor's fare."

During August and September he was literally quite alone in Washington, for the President and all the cabinet were out of the city. Much work outside the regular business of his office fell to his lot. The "Hundred Days" of Napoleon had caused a mighty stir: "The royal European hunt of the beast they called a usurper, is at an end," he wrote Adams, "and Wellington has got the brush." "For my mere self," he told the President, "striving to gather up as much of consolation as possible for our own country out of the melancholy fortunes of France, and the present overthrow of the principle of self-government abroad, I am giving way to hopes, that the English in driving Napoleon from his throne, have, in effect, driven a friend of their own, and a foe of ours, from every court in Europe."

Many of the questions avoided by the treaty of Ghent needed further examination; he briefed them for Madison. He drew up a proclamation for the President's signature repealing discriminating duties against Great Britain, and dealt in his name with foreign ministers. The state of the navy, the affairs of the land office, the demobilization of the army all came under his surveillance.

The return of Gallatin and Bayard, "our long looked-for diplomatic wanderers," in September was the signal for renewed hope of clearing up the war issues. "A peep behind the British curtain at the fisheries, impressment and the West India trade, will be a treat," Rush wrote the President. He was becoming absorbed in our foreign relations. He gave Madison frequent accounts of Latin American affairs, and of the proposal of a commercial treaty with England as it was talked of in Washington. But the time was not yet arrived when he could make such problems the main concern of his career. His principal preoccupation was still the law, and in the midst of his vacation stewardship of the government he brought his studies to an interesting fruition. A letter to Adams of October 2 describes his reading:

I have been obliged within the last year or two to be very much of a law student. The solitude of Washington during the present and past season, has favored the habit; and for three or four months I have been reading and reading until I have found myself alternately a languid book-worm, and a heated enthusiast. The last three volumes of Robinson's admiralty reports systematically; Pothier on contracts; Vattel through and through, (for the second time since I came to Washington;) both volumes of Brownes lectures upon civil and admiralty law, a good deal of incidental law reading, with lastly "Wheaton on Captures," have been my achievements in the mere professional line since I returned from my jaunt to Philadelphia. Gibbon records of himself, that he once "devoured a hundred pages of Cluvers Italy, a closely printed folio abounding with quotations, in a single day." I have no conception of such rapid reading as this; but I at least find that I can read a law book through in a much shorter time than I could when a younger man.

His reading of Wheaton's *Digest of the Law of Maritime Captures and Prizes,* published that summer in New York, crystallized some ideas he had been toying with for a long while. In a "paroxysm of enthusiasm" he spent two weeks composing a "little pamphlet," on legal institutions, which he published without signature in September 1815, under the title, *American Jurisprudence, Written and Published at Washington, being a few reflections suggested on reading "Wheaton on Captures."*

"I have some tremblings for its fate," he told Adams. "It is by no means clear to me that the profession in our own country will relish it. I have endeavoured, it is true, to fight a little battle for them all; but I am not sure that other sentiments which it contains may not do away in their eyes any imaginary merit resulting from such an attempt."

The burden of *American Jurisprudence* was the superiority of American public law over English and Continental codes. Though it was relatively brief, Rush set such store by it that it must be seriously considered; it was a function of the same national spirit and enthusiasm that had led him to edit the *Laws of the United States.*

The profession of law, he intimated, was the best expression of the American national character. The "law-mind of the United States" had forerun the general condition of literature, for though the country had not yet attained "the age that can feed in any extent the merely classic mind into fullness and perfection," it had enjoyed from its earliest times "the luxury of liberty," and therefore had bred lawyers. Their progress had marked the intellectual advance of the country. Free institutions implied no other regulation or limit but the law; hence the habit of bringing everything to the courts. Everyone goes to law, Rush declared. The low costs, the universal privilege, encouraged it, with the result that the courts had become the guardians of liberties.

In England, courts were subservient to the legislature; in America they were equal. In England, courts did not interfere with the government; in America they interfered as "terrible legal battering rams" to prevent injustice and enforce civil liberties. This had given American statesmanship its jurisprudential tone, and had stimulated our public men, who alone had dared reassert doctrines of international morality in London and Paris.

American law was composed of English common law, English statute law, American statute law, and the great multitude of court decisions. It was a comprehensive code, the vast extent of which was "the evidence of our freedom, the unavoidable result of our wants." In making innovations the United States had advanced far beyond the judicial wisdom of England by making "wholesome amendments," getting rid of "that fudal [*sic*] turn, and of those perplexed and cumbrous forms of the Norman day which so long disfigured the admirable system upon which, by force or artifice, they were incorporated." The liberality of our criminal code was a grateful contrast to the awesome cruelties of the British.

America had never "subdivided" her legal profession as England had, her lawyers each an expert in one specialty. Hence American lawyers had a better understanding of the science of the law, which was in its essence a unit, an integral whole. This broad over-view of all jurisprudence produced such opinions as Marshall's, those "national treasures" which were so greatly elevating to our public spirit, so expressive of the creative ability of the American legal mind.

Because of its brevity, and the generality of its language, the essay does not strike the modern reader as particularly important in the history of our law, but it is pleasantly written, with flashes of wit and effective metaphors, it is full of provocative interpretations and imaginative suggestions. One wishes that Rush might have elaborated it into a larger work, with cases and comments to illuminate his points; then it might have helped us understand the spirit of the legal generation which Wilson and Marshall had taught and which Kent and Story were to epitomize. He did contemplate such a work; "If ever I come to a year or two of comparative leisure, after the toil of study and the bustle of affairs shall have in a degree gone by with me," he told Adams, "I have in view the plan of a work upon jurisprudence, of which some of the materials are already laid up while others are to be collected, and of which the little tract knocked off at a heat, last month, is but in part the vestibule."

From the welter of sectionalism, party strife, and political immorality of the war period, from the undistinguished leadership, ill-defined antagonisms, and vague aspirations, there began to emerge in 1816 a spirited national feeling, which affected Rush as it did most of his contemporaries, and yet was not at once clear in its fullest implications. The Attorney-General who had edited the legal code of the nation, and had claimed for American jurisprudence a moral superiority over all other systems, might have been expected to exert effective leadership in the nationalistic movement in legal thought. Rush did have a place in this movement, but it was not so important as it could have been, for he refused at a crucial moment to follow the logical development of his convictions.

The sovereignty of the United States had been seriously questioned in the war period. Not only was the political phase of that sovereignty constricted by the Jeffersonian theories of a limited government, and by the anti-war Hartford Convention, which published a report implying the power of the states to nullify acts of the federal government; but sovereignty at law (as opposed to the political concept) was also resisted, even vitiated by the willingness of anti-war merchants to trade with the enemy. Since there was no federal statute defining this as a crime, the federal courts were completely unable to take jurisdiction over even the most flagrant examples of the flouting of national sovereignty. This situation reduced the government to a state of helplessness that appeared scandalous to the administration; but nothing could be done without raising an old and sore question, namely: Did the federal courts have the right to try persons for offenses that were criminal according to the English common law, but had never been made so by federal statutes?

This question had arisen very soon after the adoption of the Constitution. The earliest justices of the Supreme Court had entertained common-law indictments, the Seventh Amendment had appeared to allow them; but in 1798 Justice Chase had suddenly denounced the practice and refused to try cases not involving statutory crimes. His decision made the whole matter a political issue, Federalists upholding, Republicans opposing, the doctrine of a national common law. For a number of years public excitement ran high on the matter. Then in Jefferson's presidency some Federalist editors and lawyers were indicted at common law for libel against the President, a political move which so shocked Federalists and Republicans alike that both turned against the doctrine. The only one of these cases that ever reached the Supreme Court was *United States* vs. *Hudson and Goodwin* (7 Cranch 32) in 1812, which Attorney-General Pinkney, on the grounds that all the other similar cases had been decided, declined to argue. The Court there upon declared summarily against the indictments, remarking that the question had been "long since settled in public opinion."

Justice Story was deeply mortified by this decision, by which he felt "The Courts are cripples; offenders, conspirators and traitors, are enabled to carry on their purposes almost without check." Rush was not entirely in agreement, though it is difficult to discern just what his opinion was. It was the Hudson case which moved him to publish his letter on treason in the Boston *Patriot* mentioned above, which advocated indictments of the crime of trading with the enemy under the law of treason, which was certainly a federal statutory crime; this indicates he was anxious to have the offense punished in some effective way. But at the same time (July 1814) he wrote a public letter to the

United States Attorney in Massachusetts in which he expressed complete approval of the Hudson rule. He argued that the admission of common-law indictments would mean admission also of common-law punishments, a code so cruel that it had no place in American jurisprudence.

But Story was determined to have a better elucidation of this point. He wrote Rush in August 1814 that he hoped Congress would at its next session remedy the defects of the federal criminal statutes, and urged him to study the subject of common-law jurisdiction so that the Court could hear argument on it at their coming term. But Bladensburg with its demoralization of the government occurred a few days later, and when Court did meet Rush was too ill to attend its sessions. Nothing therefore was done in 1815 beyond the Hudson case.

In his *American Jurisprudence* Rush did not omit the question. The states all shared together "an entire substratum of common law as the broad foundation on which every thing else is built," he wrote, and continued:

But the extent of this law, its beginning, its termination; upon what subjects precisely it operates and where it falls short; where the analogy of situation holds and where not, with the shades under which it may do the one or the other, (witness the great argument of Hamilton in Croswel's case at Albany, that in the case of Blight's assignees at Washington so far as prerogative was implicated, with numerous others that might be referred to,) these start questions upon which the nicest discriminations of ingenuity and learning have been for a century at work. Often therefore the American lawyer has gone through but half his task when he has informed himself of what the common law is. The remaining and perhaps more difficult branch of inquiry is, whether it does or does not apply to his case. Notwithstanding the determination of the supreme court in the case of the United States vs. Hudson and Goodwin, it is still by no means certain that that tribunal would not sustain another and more full argument at this day on the question in its nature so extensive and fundamental as whether or not the federal government draws to itself the common law of England in criminal matters.

Note that Rush did not take any firm ground on the issue, but he did speak in terms that seemed to indicate a willingness to open the question. That year Story, sitting on the Circuit Court in Massachusetts, tried a case of common-law indictment for piracy, *United States* vs. *Coolidge*, but his colleagues disagreed, so it came by writ of certiorari to the Supreme Court. Here at last was a test case that might overthrow the Hudson doctrine and restore federal sovereignty in an effective way. All that was really needed was an argument by the Attorney-General to produce an authoritative ruling. Rush's opportunity was an enviable one.

But, for reasons which his papers do not disclose, he declined to argue, as Pinkney had in *United States* vs. *Hudson*. Rush declared he thought the Hudson doctrine was controlling. Story was greatly disappointed. Johnson, J., delivered a brief decision in which he mentioned the disagreement among the justices which existed, and regretted the absence of "solemn argument," but in the absence of it refused to review the Hudson case.

This ended the matter, leaving one of the most serious questions of American public law hanging in uncertainty. What could have caused Rush thus to ignore the most promising occasion to increase the sovereign powers of the federal government likely to come his way? The only suggestion his letters of this time contain is unsatisfactory, but worth noting. Judge Cranch had been publishing from time to time the decisions of the Supreme Court. He was several years behind in 1816, yet his reports were the only information available, for no official reporter had been appointed as yet. Members of the bench and bar had only a general knowledge of what the decisions were. So casual were the formal attentions paid the records that Story once inadvertently took the manuscript of one whole term's cases home with him to Massachusetts! Under such conditions the doctrine of *stare decisis*, the consistency of the decisions from one term to the next, was not easy to preserve. Rush, desirous of securing a court reporter, anxious to spread information concerning the law, and recently contemplating a work on the body of national law that had been produced, was more than usually attentive to the controlling authority of decisions. It may have been an especial care for precedents that determined him to refuse to plead against the *Hudson* doctrine in spite of the willingness of the Court (personally and officially communicated to him) to hear argument.

In the other cases of the 1816 term he had no particularly important part, not even appearing in the famous *Martin* vs. *Hunter's Lessee* (1 Wheaton 304) which was decided on March 20. Nor did the term of 1817 contain much beyond prize cases and others arising from the war, which Rush handled in a routine manner. His only references to the Court in personal letters that year concerned the death of Samuel Dexter of Massachusetts and Alexander J. Dallas of Pennsylvania, the Secretary of the Treasury, both of whom had been warm personal friends.

I

Late in the summer of 1816 the Attorney-General joined James Monroe in an excursion to Albemarle and other parts of Virginia. "Health and recreation were the double motive," he told Adams. It was excruciatingly hot: "the sun it did so beat upon us, and the dogs barked away our rest at night"; but he enjoyed his first visit to "the antient dominion." He visited Madison at Montpelier, and at Monticello saw "the venerable Jefferson, walking over his own hills with the best health, and the best enjoyments, at past seventy." The Third President's stately home he thought "in some respects superb; wonderfully artificial—a curiosity!" He returned to Washington before Monroe to watch the election and send news of its progress to Albemarle. His trip with the Secretary of State had cemented their personal friendship; at the moment when Monroe was a candidate for the presidency this was no small gratification to Rush. He had seen the three whom Abbé Correa, the Portuguese Minister, called "the Presidential Trinity, the past, the present and the future," and had identified himself with the succession. There are indications that he had also made certain arrangements with Monroe. There was a fellowship between these two that both felt sincerely. In 1815 when Dallas, ill of the "gout in the stomach" that in a few months killed him, had wished to retire from the Treasury, Monroe and Rush had joined in dissuading him. "Several of us," Monroe had written Rush, "have had hard service together, & it will be highly gratifying for us, to continue together to the end."

Monroe's election therefore promised to make no change in Rush's position except to improve it. But the President-elect took his time about designating cabinet positions. In January Rush wrote Adams that the newspapers were all speculating as to who would succeed to the State Department, that he himself looked for John Quincy Adams to be appointed, but "What Mr Monroe's intentions, in this respect, may be, I know not." No formal notice came to Rush concerning his own post until near the inauguration, when it was necessary for Monroe to consult with all the executive officials regarding plans for the ceremonies on March 4, which had miscarried through Clay's pettish refusal to allow the House chamber to be used. On that occasion Monroe informed Rush he was to continue as Attorney-General, that Adams was to have the State Department, and that until the latter's return Rush would be asked to administer the affairs of both offices. Monroe may have disclosed the further plans he had for Rush for the future, or the two may have had an understanding dating from their junket together through Virginia, but he made no public announcement of them, and informed the Prince Regent no successor to Adams would be appointed at once.

Immediately after his inauguration Monroe departed for a four months' tour of the country. His absence left Rush the temporary head of the executive department of the government, for he was Acting Secretary of State and Attorney-General also from March until September. The government was not well organized; Secretary Crawford, who had succeeded to the Treasury on Dallas' death, was present part of the time, as was

Crowninshield, whom Monroe continued for a while in the Navy Department; but the War Department was administered by its chief clerk as Acting Secretary, no one having as yet been appointed to head it. As a result of the lack of permanent officials little of importance could be achieved; but Rush found Monroe had left so much unfinished work at the State Department that he had all he could do keeping abreast of it.

One of the characteristics Rush displayed throughout his public career was the ability to accomplish a great amount of work in a short time. He was like John Quincy Adams in this. A rapid worker accustomed to spending twelve to fifteen hours daily at his desk, he was methodical, precise, and apparently tireless. He had an orderly filing system; every paper was neatly docketed and endorsed with a brief of its context. This was a welcome contrast to Monroe, who was impulsive, careless almost to the point of slovenliness, and worked in spurts. By dint of prodigious effort Rush was able to keep the Attorney-General's office going, to discharge the formalities of official receptions and conversations with foreign representatives, correspond frequently with the President, and run the State Department so vigorously that when Adams arrived he found business "much in arrear, but without any accumulation of it since Mr. Rush has been at the head of the Department."

Most of his preoccupations of this busy summer were matters which Rush neither originated nor finished, but which he merely pushed along as they presented themselves. One, however, a negotiation of the gravest importance, he was able to finish. Monroe and Charles Bagot, British Minister, had been carrying on conversations with a view to settling the question of armament on the Great Lakes. The War of 1812, if it had done nothing else, had certainly proved that whoever controlled the Lakes could command the western approaches to both Canada and America. The genial Bagot, universally popular in Washington, had found Monroe receptive to the British desire to reduce the armed forces. On August 2, 1816, Monroe had made proposals which Bagot communicated to England. There they were accepted, and on April 28 the British Minister informed Rush of this fact. In return Rush sent a note expressing the President's satisfaction at the understanding, agreeing that each nation should confine its naval strength "On lake Ontario to one Vessel not exceeding one hundred tons burden, and armed with one eighteen pound cannon. On the upper lakes to two Vessels not exceeding the like burden each, and armed with like force, and on the waters of lake Champlain to one Vessel not exceeding like burden and armed with like force."

Rush had very little to do with the formulation of the agreement; he came in at the end of things, when all that remained was for Britain to accept the American proposals. But through the forms of designating public documents this exchange of notes has become known as the Rush-Bagot Convention. It was originally nothing more than an agreement between the two representatives, but a year later Monroe laid the documents before the Senate, which formally ratified the conditions, thereby giving it the status of a treaty. The continuing peace between the United States and Canada, and the extension of the unfortified boundary from ocean to ocean gradually gave it a traditional character, until it became the longest-standing peace agreement between two powers, the gunboats with their feeble eighteen-pounders quaint symbols of an honorable and precious international relationship. The terms of the notes of 1817 stood unchanged for 124 years. Then the St. Lawrence Seaway Agreement of 1940–41, permitting the construction of ships of war on the Lakes, in effect altered the scope of the Convention. It had become customary to regard the ratification of 1818 as tantamount to a treaty, but the recent seaway agreement does not repeal it, though it does contravene its provisions.

Rush dealt with many other matters during the summer of 1817: he completed the treaty with Sweden which Monroe had been negotiating, and gave Jonathan Russell, our Minister there, his final instructions; he watched British affairs in Florida, which were "curious"; the treaty with Algiers demanded attention, as did the Portuguese revolt, Latin American independence, the appointment of a committee of inquiry to visit the Spanish colonies and the new states, the attempt of Bonapartists to raise a fund in America for the Mexican insurgents, and so on; but none of his work could, from the nature of his position, be conclusive. He was only "sitting on the lid" until Adams arrived and Monroe returned. In August he had from the former news of his arrival in a gay and whimsical letter from Quincy:

As a truant I believe I must bring a writ of error from your black letter decision before the Supreme Court of the United States where common law is of no authority. Feeling nevertheless the force of considerations which your kindness and friendship have forborne to urge, I shall abridge as much as possible my visit here, and as far as anticipation may be allowed to the instability of human events, you may depend upon seeing me at Washington upon this day month. As the learned are agreed that the world began at the autumnal equinox with the sun entering upon the sign of the balance, I hold it the most auspicious time for commencing existence upon my new world; and although the season is apt to be tempestuous, if I am entering upon it to ride in the whirlwind, I shall have the consolation of looking to a steady spirit in our chief who will know how to direct the storm.

By the time of Adams' arrival it had become publicly known that Rush was to succeed him at London. Just when Rush was offered the post, and when he accepted, is not disclosed by the records; but not the least of his interests in meeting Adams was the prospect of discussing with him the work of his mission. He had long had a very high opinion of Adams' abilities; had admired his *Lectures on Rhetoric*, had considered him the "leading man" of the commissioners at Ghent, his letters "perfect models of intellectual and mechanical beauty"; when he had been suggested for Monroe's cabinet Rush had described "his genius, his principles, and his pen" as "most conspicuously, number one, for the elevated and difficult duties of our own foreign office."

Adams was as good as his word. He arrived in Washington on the twentieth of September, and went at once in search of

Rush who, having closed his house and sent his family to Annapolis to await departure, was living at the Franklin Tavern. This was the tavern, by the way, of William O'Neil, whose daughter Peggy was then Mrs. Timberlake, living next door to the Franklin and already a celebrated beauty of the city with some of her notorious conquests behind her. Adams and Rush called on the President, and then began to study together the problems of the Department of State.

At Adams' request, Rush postponed his departure until all current problems of the department could be discussed. The two worked together all through October; it was an experience that gave Rush personal acquaintance with the man who for the next decade was to do more than anyone else to shape his career.

Among all the problems before them none was more difficult than the instructions the Secretary was planning for the English mission. Adams, reflecting "upon a general principle for drafting instructions for Ministers going abroad," determined to make this document the example he would follow in other cases. "I shall be at no loss for want of matter," he noted. Rush was consulted, and the two mulled over the problems of the mission for many hours. "I told him," Adams pleasantly wrote in his diary, "I believed he must do as Sully did when he was sent to England by Henry the Fourth of France, and draw up his own instructions. At all events, I asked him to make a minute of all the subjects upon which he wished for instructions, which he promised." The document was finally finished on the sixth of November, and nothing more remained of official business to delay Rush's departure.

The navy had just launched two new frigates-of-war in 1817. One of these, the *Franklin*, was preparing to take its shake-down cruise to the Mediterranean that winter, where it would remain to relieve Commodore Chauncey. Rush conceived the notion of crossing to England in her, an unorthodox way for an American minister to travel, but in this instance convenient and possibly not without significance. Adams was at first reluctant. "I intimated to Rush himself a doubt whether some inconvenience to himself might not result from the impression which might be made by his going in that vessel; but he had set his heart upon going in her, and anticipated rather with exultation the impression that it would make in England." But as he reflected longer on the reactions in London to an American minister landing from a line-of-battle ship, a "bulwark of our holy religion," the Secretary began to see an object lesson to Britain on it.

The *Franklin* was at Annapolis where Rush could board her easily from the home of his wife's relations. On the sixth of November he said his farewells in Washington, but when he reached Annapolis he encountered interminable delays in provisioning and equipping the vessel. His own stores had been laid in at a cost of five hundred dollars advanced against his salary; now with one postponement after another he had to borrow another hundred and fifty dollars from his brother James. The provisions for his own party included food, wine, beer, livestock, fowls, vegetables, milk boiled and sealed hermetically, apples, flour, chests of dried fruits, medicines, and salted meat. It seemed enough for the whole crew. Finally after many vexations the ship was ready, and on the nineteenth the Rushes, complete with four children, a secretary, three servants, and a mocking bird (the gift of Mr. Secretary Crawford to Lady Auckland) stepped on board.

IV

A REPUBLICAN ABROAD

The ocean, Sir Humphrey Davy once remarked, though a noble dominion for nations, was a bad place for landsmen and worst of all for philosophers. Whatever claims he may have had to philosophy, Rush was certainly a landsman in 1817. This was the first time he had ever been on shipboard. Fortunately the sea sickness that was to plague him during voyages in later years did not appear, in spite of a severe storm only a few days out. Indeed, he was far too busy to be ill. Everything about the ship fascinated him. A frigate of two thousand tons, mounting seventy-four guns, carrying a crew of more than seven hundred men, raised plenty of questions in his active mind. Commodore Stewart, commanding, found his scholarly guest as eager for instruction as the youngest midshipman, though less likely than a midshipman to seek his instruction in quiet times and places. In the midst of the raging storm, while hanging on to one of the guns that had been run into the cabin to keep them from banging about the pitching deck, Rush began an investigation of naval warfare. "Commodore," he inquired, "What would you do if we were at war and an enemy of equal force hove in sight?" "*Chase him*," the Commodore answered. Rush was amazed. Give chase, when for ten hours the whole energy of the crew had been engaged in combating the storm? "Certainly you could not fight him?" he shouted over the din in the cabin. Stewart explained. Not in the storm, he admitted, but immediately it was over. Crippled and exhausted as they were, the rigging would go up faster than it came down. Such, Rush reflected, was war. And such was the gallant American navy.

To any lover of Franklin—and what Philadelphian was not in 1817?—the Gulf Stream was an absorbing topic. Rush's interest in it was heightened on this voyage, for it appeared to play him a mischievous trick. Laying a course direct for England, the *Franklin* left the Capes of the Chesapeake on a Sunday. To the amazement of everyone on board, a landfall was made the following Friday. Through some unaccountable error in navigation, doubtless exaggerated by the storm, the ship had reached Bermuda, hundreds of miles off course! The Minister considered this new and revealing evidence of the currents of the Gulf Stream; more likely it suggests a comment on Commodore Stewart's reputation as a navigator.

After four weeks' sailing without sighting another vessel they reached the Channel the fourteenth of December. Here nights were long, days damp, dismal, and overcast. No sights could be taken, no ship was spoken, no pilot came out to hail. There was much apprehension on the after deck, hardly allayed when it was discovered that in spite of their considerable records of service, not one of the officers aboard the *Franklin* had ever before been in the Channel. They proceeded by soundings, studying the scrapings which the lead brought up, hoping to sight Portsmouth or Cowes before disaster overtook them. Finally a pilot appeared, gloomy, taciturn, and moody, but successful in maneuvering the vessel through the difficult Needles. When they anchored at Cowes they learned the pilot was one who had been expelled from the guild for constant intoxication, and all the while the great frigate was in his charge had been drunk as a lord.

With such untoward incidents behind him Rush might have congratulated himself on keeping his family alive and reaching England, but his difficulties were not yet over. For some reason no order had been received from London to pass his baggage on diplomatic courtesy through the customs, so two days longer he had to remain on board, finally landing without baggage, to put up at the Georges Inn at Portsmouth until something could be done. A vigorous protest might have gained him exemption, but he disliked to begin his mission with a complaint, however trivial. The customs examiners at last decided to allow his trunks to enter, holding back one only as a bond. They happened to choose one packed with books. Any other selection would have annoyed Rush less.

A post chaise speeding over "roads like a floor" took the party to London. It was more than a one-day trip, necessitating a stop-over at Godalming where as a sort of thematic finale to a journey as filled with curious episodes as one journey might well be, Mr. Crawford's mocking bird expired. Rush had done his best, nursing it through all the long voyage, but either the rigors of the climate were too much for it, or perhaps more temperamental than its custodian it died of exasperation. Deprived of this member the family reached London on the evening of the twenty-first of December, in time to have dinner with Rush's sister, Mrs. Cuthbert, now a permanent resident of London.

On the twenty-third the new Minister paid his first call on Lord Castlereagh—"there was a simplicity in his manner, the best, and most attractive characteristic of a first interview"—and then set about to see the sights of London.

It was December, that is to say, everyone was out of town. The Prince Regent was at Brighton, Castlereagh was going there, English society was at home in country estates. Rush was soon to learn about the English seasons. September marked an era in the year, for it was the beginning of hunting. Once when he and Gallatin were negotiating with two British plenipotentiaries Gallatin suggested a meeting on the first of September. "Spare us!" cried the Englishmen. "It is the first day of partridge-shooting!" All through the fall and winter till after the Christmas festivities were over on Twelfth Night, the English gentry were to be found only in the counties.

The fog, another feature of London's December, lay over the city like a pall. Daylight began at nine, was over at four. In the murk and mist, "opake, dingy yellow," carriages crashed into each other, thieves plied their trade, pedestrians were run down or lost their way. Rush was "tempted to ask, how the English became great with so little daylight?" But even a London fog will lift, and on clement days he went enthusiastically about his sightseeing.

Everything was new to him. He had known only three or

four cities well in his life thus far: Philadelphia, Washington, Baltimore, Annapolis; none of these had prepared him for London. Tremendous in size, devoid (as he thought) of architectural beauty, planless, chaotic, and sprawling, it was of absorbing interest. His insatiable curiosity led him into every corner of the city; ultimately he came to know it as well as any native. He began at once to keep a journal, a task he had never before set himself but which for the next eight years he was to pursue with more or less regularity. Several times a week he would write long and detailed entries. He did not neglect his diplomatic work in what he wrote, but that, more effectively and more fully recorded in his dispatches, was obviously not the main purpose of his diary. The chief place he gave to the social and business life of the metropolis, his conversations with persons in public or cultural activities in the city, his experiences in traveling about the countryside. From his journals there emerges a colorful picture of England under the Regent, and of course a revealing picture of Rush himself. They were to form the basis of his subsequent publications, *Memoranda of a Residence at the Court of London*, the purpose of which was to improve Anglo-American relations; but in the jottings he made Rush was not so conscious of this ultimate theme. He wrote for the day only; his original journals are more vivid, less restrained than the published versions. They reveal the constant excitement of the writer; obviously Rush was wonderfully stimulated by the things he was seeing and learning in England.

For despite the half-remembered oratory of his Fourth of July speech in 1812, he went to England in 1817 prepared not only to learn, but to admire as well. As American Minister this was Rush's most distinctive characteristic. At a time when Americans and English were both suffused with mutual hates and resentments bequeathed them by the recent war, during a critical period in England, as an inflexible Tory party struggled with new industrial phenomena, his warm enthusiasm was an acceptable change from the austere and unfriendly appearance

John Quincy Adams had been unable to avoid giving. Not the least reason for his success in his mission was his personal enjoyment in it, his intellectual sympathy with the English.

The things that interested an American abroad in the early nineteenth century were things that had an importance for his own country—commerce, trade, finance, and the national policies regarding them. Yet England was a country of anomalies, which in the mind of a man like Rush were her most challenging features.

The stranger sees in England, prosperity the most amazing, with what seems to strike at the roots of all prosperity. He sees the most profuse expenditure, not only by the nobles alone, but large classes besides; and, throughout classes far larger, the most resolute industry supplying its demands and repairing its waste; taxation strained to the utmost, with an ability unparalleled to meet it; pauperism that is startling, with public and private charity unfailing, to feed, clothe, and house it; the boldest freedom, with submission to law; ignorance and crime so widely diffused as to appal, with genius and learning and virtue to reassure; intestine commotions predicted, and never happening; constant complaints of poverty and suffering, with constant increase in aggregate wealth and power.

London was the commercial capital of the world. This was a new experience in more ways than one. America had no commercial capital. Her trade was conducted through five or six seaboard cities from Boston to New Orleans. There was no single *entrepôt*. But London was the hub of trade for all the Empire. However empty the West End might be out of season, east of Temple Bar activity never ceased. Coal wagons, carts, vehicles of every sort thronged the streets in two constant streams of traffic, the horses coming so near the crowded sidewalks that "their hoofs, and the great wheels of the waggons, are only a few inches from them." The Thames at the foot of the hill was a black forest of masts and spars, as choked up with vessels as Cheapside and Fleet Street with vehicles and people. The shops stood "side by side, for entire miles." Even in the West End, where he had expected beautiful isolated mansions fitting the residences of the richest people in the richest city of Europe, Rush found "haberdashers' shops, poulterers' shops, the leaden stalls of fishmongers, and the slaughtering blocks of butchers, in the near vicinity of a nobleman's mansion and a king's palace," shops of all kinds where every conceivable article was displayed, "and all made in England, which struck me the more, coming from a country where few things are made."

The wealth of the "mechanics, artisans, and others, engaged in the common walks of business" was truly incredible. There were retail haberdashers who cleared thirty thousand pounds a year, brewers whose buildings and fixtures cost half a million pounds, silversmiths who were worth as much; there was a person in Exeter Change who made a hundred thousand pounds by selling razors, there were job-horse men who held in government bonds more than a hundred thousand pounds, confectioners and woolen drapers who had even more.

The working classes looked healthy, which was surprising in the crowded and dirty city, and were temperate in their habits. This Rush, who had inherited his father's temperance sentiments, thought must be partly the effect of the new tea houses springing up all over the city which, while they did not reclaim old drunkards, "diminished the stock of new by lessening the appetite for ardent spirits." The working people were to be found after the day's labor was over in the many parks about the city. These parks, a medical friend remarked, were the "lungs of London," little retreats, "many of them hidden amidst foliage, and showing the neatness that seems stamped upon every thing rural in England," which served the citizens "as places in which to breathe, after the pent-up air of confined streets and counting-rooms."

All about him Rush saw the picture of British opulence, the "anatomy" of British power, a power as venerable as the Tudor monarchs. Every building, every room, seemed to have such associations with the past as America could not afford. His country's heroes were of Rush's own time, or within his memory; Britain's were of antiquity. To be placed in a sort of tactile contact with Shakespeare, Cromwell, Milton, Pitt, and all the thousand others who represented England to him was a constant source of wonderment and veneration. Jeremy Bentham, showing him a house in which Milton had lived, found Rush so moved that he obtained for him a carved baluster from the staircase "which there was reason to think the hand of the great bard had often grasped." He dined with the Chancellor of the Exchequer in a room in which the elder Pitt had dined; Carlton House was for him peopled with the ghosts of a glorious past; portraits of men whose names were landmarks in the history of English law lined the walls at Lord Hardwicke's when Rush dined there. He found himself writing a treaty in a room in which the Duke of Monmouth had lived, at a desk on which Edward Gibbon had labored. "The English historical names as met in daily society, vividly arrest the attention of Americans," he remarked in his journal. The sure way to his heart was an anecdote of a famous person.

House-hunting was a discouraging task in London. A minister had to live in the West End, maintain a certain state, be prepared to give dinners and receive calls; but Rush's salary was small, almost the smallest of any of the diplomatic corps, and he had no private means. Rents ran from four hundred pounds up to many thousand for the year. This presented a real problem. After much vexation he settled his family in Marylebone, a new part of London where other ministers and ambassadors lived, which with its wide streets crossing at right angles to each other reminded him of Philadelphia. His house cost him four hundred and fifty guineas a year, a terrible drain, but he reminded himself that it was not for those "honoured by being selected to serve the Republic abroad, to complain."

While he was busy learning his way about, the real work of his mission had not begun, for little could be done officially before his presentation to the Prince. He had plenty of miscellaneous matters, however, to occupy his time. There were private claims which had to be presented in routine ways to the government, there were Americans resident or traveling in England who claimed continual attention, there were cranks who called to advise him about newspaper attacks on America or the dangers of British espionage. His letter packet always contained some requests for advice about emigrating to America, which annoyed Rush. "The bad subjects of Britain we do not want; the good, it is no part of my province to be instrumental in drawing away."

Finally after six weeks he received an appointment from the Prince Regent for the twelfth of February, preceding a Thursday afternoon levee. He was apprehensive about his conduct on the important occasion. Meeting the First Gentleman of Europe had unsettled many a diplomat more experienced in the ways of courts, and for Rush this was the newest of all his new experiences. He learned that the Regent did not like set speeches and preferred simplicity, but what was simplicity in terms of Carlton House? He fell back on some first principles: "A competent knowledge of the world may guide any one in the common walks of life; more especially if he carry with him the cardinal maxim of good-breeding in all countries—a wish to please and an unwillingness to offend." Armed with what self-possession he could muster he passed through the ordeal without mishap. He found the Prince gracious and kindly, as anxious as he for things to go right.

The ceremonies of the court, presentation and the many levees that followed, Rush thoroughly enjoyed. He had an eye for pageantry and color, and here amid sights which "the united capitals of Europe could not match" he found a magnificence and a graciousness that testified to English beauty as well as to her opulence and power. "Like old English buildings, and Shakespeare," he surprisingly remarked, "it carried the feelings with it."

Sometimes his democratic predilections reproached him for his susceptibility to the trappings of autocracy and royalty. He rationalized a defense; whether or not America ought to send ministers to Europe might be a debatable question, but certainly once sent they should "offer all the appropriate marks of respect which the usages of the world accord to sovereigns and those in immediate connexion with them." One qualification an American minister needed in England in 1818 was a tolerance of these forms of monarchy which were so much the target of American jibes against the Old World. In Rush there was more than tolerance; there was a sincere if somewhat sheepish relish.

Once he had been presented, his position as a fully accredited member of the diplomatic corps was established. The round of calls and dinners, so important a part of diplomatic work, began immediately. To the American Minister, particularly if he were of a sociable turn and gracious manners, all the houses of London were open, from Buckingham Palace and Carlton House, where he had entrée at the private doors, to those of the diplomatic corps, the cabinet ministers, the members of Parliament, and, most interesting of all, those of the leaders of London's literary and intellectual world. It was a remarkable opportunity for Rush, this carte blanche; it enabled him to study intimately and carefully those mainsprings of national character which had been responsible for what he considered the English miracle of commercial and naval supremacy.

Most entertaining and in a way most informative of all his social life was the intercourse he had with the aristocracy. The typical American attitude toward the British aristocracy was still formulated in the democratic environment of the American spirit, a compound of immense if surreptitious curiosity, fascination with titles and their owners, and suspicion that the noble class was fundamentally cruel and certainly expensive, contributing little useful to the nation. Rush soon discovered that theirs was more than an ornamental rôle.

In France [he wrote], before the Revolution, the noble families were computed at thirty thousand. In England, they may perhaps be computed at six or eight hundred. This handful does more of the every-day business of the country, than the thirty thousand in France. In France, they did the work of chivalry; they fought in the army and the navy. In England, besides this, you trace them not merely as patrons of the arts, but in road companies, canal companies, benevolent and public institutions of all kinds, to say nothing of their share in politics; in the latter, not simply as cabinet ministers, but speakers, committee-men, and hard-workers otherwise.

Whenever one went to a subscription dinner, whether for a Bible society, an infirmary for diseases of the eye, for the relief of decayed artists, a hospital for the care of the deaf and dumb, or a thousand and one other subjects of philanthropy, a peer was in the chair, another gave a toast, even a royal duke might be present. London's annual benefit banquets, those occasions that filled every tavern, hotel, or public house during the month of May, were the hobbies of the peerage. Rush attended them with relish. The Foreign Bible Society was presided over by Lord Teignmouth, with whom he worked in developing the Society's American interest; the Lord Mayor gave a dinner; the Royal Academy, where Rush was greatly moved to see his compatriot, old Benjamin West, in the president's chair as Sir Joshua Reynolds' successor, invited the diplomatic corps to its annual banquet, and elicited a speech from the American Minister. At a Burns Monument dinner Rush sat next to the Duke of York. Both had to earn their meal with addresses. "Do you give speeches at your public dinners in the States, as we're forced to here in England?" his Royal Highness wanted to know. Not hitherto, Rush replied, but it was a custom which tended to improve the character of public dinners by introducing excitements beyond those merely jovial, and ought to be encouraged. The Duke assented. He was, after all, a gentleman.

Rush marveled at the capacity to enjoy, to amuse, to trifle, to display riches and relieve poverty, to turn from the gaming tables to the annual banquets. It was the more remarkable, as the gentry of London pursued a rigorous schedule that would have exhausted persons of weaker fiber. Society, which included the diplomatic corps, consisted of a group of cliques and "crowds" that spent themselves in constant gatherings of innumerable kinds. They lived round the clock. For the diplomatic circle Lady Castlereagh gave a weekly supper after the Opera, which did not finish till midnight.

Parties beginning at that hour, last until two or three. Most of those who have been at them, do not rise until towards noon the next day. About two, commences the roll of carriages. At six in the evening, the *morning* ends. Then, scarcely sooner, the throngs of carriages, with gentlemen and ladies on horseback, disappear from the streets and parks, the hour of preparation for dinner being at hand.

Most of all Rush enjoyed the private dinners. These gave him the happiest memories of his life, memories of "hospitalities, that can neither pass from the mind, nor grow cold on the heart." He found them larger than he had known; Britishers did not follow Mr. Jefferson's rule of inviting "never fewer than the Graces nor more than the Muses," but usually had twelve to sixteen. At dinner the reservations and diffidence of the British disappeared, conversation was a wonderful and perfected art, which moved along under common contributions and restraints. "There is no ambition of victory. To give pleasure, not to try strength, is the aim." All dinners were alike in pattern, yet variations in the richness of the service or in the quality of the guests gave a savor to each one.

Of the scores of houses at which he was entertained, Rush noticed many things in common. The first and most remarkable characteristic was the opulence of the nobility. Wealth, prodigious and untold wealth, was apparent in the furnishings of every room. The portraits on the walls, the carpets on the floors, the vases, the mirrors, the tapestries left him agape. Silver services in profusion were on every table; the possessors were long accustomed to it and unconcerned,

. . . but the foreigner sees in it all, national as well as individual riches. Whence proceed, he asks himself, the incomes, so large, so increasing, that retain, and acquire in fresh accumulation, luxuries so costly, but from the land? and what would be the land with all the works upon it, what the crops on its surface, the mines underneath, but for the manufactures and trade which bring all into value by a vast and ever increasing demand; increasing at home as abroad, increasing in war as in peace?

This opulence was one of the manifestations of the greatness of Britain. It was a luxury far in the future for America, if indeed it ever had a place in her destiny.

Dinner conversation was in French. This, for the diplomatic circle, was the usual language, and once the unaccustomed habit was mastered, Rush began to learn as he never had known before the art of conversation. He was a little startled to discover that affairs of state were not taboo. Some things emerged at the table or in the hour (never longer) in the drawing room afterward which would not have come his way otherwise. The Neapolitan Minister, for example, introduced the subject of America's participation in the Black Sea trade—"all we desired was the opportunity" Rush told him—and someone else proposed the possibility of the United States acquiring an island possession in the Mediterranean. Why didn't America accept suggestions about affiliating with the Holy Alliance? This was a particular challenge to the Minister to discourse on the differences between the Old World and the New. In the midst of difficult and tortuous negotiations with Castlereagh about the West Indies Trade, which involved the preservation of the British colonial system, Rush had the subject thrown at him at dinner; but most surprising of all, when the American army occupied Pensacola he found himself questioned in social gatherings, despite the well-known serious tension between his government and Spain and England.

Simplicity was the quality he discovered most admirable in the aristocracy. There was a poise, a graciousness, an ease, a desire to please, that characterized everyone from the wonderful old Queen and the Royal Family on down. Even the royal dukes, those numerous and eccentric sons of George III, whom the world's opinion did not treat kindly, Rush found amiable, informed, and not unattractive. Cumberland inquired about the American language, how did it differ from the English in pronunciation and idiom? His duchess mentioned Mr. and Mrs. Adams, whom she had known in Berlin. The Whiggish Sussex paid a call, was eloquent in his ardor for constitutional liberty

—"I had not been prepared for quite as much in a prince of the blood, and prized it the more"—he spoke of Gibbon, of Addison, of the nonsense of using French as the international language, and displayed his own familiarity with many tongues.

The Family, like everyone else in London society, evinced a lively interest in America. Once in one of the palaces of George III (still living, though hopelessly insane) Princess Sophia Mathilda spoke with admiration of Washington, and the flavor of the situation did not escape Rush. Part of this interest was, of course, but the normal conversation an American minister met with among polite people, but part also was due to the changing opinion of America in educated circles of England. Republicanism was having its effect among those beneficiaries of the Metternich system, who were coming to recognize a theory as well as a threat. Once at a dinner with Lord Bathurst, when both the Duke of York and the Duke of Gloucester were present, talk turned on the United States. Climate, geography, government, products, steamboats, and slavery were discussed; on a point in geography one of the princes corrected an error Rush made. Both dukes were puzzled by the Senate and the Supreme Court in our constitution; Bathurst was hopeful of securing international coöperation in the affairs of the African Colonization Society. A constant source of amusement was the difference in language. Harrowby, Lord President of the Council and linquist of ability, was particularly attracted by the Americanism "lengthy."

Of course the navy was a favorite topic of conversation, and Rush acquired an interest in maritime affairs that was never to leave him. He was always delighted to record in his journals anecdotes he had heard of British naval history and the exploits of English officers, particularly of the noble classes, and he sought in the British nation those resources and that spirit which had been responsible for over two hundred years of naval tradition. The French wars had not diminished her naval strength, indeed they had enhanced it; she emerged in 1815 stronger on the sea than she had ever been. All the nations of Europe singly or combined could not make a force to equal hers. France and Russia were both anxious to build up their navies but had neither the essential sources of power nor the seamen trained in mercantile marine. Both together could not make as good a showing as the United States. As for steam, " 'that walks,' as Mr. Canning said, 'like a giant on the water, controlling winds and waves,' " Britain would introduce it to the world rather than be subjected by it.

The American navy by its exploits in the Mediterranean and in the late war had gained great respect in England, and the commercial position of the United States was being carefully studied. Britain and America were, the Chancellor of the Exchequer said, the two greatest maritime nations of the world. Rush was more avid on this point than he permitted his English friends to perceive. He followed closely everything published or said about naval policy, believing the day had come "when great Britain not only feels, but is willing openly to acknowledge the present superiority of our skill upon the ocean." This he confided to William Shaler, our consul at Algiers and longtime friend, and he added the assurance that America's navy would soon outdistance England's in other things besides skill.

This nation may build as we do; equip as we do; man, and work the guns, and train their men as we do. All will not answer while the energy of soul that springs from voluntary enlistment is wanting to their men, and that lofty-minded patriotism to their officers, which I firmly believe characterises, and will ever continue to characterise, in so much higher a degree, ours. Other things being equal, these moral considerations must keep the scale in our favor.

The unexpected expressions of regard for his country were always inspiriting to Rush; in a land that represented all he hoped America would one day become it was heartening to find such admiration for our still tentative achievements. But even the gratification of this patronage did not dissuade him from the conviction that America was morally superior to England. Her development in his lifetime was a proof of this.

The last forty years have witnessed . . . steady advance, in prosperity and power. Europe and the world behold both in proofs as irresistible. The enlightened portion of the world will also infer, that a nation with a foreign commerce overshadowing that of the greatest nations of Europe, England excepted; whose whole tonnage. . . already exceeds fifteen hundred thousand; a nation throughout whose borders the public liberty and prosperity have long been diffusing the means of private comfort and the lights of general education,—the enlightened everywhere will infer, that such a nation cannot be wanting in adequate intellectual advancement or social refinements, any more than in political power. They follow through the indissoluble connexion between causes and effects. Ingenuity and ill-nature hunting for exceptions, may find them; but the great field of excellence remains. It will continue to widen, until Britain herself, encompassed as she is with glory, will in time count it her chiefest, to have been the original stock of such a people.

The aristocracy, with its opulence, its charities, its projects, its liberal interests, and its curiosity concerning America, was but a small part of England. Its capital was London, but London was also the capital of British finance, British law, British science and art, the home of the great spirits of English liberalism and reform, the capital of the English-speaking mind. More and more Rush turned to these. His experience in Washington, his legal training, his intellectual animation, sought its natural level among men of his own type.

Nothing of public affairs so interested him as the financial success of the government. It seemed incredible that a nation which had just fought a twenty-year war, which had only a small indigenous territory, and had no particular reputation for efficiency and good management should be in the best financial condition of all the powers of Europe. Adams had expressed several times a little too publicly the conviction that only this miraculous prosperity of the government held the tattered fabric of the Tory "system" together. Rush was not disposed to criticize on the same grounds, but he did appreciate the importance of the financial success of the ministry. He had had experience of government budgets, he knew the problems, but not until Parliament adjourned in 1818 did he become conscious of the splendid opportunity for study in this subject. When he attended the dissolution ceremony and heard the Speaker observe that the revenue was increasing, Rush sought the facts. What was the source of the revenue? How much did each type of taxation yield? What were the exports and imports, the expenditures for arms and civil service? He was dismayed to discover that no one could estimate within fifty million pounds the extent of the national debt, though he guessed it to be eight hundred million, but still more surprising was the fact that British resources had increased even more than the debt, and the government could, at any moment, borrow from British capitalists sums larger than were ever raised before, could indeed on the strength of her credit amass a greater sum than all the rest of Europe put together. The opulence of Britain was best reflected in these government figures. What paralyzed other nations' resources seemed to fructify England's; she had learned how to unite commerce with war so that both would flourish together.

One reason, Rush decided, was that Britain's wars were never fought in Britain. "Moscow may be burned; Vienna, Berlin, Paris sacked; but it is always, said Franklin, peace in London." That war increased the wealth of Britain was the law of her insular position and her maritime supremacy. Mr. Vansittart, Chancellor of the Exchequer, bore the brunt of much of Rush's curiosity. What were the best books to study on English finances? Mr. Vansittart recommended Sir John Sinclair's, so Rush read it and sought out the author. He found him instructive and entertaining, an authority not only on British finances but on British agriculture as well, anxious to develop correspondence with American societies.

Rush's first love was the law; now he had a chance to study the English legal institutions of which he had written in *American Jurisprudence*. His impressions were somewhat more favorable than they had been then, his attention always alert. As he traveled in Kent he remarked the outward signs of the difference of this part of England, where *gravel kind* inheritance divided estates, from the rest of the country which adhered to primogeniture. The several attempts at assassination of officials or the Royal Family brought the realization that even assassins were not denied the protection of the law. "Whether the life of their King or the lowest subject be struck at, let the law have its course is the cry in England. Their code is sanguinary, but all are bound by it, all look up to it." Even the crowds in the streets seemed to conduct themselves with an inherent respect for orderly and correct procedure.

Some of his most prized acquaintances were lawyers and judges. One in particular was to prove an enduring friend. He was attending a reception at St. James's Palace when a stranger came up to him. With a stern look he announced, "I'm going to bring a bill into Parliament, making it indictable in any stranger, whether ambassador from a republic, kingdom or popedom, ever to leave his card without his address upon it; how do you do, Mr. Rush, how do you do? I've been trying to find you everywhere—I'm Lord Erskine!" Urbane, witty, jovial, the great Chancellor, then nearly seventy, was vastly appealing to the American. He illustrated, Rush wrote, the fable of youth peeping through the mask of age. "It was a treat to see so much genius with so much playfulness; such a social flow from one whose powerful eloquence had been felt by the English nation, and helped to change, on some fundamental points, the English law." Lord Erskine was a constant caller at the Rushes', a wise counselor to the Minister in moments of despair. Best of all were his anecdotes of Burke, Pitt, Fox, and the others of a generation gone by, men with whom Erskine had tilted when he was Rush's age.

Brougham, too, was delightful. His erratic and stimulating conversation left Rush breathless on their first meeting, which occurred at Jeremy Bentham's:

There was a quickness in his bodily movements indicative of the quickness of his thoughts. He showed in conversation the universality and discipline that he exhibits in Parliament and the

Courts of Law. The affairs of South America, English authors, Johnson, Pope, Swift, Milton, Dryden, Addison, (the criticisms of the last on Paradise Lost, he thought poor things); anecdotes of the living Judges of England; of Lord Chancellors, living and dead; the errors in Burrow's Reports, not always those of the reporter, he said; the Universities of Oxford and Cambridge; the Constitution of the United States—these were topics that he touched with the promptitude and power of a master. He quoted from the ancient classics, and poets of modern Italy, (the latter in the original also,) not with the ostentation of scholarship, which he is above, but as if they came out whether he would or no amidst the multitude of his ideas and illustrations. He handled nothing at length, but with a happy brevity; the rarest art in conversation, when loaded with subject matter like his. Sometimes he despatched a subject in a parenthesis; sometimes by a word, that told like a blow.

There was one subject which awed all foreign visitors and amused all Englishmen during that season; it was the famous wager-of-battle case, *Ashford* vs. *Thornton*. Ashford had accused Thornton of the murder of one of his family; Thornton responded with an appeal to the ancient right of trial by battle which though it had not been claimed for many centuries, indeed had not been thought of except by antiquaries and novelists, had never been repealed by statute and so presumably was still in the legal code. The Court of King's Bench conducted the trial with grave decorum. Rush had a place on the judges' bench, where he watched Lord Ellenborough in the seat of Coke, Hale, and Mansfield gravely hear learned argument whether a trial by battle could take place in the nineteenth century. It was a field day for English law. The court ultimately decided the battle was valid, never having been repealed. "Free government," Rush reflected, "is complex, and works slowly; tyranny is simple, and does its work at once." Of course in the end no battle was fought, for the law was as replete with technical flaws as it was with absurd survivals. "But the case marks an incident in English jurisprudence," the Minister noted, "having come near to converting the Court of the King's Bench into another Lyceum of Mendoza."

Of all the friends he made in Europe, few were so rich in knowledge, so full of entertainment, so ingenious, as the jolly and learned Sir Humphrey Davy, greatest figure in London's scientific world in 1818, chemist, philosopher, humanitarian. Rush was enchanted on first meeting, found him universal in his tastes, a scholar who epitomized everything good in English science, as well as a man of affairs influential in government policy. Among Davy's many concerns was the projected North Pole expedition, for which he was adviser to the Admiralty. He took Rush with him to inspect the polar ships fitting out at the Navy Yard at Deptford. They also inspected the dockyard, which Rush compared with America's, the Naval Observatory, and the seamen's hospital at Greenwich. The last was as grand as a palace: "Domes; single and double rows of columns; flights of solid steps; Corinthian porticoes—met the eye on all sides." Somewhat cynically the American Minister reflected that since most of the sailors on English naval vessels were impressed into service, it was only right that the government should thus care for them when they were no longer able to work.

Interest like Davy's in American science and humanitarian reforms Rush met also in William Wilberforce, whose fame as a philanthropist, abolitionist, and Methodist tractarian was as great in America as in England. Sir Benjamin Hobhouse likewise, president of the Agricultural Society at Bath, seconded all efforts for international coöperation. He had long desired "that the agriculturists of the two countries should correspond, exchanging observations, and the results of their experiments." He had already had much correspondence with Richard Peters, president of the Agricultural Society of Philadelphia.

The venerable Jeremy Bentham gave Rush great pleasure in his "unique, romantic little homestead" in the midst of the slums of Westminster. A quiet, unobtrusive person, Bentham displayed in conversation none of the involutions of style and esoteric diction of his printed works: these, Rush judged, were the faults of solitude. His observations on the United States were especially interesting to the Minister:

"Keep your salaries low," said he; "it is one of the secrets of your Government.—But what is this," he inquired, "called a Board of Navy Commissioners that you have lately set up? I don't understand it." I explained it to him. "I can't say that I like it," he replied; "the simplicity of your public departments has heretofore been one of their recommendations, but *boards* make *skreens:* if any thing goes wrong, you don't know where to find the offender; it was the board that did it, not one of the members; always the *board*, the *board!*"

In close sympathy with the liberals except in party politics was Alexander Baring, head of the firm of Brothers Baring & Co., the most important banker in England. Baring was a man of many activities. Intimate adviser of the Duke of Wellington, largely responsible for the adjustment of the French indemnity in 1818, he used his preëminent position in the world of finance to exert every influence he could to preserve world peace. Among the best-informed men in England, he was later (as Lord Ashburton) to play an important part in preventing war between England and America. Rush's acquaintance with him began on Baring's return from an extended visit to Paris, bringing with him an introduction from Gallatin. "You will find him a true and loyal Englishman but perfectly well informed on the subject of America," Rush read, "and with more friendly and liberal dispositions towards her than any of his countrymen, at least within the circle of my acquaintance." Baring's firm served as the bankers for the United States in London, which necessitated frequent conferences. All American legations and consulates in Europe banked with him, and one of Rush's routine duties was to adjust the credit of American continental establishments through him, for the London legation was a sort of clearing house for current accounts that would all be rendered to Washington quarterly. But Rush's connection with the versatile capitalist was soon to become much broader than a business relationship. The friendship begun in 1818 was to last until Ashburton's death thirty years later, and to prove continually a source of the greatest satisfaction to the American.

Resources for study and the acquisition of information Rush

found much more numerous in London than they had been in Washington. The newspapers particularly interested him. He could not have agreed, had he heard it, with the Duke of Wellington's remark, "owing to the ignorance and presumption and licentiousness of the Press, the most ignorant people in the world of military and political affairs are the people of England." He could scarcely credit that although he lived north of Portman Square, three miles from the House of Commons, the papers arrived at nine in the morning containing a complete account of the debates of the previous night.

Not only parliamentary debates but also the sittings and judgments of the law courts were subjected to the same public notice by the press. When Rush remarked to a judge on the smallness of the chambers for the court, he was told, "We sit every day in the newspapers!" There was a fearlessness in the press that would have put all London in a flame in the days of Wilkes or "Junius." "There are countries in which the press is more free, by law, than with the English," he noted, "for although they impose no previous restraints, their definition of libel is inherently vague. But perhaps nowhere has the press so much latitude."

"Every thing goes into the newspapers," he added: social news, private dinners, the goings and comings of the great and near-great; styles and fashions, tastes, opinions, and prejudices. Madame de Staël jeered at the English, living "with a window in their bosoms." Rush was to learn that some of the papers were for sale to foreign powers; he himself suffered bitterly at the hands of the Spanish in 1818 who were said to have bought five papers for the purpose of discrediting American expansion in Florida and winning the British public to their support against the rebellious South American colonies.

Clubs were particularly attractive to a man of Rush's friendly nature. Their antiquity was surprising to him; he learned with awe that the lights of White's had been burning continuously since the reign of Charles II. But neither this nor their social activities concerned him so much as their useful character. "The

London Clubs of the higher order are not associations for mere conviviality, but for intercourse upon a far broader scale; political, literary, scientific, dramatic, and objects more diversified." He had the freedom of several bestowed upon him, among them the United Service Club, splendid rendezvous of army and navy officers, the Traveller's and the Alfred. Sir Humphrey Davy gave him access to the library and the reading rooms of the Royal Institution where he, Brande, and Milligan were delivering their well-attended lectures.

All in all, it was an exciting place to live. For an American who was formulating the doctrines of a national "system" it was a wonderful experience, for it gave what seemed to be the true guides to national opulence. The planning of society, the charting of its future, the fostering of its arts and inventions, the mapping of the course along which riches lay, the social organization of a great people, required of a man who intended to take part in it a rigorous study, an appreciation of the best materials, a tolerance of differences, a willingness to accept the lessons that observations and reflection taught. Rush had known in America some of the problems of administration, but his experiences had been limited. Limited, not as one measures a public career, for indeed the passage from Treasury to Justice to State Department had varied his contacts and enriched his interests. But measured by the standard of a planned society, and the equipment necessary to men who would plan it, it had left many gaps. In England he was aloof from problems of administration, yet in a position that enabled him to view the whole picture of English opulence, English law, English finance, English letters, her navy, her industry, her liberalism, her constitution, her agriculture, her commerce, her nobility and her poverty, her municipal life, her laboring classes and her peasantry. It was the richest country in the world, the model for American ambition, the guide for her future, a fruitful laboratory for the student of national systems.

"A wise nation," Rush wrote Shaler at Algiers, "like a wise man, seeing how an adversary has got upon the vantage ground, will first imitate that he may in time surpass him."

V

AMERICA AND ENGLAND

The attractions of London formed a colorful backdrop for scenes in the diplomatic drama Rush was to play, but even in his most enthusiastic moments he could never forget the underlying animosities between his nation and Great Britain. Not three years had passed since public opinion in both countries had been inflamed with deep and bitter hatred; very little propaganda would be needed to bring anger and resentment again to the surface. Rush knew very well that the first crisis in their relations would set off a popular explosion.

True enough, the Tory government was stronger in 1818 than it had been even a year earlier, and in their firmer position the ministers were showing a desire to conciliate. Gallatin wrote from Paris that Whitehall displayed "a more favorable disposition towards the United States than had existed at any former period. At all events they have not for the present any wish to quarrel with us." In Washington, too, there was hope of a more amiable relationship. Time was working on Rush's side, and time, as Castlereagh remarked, could do much more to settle questions in dispute than diplomats. As the animus of 1815 faded farther away into the past, the possibility of a general treaty of the sort Adams had long had in mind seemed more plausible.

Here again the temperamental differences between Adams and Rush come to the fore. More placid as he was less discriminating, more graceful in social intercourse, more sympathetic to England, more susceptible to those elegancies and entertainments which had bored and sometimes shocked his predecessor, Rush was better able to sense subtle changes in public attitudes than Adams had been, and could deal quite freely with some whom Adams had alienated or repelled by his frigid austerity; thus as time was his ally, so likewise his personal characteristics helped Rush eventually to win a measure of that success which in 1817 seemed so far off.

As a diplomat Rush was an interesting contrast to both Adams and Gallatin. These two, poles apart in every way, had disagreed at Ghent, discovering their personalities incompatible, their methods entirely opposed. The urbane Swiss, however much he admired the American character on the frontiers of Pennsylvania or Virginia, considered it unsuited to European courts. He had, his son wrote, "a strong belief in the superiority of European intellect" over untrained American-born politicians, who were "a lot of rough colts who want breaking in." Adams he underrated, thinking "little of his talents and less of his manners." But a quality Gallatin lacked Adams had in high degree, namely, a sturdy American bias in his thinking, the bold faith in American destiny that could assert at once priority in the Western hemisphere and isolation from European political concerns. Adams' ambitions and his emotions were indigenous to America: all his travels and long residence in four European courts, far from diluting, had rather strengthened his nationalism; Gallatin's bias was international and European; his long residence and public service in America had changed him very little from the citizen of cosmopolitan Geneva. Their mutual lack of understanding resulted from the fundamental difference between Puritan Yankee and Puritan Swiss.

Rush was neither Back Bay Puritan nor urbane Genevan, but his plastic nature permitted him to combine the personal ease and gracious manners of Gallatin with the intense nationalism of Adams, and while he left no such impress upon the history of his times, though his career was equally long and busy as theirs, he was to accomplish some things that neither of his greater contemporaries alone was able to do.

Certainly Rush's attitude toward Adams as Secretary of State was far different from Gallatin's. The latter found the Secretary's communications disagreeable or annoying, resented what he thought were "Yankee tricks"; but Rush discovered in Adams, as he had in Monroe, an inspiration. A statesman of profound and various knowledge he thought him, a man gifted by inheritance, trained in service, "accomplished as a scholar, fervent as a patriot, and virtuous as a man." It was the strength of mind, the conscientious devotion, and the earnestness of the Secretary in Washington that motivated Rush, and if he moved more easily among Londoners of all ranks, winning victories that had been beyond Adams' reach, it was in part at least because he stood on the firm platform his chief had built for him.

Every day he gave to official business Rush ran into Anglo-American conflicts of many sorts, some the merest trivialities, others involving the very structure of the imperial system or the integrity of the American republic. There were private claims of American citizens against the British government, hundreds of them great and small; there were antagonisms of commercial interests intensified rather than allayed by the Convention of 1815; there was the vexing problem of slaves carried off by the British army and navy in the war; there were the old issues of impressment and fishing rights, which the Treaty of Ghent had failed to solve; there were boundary controversies, rivalries for the trade of the rebelling colonies of South America; these all disclosed the underlying "natural" antagonisms between two nations whose territorial possessions were contiguous, whose maritime aspirations clashed, whose common heritage of language and tradition beclouded rather than clarified the thinking of both.

Of these many problems there appeared no easy solution. Some were as old as American independence itself, some were the products of the War of 1812, still others had not yet become real but were visible in the future. Each one, however trivial or particular in itself, seemed to carry implications for the general picture of relationships which made its separate resolution impossible. This indeed was one of the serious difficulties. Even the most routine private claim that Rush had to present was likely to raise questions that soon brought the imperial system or the European alliance into the conversation. It was necessary to find some principles or rules by which various levels of controversy could be distinguished, to adopt procedures which would facilitate the handling of minor matters while the major were slowly addressed and possibly solved.

Distinctions like this were hard to make, but Rush perceived in the policies of Castlereagh a desire for good feeling that accorded with his own wishes. Where Adams had been suspicious and wary, he was willing to be open and hopeful. Nowhere was this better revealed than in his handling of private claims. These troublesome matters had to be pressed constantly, yet pressed if possible in such a way as to introduce no commercial or political issues beyond the private claim itself. Rush's method was to bring them one by one before the government, usually to Castlereagh's secretary, Mr. Joseph Planta, with the utmost politeness, stressing no principle but only the specific terms of the claim. Though some had persisted for a generation he got a surprising number of them settled, and as the years passed it became easier to remove this source of animosity. The help of Colonel Thomas Aspinwall, consul of the United States at London, who grew to be an intimate friend, was invaluable in this business.

And so through personalities rather than principles or rules progress was made. As he found the claims problem clearing up before his patient labors, Rush began also to feel optimistic about larger matters. As his acquaintance with Castlereagh ripened, he realized how sincerely that minister desired to improve Anglo-American relations. His good will and poised judgment was the counterweight to the welter of popular antagonisms and resentment. This had even impressed Adams, though it had never overcome his suspicions, and as Minister he had been wont to view every overture as an example of the studied hypocrisy of the British character. But in Rush, Castlereagh had not only an admirer who would place in him confidence and trust, but one who would communicate some of his feeling to Washington. He began with no preconceived opinions of British character, he ended with almost extravagant regard for the British statesman.

Robert Stewart, Viscount Castlereagh, was in his forty-sixth year in 1818, a slender, handsome man, "smiling, inscrutable and splendid," austere and reserved but capable of inspiring in others real affection. He could be winning when he chose to unbend. Rush was among those with whom, for the manners of the day, he was informal and easy. In their very first interview he was simple and straightforward, remarking that he preferred to conduct business with foreign representatives by conversations, "a course which saved time and was in other ways preferable as a general one to official notes." He was invariably frank in conversation, always committing himself a little farther than Rush had expected him to. Furthermore, in spite of his preoccupation with the business of Europe surrounding the conference of Aix-la-Chapelle in 1818 he was frequently available to the Minister. In the course of his first twelve months in London Rush had no less than thirteen fully planned interviews in addition to numerous conversations at dinners and on casual meetings. Nothing so perfectly reveals the new spirit Castlereagh brought to the settlement of the American relation than the quality of these conversations. Rush found every one a helpful, pleasant discussion the cumulative effect of which was not only to clear the air but also to establish the best type of mutual regard. He deeply appreciated "the candid and liberal spirit" in which the Foreign Secretary viewed American affairs:

Let those who would doubt it consult the archives of the two nations since the end of our revolutionary war, and point out the British statesman, of any class or party, who, up to the period of his death, made more advances, or did more in fact, toward placing their relations upon an amicable footing.

The whole diplomatic corps shared Rush's respect for Castlereagh's manners and affability.

If anything intrinsically unpleasant ever arose in the transaction of international business with them, he threw around it every mitigation which blandness of manner could impart; whilst to announce or promote what was agreeable, seemed always to give him pleasure. His personal attentions to them, were shown in ways which appeared to put out of view their coming from an official source, by the impression they made on the heart.

It was the Foreign Secretary's position in continental affairs that most interested the American Minister after his own concerns. Always sensitive as Rush was to the personal color and human values of the leaders of the world, he was aware of the earnestness and devotion of Castlereagh; he knew the isolation in which he lived, and knew also that this was the result not of a propensity to solitude but of absorption with his tasks and conscientiousness in his duties. He saw him not only in the Foreign Office but also in his home at Cray Cottage, where his delight in things rural struck a responsive chord; he saw him as a whole man, an able and tireless public servant, whose application and energy had given him a thorough comprehension of international politics. As always Rush was willing to learn; it was a valued privilege to associate with the Minister who in a rare burst of personal revelation exclaimed to his sovereign, "Sir! It is necessary to say good-bye to Europe; you and I alone know it and have saved it; no one after me understands the affairs of the Continent."

It was, naturally, with Castlereagh that most of Rush's dealings took place, and the Foreign Minister's preëminence among the cabinet members, both in Parliament and with the Prince Regent, made the others fade somewhat into the background. Lord Liverpool, the Prime Minister, he knew casually, and was not unaware of his peculiar strength. "Splendour of genius was not his characteristic," he slyly remarked, but he acknowledged that "History will view his administration as one of renown to England." After all, under Liverpool's supporting management of the Tory party in one of its most critical periods, Castlereagh had been able twice to dictate in the name of Britain the peace of Europe in the French capital. Of the other ministers he came to know Bathurst best, for he was closest to American affairs; but when he compared the British with the American administration he was not overwhelmed with the superiority of the English. Behind him was Adams, and behind Adams

Monroe, "a patriot and a sage." With this backing he felt no disadvantage.

The instructions Rush carried with him to London in 1817 were general, containing no positive order for the Minister other than to recur to the instructions given the commissioners at Ghent three years earlier. There were two treaties "unquestionably subsisting" between America and Britain: that of Ghent and the Commercial Convention of July 1815. But Ghent had avoided rather than solved the issues which caused the war; these latter still remained, while the commercial treaty was compacted for four years only, and under its provisions full satisfaction had not been obtained. The major conflicts of 1812 still persisted, therefore, and America was feeling the strain more and more as she expanded on her frontiers.

Four classes of issue were at hand, arising not so much from the two treaties as from the conditions that lay behind them. First there were disputes over our northern boundary and over fishing rights, and England's apprehension concerning American designs on Spanish Florida. Second, three questions arose under the Commercial Convention: equalizing tonnage charges and duties by appropriate legislation as called for in the treaty, renewing the whole Convention on its imminent expiration, and extending reciprocal duties to American ships trading with the British West Indies in spite of the ancient mercantilistic principles of the empire. Third, political questions of many sorts had to be solved to bring mutual understanding. Some of these involved merely differing interpretations of international law, others had grown out of the struggle for neutral rights during the war; but the most serious were the results of the isolation of America from the European concert of powers and the ignorance at Washington of the intentions of the sovereigns. Finally there were political questions that arose from rivalry on the sea and the accident of common language, chief among which was the dramatic issue of impressment.

American statesmen had long cherished the hope of seeing all these questions lumped together in one general negotiation, or at least enough of them to pave the way for definitive solutions of the remainder, and for two years before 1815 Adams had had a direction of full power to conclude

. . . a liberal and comprehensive treaty, to place the commercial intercourse between the two nations upon a footing of general reciprocity, and to settle, by positive and definite agreement, the principles with regard to the search of neutral vessels, to the list of articles of contraband, to the neutral right of trading with the enemies of a belligerent party and with their colonies, to the doctrine of blockades, and, above all, to the pretensions upon which, in the late wars, the British naval officers followed the practice of impressing men from American merchant vessels on the high seas, upon which the rights of the respective parties should in the future be understood to rest.

Under his powers Adams had presented (September 17, 1816) four considerations to Castlereagh to be embodied in a pact supplementary to those existing. He found Castlereagh willing to discuss impressment and inland trade between the United States and Canada, but the West Indies trade and questions of neutral rights on the sea in time of war he unequivocally outlawed. Adams insisted on these points with such constancy that for the remainder of his mission nothing substantial was done, although Castlereagh did (March 1817) present a draft of four articles as a basis of renewed conversations. But neither party was willing to go far enough to establish common ground, and there the matter stood when Rush arrived.

He began slowly with his many tasks. There seemed little he could do on the larger issues, so he occupied the first four months of his mission introducing special proposals, revealing himself the while to the Foreign Secretary. Two matters he brought up at his earliest opportunity. The first concerned slaves carried off in British ships after the War of 1812 for which America asked indemnity as provided in the Treaty of Ghent, but England, putting a different construction upon the phraseology of the treaty, refused payment. It was, Rush insisted, purely a matter of grammar. He proposed the selection of a third power as umpire, as suggested by the treaty, and Castlereagh acceded to the principle of mediation, indicating that the whole machinery of the Treaty of Ghent should be adopted. He urged upon Rush, and significantly this was the first British proposal for lumping various matters into one negotiation, that commissioners and umpires might consider the slave question and two of the boundary questions together in a general pact. Rush was forced to refuse on the ground that the loss of the slaves was a palpable injury, while the boundary disputes were ancient, ill-defined claims, but he closed no doors, nor did Castlereagh, who gave assurances that compensation for slaves would be acted upon separately even if the proposed mediation encountered obstacles.

The second matter of immediate importance was the reduction of duties growing out of the Commercial Convention of 1815. The Convention had provided for the equalization of duties on American and British imports in the United States and the British Isles, but Britain had not yet abolished those levies she was obligated by the treaty to remove. Rush broached this problem, and Castlereagh promised to secure compliance with the treaty, which over the course of several months he was able to do.

Meanwhile Castlereagh himself sought from the new Minister some report on the President's opinion of the four articles he had submitted concerning the West India trade. This question was critical, for unless England made some concession on it there would be no point for the Americans in renewing the Commercial Convention. Castlereagh had informed Adams that the government would be entirely unwilling to relax the provisions of the imperial system, but his four-point draft had made these concessions: that certain free ports for American ships be established in the Caribbean; the Bermuda trade be opened entirely; certain loads of cotton and tobacco be permitted annually at Turk's island; and the Canadian commerce be partially opened. Public interest in the United States on this matter was intense, and though British commercial interests represented by men like Thomas Wallace and William Huskisson were willing to throw all the colonies open to the Americans, relying on the increase in trade to make up the loss in revenue, the ministry and most of the Parliament still adhered to the letter and spirit of the mercantile system.

Rush was forced to say that the proposals would probably be considered unsatisfactory, and present as the only possible counter-proposals complete freedom in colonial trade. Castlereagh responded with an explanation of the colonial system; to this Rush answered that the American doctrine, adhered to since Washington's time, required that even the least opening of the commerce to American ships implied the right of America to participate in its regulation, and that if no satisfaction could be obtained Congress would be forced to interdict the trade altogether. What America wanted was equality, and if she could not have an equality of advantages she would enforce an equality of disadvantages.

It was not encouraging thus two months after his arrival in England to be forced to reject a proposal which, however inadequate, might have alleviated the tense feeling between the two countries; but Rush was not yet aware how determined Castlereagh was to win American good will. It was something of a surprise to him when the Foreign Secretary introduced two other problems. Apparently desiring to find some matters which could be separately treated and settled, Castlereagh mentioned conflicting claims to territory which lay outside the provisions of the Treaty of Ghent, particularly the northwest boundary and the Columbia River settlement, for both of which negotiation had been recommended in 1815 but never carried through. These, Castlereagh said, were of no immediate importance but were the source of probable future differences and might well be removed.

Rush was deeply impressed by Castlereagh's attitude. The foresightedness that would seek out causes of discord and correct them before they had come to a head he deemed liberal and large-minded statesmanship. Though he had no instructions on the points raised, he concurred in the desire for adjustment, and communicated the proposal to Adams. He recognized that its significance was not in the boundary question itself but in the intimation coming from Britain rather than America that there were questions not yet at issue between the two governments that might form part of a negotiation.

Thus by April both Rush and Castlereagh had made overtures pointing toward a general treaty. Rush in following Adams' line had got no farther than his predecessor, but Castlereagh by selecting other matters to treat of had successfully distinguished among all the issues those which the British could discuss, on which there seemed some possibility of agreement. As to the latter Rush was continually more sanguine than the situation warranted. Eventually he had to give up many points, and always they were points which Castlereagh had originally rejected or discouraged. But Rush had made an important contribution of his own. By his genial and frank manner and his willingness to trust the British minister he had succeeded in separating from the web of American policy those concerns that involved only Britain and the United States from those which were bound up with Latin America, Spain, and the Holy Alliance.

Rush had let the proposal for a general negotiation rest for several weeks, when on April 11 he saw Castlereagh at his own request and reopened the matter of a comprehensive treaty covering the whole relationship of England and America. Whatever he was expecting as the maturing of his suggestion of boundary negotiation, this was certainly more than the British Minister could agree to. For the next few months his part was continually to restrain the American, until finally he got the terms of the negotiation narrowed down into manageable form. Rush on the other hand just as vigorously resisted, pushing always for a more extensive treaty. He deemed it necessary to reach an understanding on neutral rights, blockades, and contraband before the great issue of impressment could be clarified.

In shaping the outlines of the Convention of 1818 the point of impressment was an axis about which both men revolved. Castlereagh was willing to discuss the problem in general and limitations on the taking of seamen in particular, but entirely refused to consider neutral rights or related parts of the maritime code. The British cabinet would never forego the right of a British officer to board and search an American vessel. America's policy, on the other hand, included a willingness to allow only natural citizens to serve in the merchant marine if Britain would give up its pretension to search our ships. The American Minister knew his Vattel. He informed Castlereagh that only in England did the laws of citizenship assume a perpetual allegiance on the part of subjects. The question was peculiar as between the two nations, for common langauge was at the root of it. The maritime code of England would result in a *mare clausum*, he insisted, and America was determined to defend a *mare liberum*. It was a vigorous plea Rush put forward, and he found Castlereagh sincerely anxious to have the question settled. Though both realized the unlikelihood of reaching a satisfactory compromise, the American proposal that both countries prevent each other's seamen serving in their navies and merchant marines was accepted as a tentative basis for conversation.

Further delimitation of the terms of the negotiation now devolved upon Adams who, after Congress recessed in April, was able to give a larger share of his attention to the problems. He found it difficult to believe that Castlereagh was in earnest about a settlement that had been so often refused, but there were enough signs in British policy to convince him even against his biases, and he began laying the foundations for success. Very little in the way of effective understanding between the two nations could come, he declared, until they reached an agreement on two points: the first, that whenever England and the Alliance were intending actions on the Spanish colonies which would interest the United States, he might be informed of them in advance; and the second, that the West Indian trade regulations be adjusted satisfactorily. These sources of discord could be removed only by restating the relations between England and America. Therefore he authorized Rush to propose (five weeks after he had actually done so) "an immediate general negotiation" of a new commercial treaty, including the colonial trade and other subjects already in discussion, namely, the slave question, fisheries, the western boundary, and the Columbia River mouth. He would be joined in negotiations by Gallatin, who would come over from Paris. "We entertain hopes that this measure may result in a new treaty which will remove most, if not all, of the causes of dissension between us and Great Britain," he added. The free port bill already in Parliament and the successful end to the Passamaquoddy Islands adjustment in Washington augured well for these hopes.

Thus by the end of May Adams had defined the American ground in spite of his skepticism. He continued suspicious of Castlereagh, particularly of his silence on Spanish intervention, but he felt that America, having passed a retaliatory act against the British colonial system but having at the same time offered "the hand of liberal reciprocity" to counteract it, was in a strong position. The more letters he wrote on the subject the more the Secretary seemed to fluctuate between sanguine hopes and what was almost indifference, for apparently he believed the retaliatory law equalizing the advantages of trade made it unnecessary to bargain. Gallatin, when he learned of his part, was not so discouraging. Though there would be difficulties, he had confidence in the friendly disposition of the British government.

In London Rush and Castlereagh continued their talks regarding impressment throughout June and July. They reached the expected impasse, at which the cabinet refused to give up the British right to search American vessels, and the Americans refused a settlement which would surrender the inviolability of her ships, but each continued to search for further possible grounds of agreement. When Adams' instructions arrived they were found acceptable to the cabinet, and on the twenty-third of July a general negotiation was agreed to by the British. Castlereagh made three final gestures to smooth the way: he assured Rush that the European powers had not as yet formulated any intentions of intervening in Spanish affairs, he held out some hope that the British colonial system might be modified even though it could not be destroyed, and he proposed that the Convention of 1815 be separately renewed to guard against delays or obstructions. To the last Rush acceded, with the observation that

... in the trade between two countries, the United States are likely to have their equal share as carriers, as long as the charges upon the vessels of each continues equal. That is all that the United States ask. It is the offer they make to all nations. They hold it out in a permanent statute, as the basis of their code of navigation.

Frederick Robinson and Henry Goulburn were chosen as the British plenipotentiaries. Robinson, President of the Board of Trade, afterwards Viscount Goderich and Earl of Ripon, had been one of the British commissioners at Ghent in 1815, and was therefore well known to Gallatin. He was an easy-going, affable individual, much dependent on men like Wallace and Huskisson in his administration of the Board of Trade, "advanced in his ideas," with no "insular prejudices," a delightful companion with whom both Rush and Gallatin liked to deal. Goulburn was less prominent and less "enlightened" but "very amicable and pleasant." Meanwhile Gallatin was expected momentarily, his departure waiting only the receipt of full powers. Rush was naturally delighted with the prospect of entertaining his old chief. He set aside the whole second floor of his house for his guests, not deterred by Gallatin's requirements of "a parlour, four master bed-chambers, two Servants d°, the use of a kitchen & that of a bed, table & kitchen furniture." On August 16 the Paris party arrived, among them young red-headed James Gallatin, whose lively diary throws some oblique lights on the course of the negotiation.

Since the conference at Aix-la-Chapelle had been postponed till September 20, Lord Castlereagh was still in town and anxious to have business begin before his departure. His first step was to propose two modifications of the British stand on impressment which while in themselves unacceptable gave nevertheless such encouragement that the subject was again brought within the pale of the discussion. His second move was to place the whole negotiation on an informal and friendly footing by inviting both British and American plenipotentiaries down to North Cray for a week-end. Rush, enjoying to the full the company of Gallatin, traveled the sixteen miles of Kentish countryside with delight and interest. He found Cray Cottage a worthy study in itself, with its menagerie of exotic animals, its thoroughbred sheep, and its well-tailored gardens.

Castlereagh's sincerity was revealed in his welcome. He told the plenipotentiaries he had a great interest in the negotiation, important as it was to both countries. His Majesty's government, he added,

earnestly desired that every question which had led to past misunderstandings, might be amicably adjusted at this season of peace, so as to lay a foundation of stable harmony for the future; he trusted that the aim of each country would be to advance, as far as compatible with its own rights and interests, the just rights and interests of the other. In short, said he, let us strive so to regulate our intercourse in all respects, as that each nation may be able to do its utmost towards making the other rich and happy.

Having started the conferences off, Castlereagh was not yet finished with his gestures of encouragement. On August 29 the delegates agreed that the British should spend a week preparing articles on impressment, the Americans on maritime subjects; Gallatin and Rush determined that these questions should be discussed together or not at all. Three days later a note was delivered asking Rush to call at Lord Castlereagh's home at once. Rush went in haste, to find carriages and drivers at the door, the Foreign Minister about to set off for Dover on his way to the European conference. He had put off seeing Rush until the last moment, he said, yet he had a communication of the utmost moment to make on impressment. The cabinet had after some discussion agreed finally to waive the right of a boarding officer to call for a list of the crew. The satisfaction of this news was heightened for Rush by the busy scenes of imminent departure about him. He agreed with Castlereagh, that once the principle was settled, viz., on America's engaging not to employ British seamen the practice of impressment would cease, details could be adjusted without difficulty later. Rush was delighted with such a fair prospect "of laying this great controversy at rest." As he picked his way among the traveling boxes he reflected (so he wrote President Monroe) that Castlereagh "may have deemed it best to go off, in his semi-sovereign capacity, unfettered with such prospective embarrassments upon the ocean from a quarter so formidable as the United States, in the possible contingency of England intending to take any high tone at the Congress."

Eventually he was to change his opinions of the significance of Castlereagh's absence, but certainly when conversations opened on the fourth of September everything had been done that could give genial atmosphere and hope of success to the negotiation. Castlereagh had not missed a single trick.

The Foreign Secretary's departure occurred just as the real work of negotiation was getting under way. From the fourth of September for six weeks the four plenipotentiaries met constantly to debate the twelve subjects before them, preparing between meetings articles and protocols on each question. The Convention of 1818 which emerged and was signed on the twentieth of October was a compromise. It was an improvement over the Treaty of Ghent, for it settled some issues and cleared the air on all; and it was better than Adams had hoped for. But its achievements were measured by its failures. Ultimately impressment and the West Indies trade had to be given up. Rush's disappointment at this outweighed his satisfaction at the successful conclusion of five important questions. The ideal of a comprehensive adjustment of all outstanding issues together with authoritative agreements on neutral rights and contraband trade that would write into international law for the first time acceptable definitions of these controverted points had not been reached. "It settles at best but a few of the many disputed points between the two nations," Rush told Caesar

Augustus Rodney. "We shall go on I trust husbanding our resources, pecuniary, naval, and military, as the safest means of our future welfare. All is tranquil now; but it cannot last, and among the governments of this old world we are never to look for friends."

There were solid achievements, nevertheless, of the greatest significance to both countries. The first of these was the fisheries question. Off Newfoundland lay the Grand Banks, where New Englanders had been accustomed to fish for a hundred and fifty years. This privilege had been guaranteed to Americans in the Peace of Paris following the Revolution, but the British claimed this treaty had been abrogated in 1812 under the rule that any treaties subsisting between two powers are nullified by mutual declarations of war, and therefore the whole question of the fisheries had to be considered again from the beginning. Where British territory had always furnished a base for American fishermen to gather stores or to dry their nets, they were already forbidden to trespass. The growth of population in New Brunswick and Nova Scotia had brought serious international rivalry; the Americans needed legal protection to enforce their claims. Adams argued (thinly enough) that the Treaty of 1783 was exempt from the general rules of international law, for it was not a pact between two powers, but the creation of a new nation, the independence of which was not impeached by subsequent wars or treaties. Both English and American arguments seemed merely academic in the face of the seriousness of the situation. The British plenipotentiaries were armed with memorials and resolutions of their colonials, while feeling ran so high in the New England states that the fisheries came near being a cause of war. Rush, Adams, Castlereagh, Robinson, Goulburn, and Gallatin all perceived the necessity of reaching some adjustment that could be defended to both peoples. After much discussion it was clear that each side would have to surrender something to effect a compromise. Rush hit upon a satisfactory adjustment, and on his protocol the final article was based. The United States "renounced forever" the right of fishing within three miles of colonial coasts (with stipulated exceptions), a phraseology designed to make the whole more palatable to the British public but of no practical importance to American claims, for fisheries extended beyond the three-mile coastal reserve in almost every place concerned. The word "forever" was opposed by the British, but the Americans under their instructions could not sign without it. Rush traded the renunciation clause for British concession on this point, a significant victory in his opinion.

On the whole the Americans were completely satisfied; from a weak claim they had emerged with more than anyone had expected. But popular clamor against the article rose to threatening heights in England and the colonies. This the cabinet resisted with firmness, knowing that settlement of this issue would avert an open if undeclared war; nor did they conceive that the article as it stood impaired the honor of the "essential interest" of either country.

A second achievement of the convention was the adjustment of the boundary line between the United States and Canada from the Lake of the Woods to the Rockies, which was placed at the forty-ninth parallel. The British made the same claim they had at Ghent for navigation of the Mississippi, but when accurate maps disclosed that the Mississippi nowhere touched English possessions they perforce gave it up.

As for the Columbia River mouth, and the boundary from there eastward to the mountains, no precise agreement could be made, but a temporary arrangement was concluded providing for joint settlement of the disputed territory, with equal trade and navigation rights. Rush regretted that nothing permanent had been achieved, but, as he said, "something was gained" in mutual satisfaction and the postponement of controversy. The Oregon question was to live for many years.

The fourth article of the convention extended for ten years the commercial pact of 1815, by which "reciprocal liberty of commerce" was established between America and England, based on equality of duties and tonnage charges in both nations. This was the original, simple purpose of the negotiation which Rush had been empowered to conclude regardless of other subjects on the agenda, but in his mind its renewal carried implications beyond immediate objects, for it preserved a tradition of the highest importance in American idealism.

The parts of this convention [he wrote] which establish an equality of duties, are liberal and wise. That the interest of nations is best promoted by discarding jealousies, is a truth which, in the abstract, few will question. But they should be discarded reciprocally, without any of the reservations for which favourite interests will always plead. Whether such reciprocity will ever be found compatible with the separate existence of communities, and all their separate rivalries, is the problem. The doctrine hitherto has been known but little in the practice of the world. The United States, as one of the family of nations, did their part, at the commencement of their history, towards giving it currency; not always however with the success that attended this convention. Its provisions seemed to serve as a model. Within short periods after it went into operation, Denmark, Prussia, the Netherlands, Hanover, Sweden, and the Hanseatic cities of Hamburg, Lubec, and Bremen, formed treaties with Britain, adopting wholly, or in part, its regulations. In some of the instances, I have reason to know that it was specially consulted as the guide. . . . Such appears to have been the influence of its example.

Final achievement of the pact was the arbitration of the question of slaves carried away by British forces in 1814. The Emperor Alexander, chosen umpire, decided in favor of America, and eventually after many delays the matter was settled agreeably to both nations.

This was the substance of the Convention of 1818. The problems it solved were serious, the solution of them an important step toward a permanent peace between England and America. But two great groups of questions remained unanswered. They were the ones on which Rush had spent the most labor, and by which he had set the greatest store. The first was the opening of the colonial trade to the same reciprocity that existed between America and Great Britain. In this matter the Americans were actually proposing that their ships be admitted equally with Britain's in the trade of Canada, Newfoundland, and England's island possessions in the Caribbean. Rush recognized the unlikelihood of his proposals being accepted. "It seemed unreasonable to say that Britain must not be left to foster, by high duties, as she saw fit, the productions of any part of her own dominions," he admitted. "But unless the United States took this ground, they could secure no substantial reciprocity to their own vessels in carrying on the trade to be arranged." From what had transpired between Castlereagh and Adams on this question, it was a foregone conclusion that little could be done. Britain did make some offers, in a paper carefully prepared by Lord Bathurst, but the instructions Rush and Gallatin had would admit no middle ground. Of all the questions at issue, on this one alone America would not compromise. Though he tried every possible rationalization of his arguments, Rush was shooting at the moon, and he knew it.

Even more disappointing to Rush was the failure to secure an article on impressment. This was due in part, he believed, to the absence of Castlereagh, who had proceeded with "noble fearlessness" before his departure, and who certainly would not have permitted the question to remain unsolved. But without his commanding presence, Robinson and Goulburn were unwilling to go any farther than the cabinet.

This peculiar issue, with which was associated so much tragedy, stood in a compromise attitude as negotiations opened. Rush presented two articles, that both nations should prohibit the nationals of the other from serving in their employ, and that impressment should thereupon cease. Castlereagh annexed two conditions, that the article should be revocable on short notice by either party, and that should any British officer boarding American vessels for lawful purposes in time of war find British seamen in it, he might make a procès-verbal of the fact to be presented to the American government. It will be recalled that Castlereagh had modified the latter condition just before leaving London by surrendering the right of the boarding officer to call for a list of the crew. Apparently, however, he had not reached an entire understanding with his plenipotentiaries, for their draft of an article was unacceptable to Rush and Gallatin.

The British draft embraced the exclusion of nationals, except those already enlisted; the listing of the latter, and the exchange of such lists; the renouncing of impressment, and the separation of this article from all others. Robinson expressed a profound desire to give satisfaction on the question, and as a matter of fact, considering how jealously Britain had clung to the right of boarding, how reluctantly she had given it up, this article seems an unexpected, welcome liberality.

But the Americans did not feel free to accept it. Two objections proved fatal to the plan. The first had to do with the proposal to list those British-born naturalized American citizens already serving in American vessels. Rush pointed out the inadequacy of American registry and court records, the impossibility of supplying the date and place of naturalization in every case. He made a substitute proposal, that proof of naturalization supplied by the seaman, if his name did not appear on the list of those naturalized, should be accepted by the British. This he felt ought to be satisfactory, particularly as Britain could annul the treaty at will whenever she thought it violated. The second objection was over the time of the treaty taking effect—whether at its signature or at its ratification.

Both of these objections appear now so minor as to be almost foolish. So much had been gained, so near an approach to a solution won, that differences such as these could have been eliminated by constructive statesmanship. Rush and Gallatin were not entirely to blame for the failure, because their instructions limited them on these points. Then too, the whole question had been refined so much that minor issues had assumed an importance all out of proportion to their true value. A little wisdom, a little freshness and realism, would have brushed these minutiae aside, and the principle once accepted, that impressment was to be abolished, details, as Castlereagh had hoped, would have been quickly settled.

Along with impressment, all other maritime questions were also dropped: blockades, contraband, trading with colonies of belligerents, prize courts, letters of marque. A splendid opportunity was thus lost for the formulation of a code of international law that might have wrought marvelously in the nineteenth-century world.

This world was already making changes in morality that affected impressment. Rush knew that eventually it would be abandoned as a British policy. He predicted that "the horrors of the *press-gang*, and the horrors of the *slave ship*, will be spoken of in the same way. British moralists will depore it; British orators denounce it; British legislators extirpate it; and British historians, in recording its long existence as a remnant of barbarism and tyranny, utter sentiments of sober joy at its downfall." Not a decade later, as a matter of fact, a reform administration of the Admiralty did abolish it, and though unsettled as a point of international law, impressment passed into the forgotten realm of bygone causes. In spite of the importance Rush attached to it, it was an evil peculiar to the age, brought into being by England's adversity in the time of Napoleon, persisted in because of America's inability to resist. It was already by 1818 a matter for the law books rather than the law courts. Rush's discouragement might better have been given to the failure to define neutral rights and prize claims, for these were issues that would remain as long as nations fought upon the seas.

It had been high pleasure for the Rushes to have Mr. and Mrs. Gallatin with them, even through the dullest months of the London season, in spite of an illness that afflicted Mrs. Rush in October and in spite of disappointment in their work. The collaboration of the distinguished elder statesman had strengthened Rush's morale and sharpened his wits, though the somewhat academic character of Gallatin's thinking had left its mark upon the treaty, as Adams observed. Returning to Paris before the formalities were concluded, Gallatin kept his ear to the ground to report what he could learn of the goings-on at Aix-la-Chapelle. If the Congress of Sovereigns determined to intervene between Spain and her colonies it would mean an entire change in relationship between America and England. On this serious problem hung almost every other issue.

But in his very first letter Gallatin had good news for Rush:

My correspondent at Aix la Chapelle writes to me, that Lord Castlereagh has communicated to the ministers of the other Powers what had passed, on the subject of the Spanish colonies and of the sentiments of the United States with respect to them, between him & Mr Rush, with whose frank and friendly declarations, made by order of the President, he expressed himself perfectly satisfied; and that his Lordship added his belief, that the independence of some of those colonies would be recognized during the next session of Congress, & deprecated the idea of interfering with that subject in any shape likely to produce a misunderstanding with the United States.

This was grand news for Rush. Castlereagh's earlier assurances had been welcome, but had failed to convince either the Minister or Adams. Now, however, optimistic hopes of mutual understanding seemed justified. The storm of criticism still raged out of doors; London papers were reviling the fisheries clause and the boundary settlement, Americans were discontented over the West Indies trade. But the cabinet, Castlereagh particularly, was ignoring popular protest, insisting on finding the best rather than the worst in the situation.

A severe test of the sincerity of both sides followed hard upon the heels of the Convention. Had it come a year earlier, Rush thought, armed hostilities could scarcely have been averted; but by the work of 1818 the spirit of resentment, jealousy, and anger had already been enough allayed so that an explosion could burst in the critical land of Florida yet not become the detonation of a war.

Florida, still an appendage of the crown of Spain, was in a state of lawless turmoil which the weak Spanish government was powerless to subdue. American and British trading interests struggled with one another and with the Indians; the whole region was a prize for the strongest contender. In the course of a surprise march across the border, General Andrew Jackson captured a fort, pursued Chief Billy Bowlegs into a swamp, arrested and executed as spies two British subjects, one a dignified, kindly, and righteous old Scotsman, Alexander Arbuthnot, trader, friend, and counselor to the Indians; the other a British lieutenant of marines temporarily rusticated for dueling in India, by name Robert Ambrister, in Florida seeking adventure.

The right or wrong of this affair was less important to the governments concerned than the use that could be made of it. The King of Spain, desiring help in preserving his southern empire, saw it as an opportunity to turn Europe against the United States, he also conceived it gave him an advantage in bargaining for the treaty he was negotiating with America. Opponents of the administration at Washington sought to score against Jackson by the cry of "Murder." British public opinion, already antagonistic to America, was enraged. Alone in the Washington cabinet, Adams defended the executions and Jackson's expedition, rising in two state papers to his greatest heights of argument. This imposed upon Rush the hardest job of all, for he had to convince the British ministry of the justice of the affair, and encourage at the same time the attitude of non-intervention which had been urged by Castlereagh at Aix.

The Foreign Minister was prostrated by gout following his return to London. He received Rush three times in his bedchamber, listening carefully to the proofs he offered of Arbuthnot's and Ambrister's guilt. He seemed convinced, for he wrote Bagot in January 1819 that the "unfortunate sufferers" had certainly been engaging in unwarranted activities, and had forfeited any claim to support from their government. Rush was complete satisfied with Castlereagh's liberal and calm attitude. But even the Liverpool ministry could not ignore the public excitement. Throughout the winter and spring a veritable storm raged, the opposition making the most of every trick. When the

House of Representatives in Washington conducted its investigation, and speeches denouncing Jackson were published in full in the London journals, Castlereagh was put in the faintly ridiculous position of defending the execution of two Britishers by an American general, while Americans themselves condemned it. Lord Lansdowne determined to move consideration in the House of Peers, and though he had Rush in to dine he notified Liverpool of his intention.

Two events saved the situation. A vote of censure was defeated in the House of Representatives, and the Spanish Treaty ceding Florida was signed at Washington. Rush was still worried and angry over British feeling, however; he confided his resentment to his journal on learning of the Spanish Treaty:

> The English papers raise a clamor, charging ambition and rapacity upon the United States. They say nothing of the acquisitions which England has been making in all parts of the globe, by her arms or policy, since the days of Elizabeth and Cromwell. Even if we were to show some tincture of this quality, still, as her own children, disposed to act in her own spirit, her journalists might make allowances; but, in fact, we acquire Florida by fair treaty; we give Spain the *quid pro quo* to the uttermost farthing; and the last thing that I anticipate is a complaint from a mind like Lord Castlereagh's.

That Minister, indeed, was using all his influence to keep the peace. When Lord Lansdowne in May moved consideration of the affair, Bathurst and Liverpool successfully opposed him. This marked the end of the crisis, which Rush had found painful; the transaction had "cost me much solicitude, and I hailed, with unmingled satisfaction, its favorable issue."

But it had served its purpose. It had disclosed the sincerity of the King's ministers' professed desire for improvement in American affairs—"how often," Rush remarked, "have nations been thrown into collision through slighter causes?"—and their willingness to act with "wisdom and firmness . . . to get the better of a wide-spread clamour . . ." As late as July Castlereagh told Rush that the case of Arbuthnot and Ambrister had been one of uncommon difficulty; he hoped the United States government would draw the "proper inferences" from the "conciliatory dispositions" England had revealed.

He then added these words: That had the English Cabinet felt and acted otherwise than it did, such was the temper of Parliament, and such the feeling of the country, that he believed WAR MIGHT HAVE BEEN PRODUCED BY HOLDING UP A FINGER; and he even thought that an address to the Crown might have been carried for one, BY NEARLY AN UNANIMOUS VOTE.

Years afterwards Rush repeated this conversation, ending with an appreciative sentence:

The lapse of a quarter of a century ought not to diminish the feeling properly due to a British ministry which, by its single will, resisting the nearly universal feeling of the two great parties of the kingdom, in all probability prevented a war; a war into which passion might have rushed, but for the preponderating calmness and reason in those who wielded at that epoch the executive power of England.

VI

THE OLD WORLD AND THE NEW

The free press was an undoubted blessing in Anglo-Saxon civilization, but it was as hard to live with as a candid friend. Rush was deeply wounded by the unsparing journalistic attacks upon him and the United States which the Convention of 1818 and the Arbuthnot-Ambrister Affair evoked. Ministers from other lands, accustomed to ignore the press or to buy it, were less vulnerable in this respect: so long as they could secure what they wished from the government, they cared little for irresponsible outdoor opinion. But they were career diplomats, members of a distinct profession with both national and European traditions; the American diplomat was by contrast an amateur. "Diplomacy is really not a profession, or career with us," the American consul at Leghorn wrote; one post did not lead to another, in a progression of graduated awards. We sent aboard private citizens who would return to private life, or public men who would return to face the electorate, and none, least of all gregarious Mr. Rush, was able to confine himself entirely to the esoteric negotiations of statecraft.

Every New World official in the Europe of Metternich and Alexander was a spokesman for democratic principles of social organization and republican principles of politics that gave the lie to the myth of (armed) peace and (paternalistic) liberalism of the Holy Alliance. Russell in Sweden, Irving in Madrid, Shaler in Algiers, Campbell in St. Petersburg, like Gallatin in Paris and Rush in London, were in a characteristically American fashion interested in the people as well as the government of a nation. When the people of these nations turned against the government of the United States, which should have been their spiritual and intellectual ally against absolutism and repression, it was more than a matter of practical politics, it was a challenge hurled at the theoretical moral superiority of revolutionary philosophy.

Rush was not insensitive to the discontents of the common people of England and the government's attitude toward it. He noted the stir caused by the trial of a printer for republishing Paine's *Age of Reason*, which the court declared a libel on the Holy Scriptures; Manchester workmen were in open revolt, labor disturbances were increasing, agrarian troubles spreading everywhere. Castlereagh, with all his brilliance, had little care, the American Minister recognized, for civil and political liberty. His policies and the opinion that supported him were unsympathetic to that democratic creed which was in America the tradition of government but in England the most sinister radicalism. The sensational "Cato Street Conspiracy" in the winter of 1819–20, a plot to assassinate most of the government, gave dramatic indication of the extent of the unrest. Domestic social upheaval was not a factor in diplomatic conferences, but it had a part in determining the direction American relations with the Old World would take.

He knew very well also that the opposition outside Parliament, even journalistic, expressed much better than Lansdowne and his Whiggish peers the liberalism and enlightenment of England. Despairing of winning back for himself or his country the sympathy of this reform group, and depressed by his chronic financial troubles, he wrote Monroe that he wanted to resign and return to the government in Washington.

But Monroe, innocent of moodiness himself yet infallible in dealing with it in others, answered with enthusiastic praise, heartily approving all Rush had done, and pointing out with some justice that the Convention of 1818 had laid a better foundation for good feeling than any Anglo-American transaction since the Revolution. Rush was overwhelmed by this unexpected testimony of the President's regard. It was, he wrote, the most grateful reward he could have. "It adds more than I can express to the happiness of my life. It attaches me to my mission beyond anything else that could have occurred, and I shall start afresh in its duties."

Praise came from British authority as well. Early in 1820,

when death released old George III from his pitiful half-life, resident diplomats had to present letters of credence to the Prince Regent in his new rôle. The King went beyond the formalities of the occasion to commend Rush for his success. He remarked that the American's conduct

. . . had been always in the spirit of conciliation since I had been at his Court; and that there were occasions when the exercise of such a spirit had been useful, and acceptable to this Government. He remarked further, that he would not rest content with directing his Minister (turning to Lord Castlereagh who stood by him) to tell me so, but was happy to take this opportunity of saying so to me in person.

Castlereagh, who had prompted the King's gracious speech, expressed his satisfaction to Rush.

The accession of George IV wrought no significant change in British national policies, but it did seem to signalize the new spirit in international relations. George III's had been a reign of wars; from the last years of the Seven Years' War through the American Revolution and the great struggle of two decades against France, the biography of that unhappy monarch was strewn with battlefields. The new reign coincided with the peace which had been delivered of such travail, and which the restored governments of Europe seemed so determined to perpetuate. "There never was a time in the history of the world," Lord Liverpool asserted in the House of Lords, "when so general an anxiety prevailed to preserve peace; when the causes of disturbance were so completely removed; when nations and sovereigns were more divested of ambition and the love of undue influence, and when the spirit of conciliation and the necessity for repose, were more thoroughly acknowledged and acted upon over the whole European community." To British and continental statesmen the preservation of this peace, delicately poised above conflict of wills and resentments, was the principal object of governmental policy. "Europe requires repose," Castlereagh said in conversation one night; "each state has had enough of war, and enough of glory, and ought to be content."

And then he added, "You too, YOU of America, Mr. Rush, ought also to be satisfied; you left off very well, and ought to wish for nothing but a continuance of peace."

But the European peace, conceived in reaction and supported by the military power of the Holy Alliance, had little in common with American ways of thinking. True, American statesmen were heartily in favor of peace in the abstract, and declared themselves willing to sacrifice their "peculiar interests" for "principles of justice and progressive civilization"; but deep in the hearts of Monroe, Adams, and Rush lurked the conviction that "progressive civilization" could never be achieved by the Holy Alliance or the European Alliance (which they usually considered as two blades of the same pair of scissors), and that, while the "clannish spirit of the sovereigns" prevailed, no policies truly liberal in the American sense would emerge from the armed camp of European reaction. The official view of this Adams and Rush had developed in the instructions Rush carried to London:

Europe may be said to have been recently new modeled, and its principal governments are leagued together for the purpose of maintaining through all its borders the state of things which they have established. The operation of this system in all its parts, the resistances which it has to encounter, as well in the internal struggles of each of the allied nations, as in the elements of discord never extinguished between the parties to the compact themselves, its effect upon the civil liberties of the individual subjects, and upon the political independence of each of the nations thus associated, are deserving of the most scrutinizing observation.

His scrutiny was of absorbing interest, but it caused Rush to feel aloof from the international conflicts raging about him, like a spectator at a play. He expressed the feeling, common, he supposed, to every minister of the United States abroad, "of entire independence of the combinations and movements going on among the other Powers, no matter what may be their nature." Now that sustained negotiations between America and England were over he realized how far apart the interests and purposes of the two countries really were. An index of this was the distance between him and the Foreign Minister. One night at the French Ambassador's Castlereagh met Rush going in to dinner. "Why, Mr. Rush," he said, "I have not seen you these hundred years!" "My misfortune, My Lord," Rush replied. "It is a proof," declared Castlereagh, "how smooth the waters are between our two countries"; and he might have added, it was a proof how wide the gulf was that separated the concerns of America and Europe.

The gulf had its bridges, of course. There were important factors of relationship that persisted even after the concert pitch of 1818 had subsided; some of them repeated a familiar pattern. Three in particular cost Rush and Castlereagh considerable trouble. The first was the serious question of the arming of Indians on our western frontiers by the British in Canada. The second was more threatening, though in its origins ludicrous: a clash between American sailors and British soldiers at Gibraltar. Several duels were fought, and an affair seemed likely to develop which might destroy the whole structure of Anglo-American coöperation in the Mediterranean. William Shaler, with the help of Rush, was able to smooth it out, preventing thereby ill will which at a critical moment might have removed the British influence in Spain for the ratification of the Florida Treaty. The third was the suppression of the slave trade by international policing of the seas. This subject was the most popular humanitarian issue of the day. On its behalf the energies of Wilberforce, Lansdowne, and a host of abolition societies had commanded government support, so that England throughout Rush's mission was continually seeking American collaboration and adherence to a multiparty treaty. The negotiation was a long one, included (as we shall see) in the conversations of 1824, and not finally terminated until the Webster-Ashburton Treaty of 1842.

But of far greater importance were the factors emphasizing American separatism from the European state system, factors cast in a new mold that would require new measures and new attitudes to deal with them. The Treaty of Vienna, that spectacular display of ex cathedra statesmanship, had left no place for republicanism in reconstructed Europe, and the four congresses of the clan of sovereigns from 1818 to 1822 each moved the control of power farther to the right. The Holy Alliance, under Metternich's tutelage, became the armed guardian of ancient tyrannies. The New World, where the fruits of revolution were allowed to ripen, contemplated this progress of dismal absolutism with alarm and with what Adams termed "confidence in the superiority of our political institutions." Every congress furnished an occasion for interested American diplomats on the sidelines to renew their sense of independence from the European order.

At the first stated meeting, that of Aix-la-Chapelle in 1818, the most critical question of all was raised, whether the sovereigns should intervene with military force to pacify the colonial revolts in Spanish America. Gallatin, keeping Rush informed of the deliberations, prophesied that intervention would fail; he proved to be right, and both he and Rush congratulated themselves on this favorable outcome. But neither expected it was more than a postponement of the issue, for the tone of the Congress in other matters had not been liberal. By the attempt to change the French election law and impose "a retrograde system which would check the progress of liberty" in occupied France, Gallatin was shocked and offended. "In every point of view it is very fortunate that the attempt should have failed," he averred. The American observers were not unprepared, in consequence of this policy, for the protocol of Troppau in 1820 threatening intervention of the Powers to suppress revolution anywhere, or the French intervention in Spain in 1823 following authorization of the Congress of Verona. These were but incidents in the course of policy the Alliance was explicitly adopting, a course entirely opposite to everything America stood for.

As the Alliance developed its interventionist position Castlereagh distinguished for England a separate policy opposed to intervention, which on the face of it might have won a response in America. Indications aplenty existed that the British Foreign Secretary would welcome New-World coöperation: his helpfulness in the Convention of 1818 and his amiable attitude during the Arbuthnot-Ambrister Affair; his pleas for candor and good will in diplomacy; his anxiety for an agreement on the slave-trade convention. Further assurances came at Aix-la-Chapelle, where he not only opposed intervention but secured consent for England and France to invite the United States "to take some measures in concert with them to suppress the piracies carried on under the flag of the [South American] colonies or of some persons pretending to exercise an independent jurisdiction in some portion of the colonies." He seemed on every occasion solicitous of the opinion of America, and once again to Anglophiles the vision glittered bright of even more than a full understanding with Britain.

But Rush was not naïve enough to accept these indications unquestioningly. Like Adams he recognized that England would pay no very high price for American friendship. The factors of interest separating the two nations were quite as significant as those dividing us from the European Alliance, and they occupied an even larger place in Rush's thinking.

With dismay he studied the falling off of American trade in Britain, a decline that seemed all out of proportion to the general economic depression in Europe. From 1815 to 1818 nearly five hundred American ships had arrived each year in British ports, but in 1819 there was a sudden drop. Only a handful appeared, and 1820 brought slight increase. The thread of direct commerce that had stretched across the ocean seemed to be cut. It would mean a reorganization of their trade by American merchants, for the capital available had to seek other outlets.

But wherever they turned, the Americans met British competition. Because the West Indies question remained unsolved Americans were still at a ruinous disadvantage in the Caribbean trade. Rush made another vigorous effort at adjustment there, presenting to Castlereagh a new *projet* based on the negotiation of 1818 providing for important compromises on every disputed point. The President was anxious, he assured the Secretary, to see the trade "opened upon a footing of entire and liberal reciprocity, rather than suffer it to stagnate; or to be crippled by countervailing laws and regulations." Nothing came of the effort, however, so British commercial superiority was maintained.

As in the West Indies, so in the harbors and bays of South America British and Americans met as competitors, with the advantage England's. Rebellion opened opulent markets and rich productive regions that England captured with twin weapons from her industrial armory: the cotton gin and the cannon. Americans had made some efforts to join in the adoption of Spain's fugitive children, private aid had proceeded on a small scale. But the merchants of New York, New Orleans, Charleston, and Philadelphia could not overcome the convincing salesmanship of the presence of the British navy.

Admiral Cochrane, he of bitter memory in Washington, had a squadron of a dozen royal ships in Latin American waters, where he engaged in lucrative liberation. Rush and Shaler, exchanging what information they had concerning this "new field" for American expansion, lamented the opportunities already missed, others being neglected. Brazil was gone to Britain, a Washington correspondent told Shaler; "an ambassador is of about as much use at that place, as at Timbuctoo." Everywhere else England's navy had got the jump on us. Rush realistically considered this the nub of the matter. He forwarded to his friend at Algiers a pamphlet recently printed on naval techniques, discovering in the science a threat to American commercial ambitions. "Every thing which touches this subject, whether immediately or remotely, I am in the habit of viewing as of the highest publick importance," he wrote. By failing to match England's building and training program we were allowing our strength on the sea to dwindle, by failing to use our ships the same way, for the same purposes, we were losing the new southern economic empire.

This whole shifting picture of the intercourse between England and America was before Rush constantly. Every incident seemed to clarify the fact of change and the need for a revision of policies. In the midst of challenging problems Castlereagh's encouragement for coöperation offered America only Britain's leadership, with but small promise of satisfaction on outstanding issues between them. The conviction of an independent destiny was stronger than this, and was reinforced by every contact. Both bent on peace, the two nations would follow different roads to reach their goal.

The separation of America from the Old World was the underlying, controlling fact of Rush's situation from 1819 to 1825. In this respect his eight years' residence at the Court of London divides itself into two periods. The first year, with the Commercial Convention, belongs to the era of post-war settlement that began at Ghent and Vienna. The theme of this era was general peace; the diplomats in these years were directed sometimes by forces they neither represented nor comprehended to the reconciling of differences and the harmonizing of ends. Thus peace between America and Britain had been established without real agreement on the issues outstanding between them that had caused a war, but the Commercial Convention and the several commissions set up by the Treaty of Ghent gradually solved some problems and erased crucial differences. This era lasted through 1819.

Then began a new period, in which the forces within each nation pulled in opposite directions, and for the theme of world peace substituted a new pattern of conflicting national interests. The general was replaced by the specific; after a period of exhaustion and confusion, a welcome period of recuperation, there began again the old game of power politics, increasing in tension and tempo as each nation recovered its old ambitions or reasserted new. Probably it was inevitable, certainly it was not to be halted or controlled by any individual or any group, for it was a political expression of deep, complex currents within nations and peoples. A diplomat in such circumstances can do no other than the nation itself, which must state and effectuate, not abstractions of universal morality, but "practical conceptions of national interest arising from some immediate exigency or standing out vividly in historical perspective." These practical considerations are not formulated by statesmen. They are expressed and interpreted by them, but they have their origin in "the hopes and fears, the aims of security or aggrandizement, which have become dominant in the national consciousness . . ." Rush's job in the diplomatic environment of George IV's reign was to voice the national interest of America.

It gives some insight into his mind to realize that he did so with fair success. Had he left none of the revealing diaries and letters that help us evaluate him as a statesman, we could still judge him on the basis of accomplishment. That he resisted the overtures of England for American coöperation in these years, that he observed and reported the crystallizing of the policies of the European Alliance, that he conducted the negotiation of particular disputes not on the basis of world policy but rather on that of American aspirations and expansionist claims, all disclose the extent to which he accepted the ruling ideas of his generation and his nation.

During the years 1819 to 1825 England's separation from the European coalition was completed, the reactionary character of the Alliance was settled, France's power was reëstablished, Spain's empire was lost. Confronted with bewildering alternatives, America chose the only one which was sharp and clear in its outlines: a national policy independent and distinct from European or British leadership. It was the decision which permitted the revolutionary plant to reach maturity, and it was a decision first made not by statesmen but by the people themselves, pursuing their own internal concerns energetically and confidently, with eyes turned west and north rather than east and south. The political climax from the American point of view came in the celebrated doctrines of separatism pronounced by Monroe in December 1823.

The events which fulfilled this underlying historical purpose were not interrelated on an obvious plane, nor did all of them concern Richard Rush. Those which did cross his career, however, were crucial. They were the Spanish Treaty, the accession of Canning to the Foreign Office, the Greek revolt, the Monroe Doctrine, finally the discussions of 1824 with British commissioners that failed to reach a treaty. One after another they successively defined and emphasized the new international order, so that slowly the emerging alignments of power became crystal clear.

The first issue on which these developments turned was the collapse of the Spanish empire. By 1819 the Latin American revolts had become a subject of the keenest interest to every European power, the principal issue in international relations. The nations of the Alliance, presuming to defend legitimacy, were challenged on their own ground. England was torn between commercial interest and political commitments, America was confronted with an opportunity to realize some of her expansionist dreams at once. But her opportunity was limited by English and European attitudes. If she consulted only her own ambitions, she would be defying the power of Europe, but if she allowed England and Europe to control her course, she would be turning aside from what many Americans already considered her continental destiny.

Our Spanish relation had been brought to a climax by Jackson's raids in Florida, which occurred in the midst of negotiations at Washington for a transcontinental treaty adjusting the boundary line between Spain's colonies and the United States from Atlantic to Pacific, and ceding Florida to America. The weakness of the empire, the refusal of England or continental powers to come to its aid, constrained Madrid to accept Adams' explanation of Jackson's conduct and to continue the arduous negotiations. Though Rush had heard reports of Spanish belligerence, which he communicated to Washington, Gallatin assured him they were based on nothing more than "the cupidity of persons formerly concerned in privateers, and who wished to be ready to prey on our commerce in case of hostilities taking place between us and Spain." However foolish statesmen at Madrid might be, he continued, folly would not go so far as to commence war with the United States at that moment; indeed every step of Spain indicated a disposition to preserve peace.

... the determination to cede Florida to us though not on admissible terms, an application made to France, (since our rejection of the mediation of Great Britain,) that she should interpose her good offices, and various other occurrences might be adduced as evidences of that disposition. If you add to these the critical situation of Spain with respect to all her American colonies, and the still doubtful issue of her protracted negociations with Portugal, it appears almost impossible that there should be any solid foundation for those rumors of an approaching rupture with us, which have been spread both in England & in France.

Rush was greatly concerned about these rumors, as he tried to learn England's attitude toward our proposed treaty. Gallatin advised him as early as March 1818 that Britain would try to prevent our acquisition of Florida; as news of the progress of the Adams-Onis conversations crossed the seas, London journalists became excited. "They are for the great allies watching & keeping us in order," Rush wrote Monroe. "Should it ever be a question whether one or more of them might be suffered to break down our independence, or even annihilate us as a people, we may easily guess if there would be any interference for our protection?" He heard, he added, that the fiery Spanish Ambassador, the Duke of San Carlos, had the newspapers brought to him every morning while still in bed. "If Spain be kindly dealt with, he takes his dish of tea with a relish; but if the United States, he springs up, and hurries across the floor, brandishing his wishes that the writer's head was off!"

Through the summer and fall of 1818 England's attitude toward Spain and America was uncertain. Our rejection of her mediation made even more serious Spain's application to the Holy Alliance, and when armed intervention was refused at Aix-la-Chapelle there still remained the question of agreement on principles. In February 1819, Rush and Castlereagh talked the issue over. Emphasizing America's neutrality in the colonial revolts, Rush declared we had performed scrupulously the duties of a neutral party, but now the time had come when justice to Spain, to the new independent governments, and to European interests required recognition of Latin American nations. He announced the President's intention of recognizing the government at Buenos Aires at once. Castlereagh responded with a frank statement that England had no intention of recognizing the colonies, that he considered it as necessary to appease this controversy as to appease all others which threatened world peace, that he could contemplate no other solution than restoration of Spanish supremacy, that while he opposed intervention by force, England's "moral power of opinion" would support Spain's determination to regain the colonies by her own efforts on her own terms. He regretted that Britain and America were not in agreement on the whole issue. As for aid privately given the South American colonies by British citizens, nothing could be done by Parliament to suppress it as yet, but certainly they proceeded at their own risk, and would not receive the protection of the British government.

The extreme differences in the points of view represented were soon to be refined away by the progress of events. Five weeks later Castlereagh informed Rush that the prospect of mediation was definitely at an end, Spain having declined all offers. "He remarked that the inference from all was, that Spain had now resolved to rely upon her own efforts by sea and land, and on the supplies of her own treasury, for putting down rebellion throughout all the dominions of Ferdinand." While this changed not at all the position of the United States, it did, as Rush recognized, eliminate the possibility of England's appearing in behalf of Spain in mediation that would prevent our Florida Treaty from going through.

This conversation was on March 21, 1819. Just four days later news reached London that the Treaty had been signed in Washington and ratified at once by the Senate. There was an immediate outcry against America in the English press, pro-Spanish interests were angered, liberals who hoped for peace accused the United States of international piracy. But, as Rush expected, no complaint came from Castlereagh. England not appearing as mediator, her interests lay elsewhere than interposing difficulties in the way of Spanish-American friendship. A few weeks later the Duke of San Carlos gave a dinner for the diplomatic corps, where he took occasion conspicuously to congratulate Rush.

His approach to me for this purpose a minute or two after I entered the room, as his guest, was with a grace noticed by some of the diplomatic corps; none of whom, probably, were strangers to the diplomatic coolness between the two nations at Washington, before the treaty was concluded.

The end was not yet, however, for only America had ratified. The Treaty provided that ratification by both parties had to take place within six months of the signing, that is, by August 22, 1819, for it to have effect. The Spanish King, Ferdinand VII, though his word had been pledged to "approve, ratify, and fulfill whatsoever might be stipulated and signed," was making difficulties. For nineteen uneasy months muddled politics at Madrid drew the attention of European foreign offices and American ministers. Pressure one way or another from England, Rush thought, would come near ending the whole matter. He was constantly on the alert, therefore, to learn Castlereagh's attitude.

Rumors flew thick and fast that spring and summer. It was hard to tell just what Britain was doing. The Foreign Office took very seriously Rush's announcement regarding recognition of Buenos Aires: a special courier was dispatched to Madrid with the news. Soon thereafter Parliament passed the Foreign Enlistment Bill intended to prevent private aid to the South American revolutionists (May 1819), during the debates on which Castlereagh surprisingly declared the government owed the House and country an apology for not adopting the measure earlier. It was meant, Rush believed, as "something in favor of Spain, nominally at least," an earnest of England's good will toward Ferdinand. There was frequent talk of England or France receiving Cuba from Spain in exchange for positive aid, and though Onis denied this when he stopped in London on his return trip from Washington, and San Carlos scoffed at it, the rumor persisted. Most serious of all was the surmise that England was encouraging Spain not to ratify within the stipulated time limit. If this were true it would change the tone of America's relation to Britain and make Castlereagh's protestations concerning frankness in diplomacy an obvious sham.

So many of the diplomatic corps suggested this to Rush that he finally put a point-blank question to Castlereagh. He received a point-blank answer. The difficulties, the Foreign Secretary said, whatever they were, "rested with Spain entirely"; His Majesty's government "neither had done, nor would do, any thing whatever to prevent or retard, its ratification." This unqualified assurance Rush relayed at once to Adams, to Gallatin, to Shaler, and to Forsyth, our new ambassador to Madrid, on the eleventh of August. But that there were difficulties behind the scenes at the Spanish capital was obvious, for though Forsyth made the strongest representations of the fatal consequences that would ensue the nullifying of the Treaty if ratification did not occur, Ferdinand still delayed. August 22 passed without action; the Treaty was therefore inoperative.

Castlereagh took pains to exhibit to Rush proof positive that England had advised ratification. France, too, and even Russia, satisfied Monroe they had had no hand in Ferdinand's surprising obstinacy. As he observed the English picture Rush convinced himself this was true, for in spite of the Foreign Enlistment Bill a huge expedition was fitting out at Dublin under General Devereaux (of Baltimore, Maryland) to go to the aid of Venezuela, and British authorities did nothing to enforce the enlistment law.

Spain was actually delaying in hope of securing from America a promise not to aid or recognize the South American colonies. Her explanations of her position were so inadequate that Monroe, submitting the documents to Congress in December, termed them a new and serious injury, threatening that the United States might proceed to carry the Treaty into specific execution, for "any measures on the part of the United States which a strong sense of injury and a proper regard for the rights and interests of the nation may dictate" were justified to maintain national honor. No commitment could be given regarding the revolutionary governments. Rush communicated this position to Castlereagh, who made no particular comment.

In January 1820, a revolt of the army in Spain forced the King to accept the liberal constitution of 1812. News of this reached London in May, and formed a topic of conversation for Rush among the pallbearers at the funeral of Sir Benjamin West. Prospects were somewhat better as a result of the new government. Monroe once more stated the American position, Castlereagh and Liverpool both vigorously denied any intention of moving in behalf of Ferdinand against the Spanish republicans. Leaders in Spain realized that to continue the delay would be to incur extensive damages for injuries; finally in October the Cortes and the King yielded. On the twentieth of the month San Carlos informed Rush that the Treaty had been ratified. Forthwith he dispatched a courier to Liverpool with a letter "to go by the first ship, for the chance of conveying the information to Washington, before it can arrive direct from Madrid."

Early in 1821, when the Senate passed its ratification a second time, the Treaty became law. The satisfaction with which Americans greeted this conclusion was unallayed by scruples of international delicacy. The far-flung boundary extending our territory to the South Sea added a dramatic persuasion to the widened view of a continental destiny. There were two ways of looking at American expansionism: English opinion might cry piracy and rapacity, might accuse the United States of territorial aggrandizement; but to Americans the capitulation of Spain was a triumph of the New World over the Old, of liberalism over reaction, of American policy cast in American, not European molds.

I

The separation of England's policy from those powers that may by 1820 be called the Neo-Holy Alliance complicated rather than simplified America's diplomatic problem. A united European system was a concrete entity to be categorically resisted; a Europe at odds within itself, torn by state competition and conflict, could not be treated categorically. Europe and England, pulling apart from each other, both offered friendship to America, no longer for the ends of peace but now for the ends of power. Rush began to feel more and more Britain's lack of sympathy for American aspirations, the dominance of strictly national motives in her polity. He could not regard her separation as actual dissent from the principles of the Continental Alliance; rather he deemed England "positively or negatively, auxiliary to the evils with which this Alliance under the mark of Christianity has already affected the old, and is now menacing the new world." The feeling grew; watchfulness passed into outright suspicion.

This suspicion was fostered by the Spanish affair, in spite of the unquestionable proof Castlereagh furnished of Britain's encouragement for ratification of the Treaty. Acceptable as this proof was to Rush, it had no very deep effect upon the issues of understanding and agreement. England and the United States had separate, possibly conflicting interests in Spain's imperial dissolution, and if this were not enough European affairs emphasized the dichotomy.

In May 1820, in a notable state paper, Castlereagh stated England's position to the Alliance, espousing more positively than before the doctrine of non-intervention. This had implications for Spanish-American relations, but Rush did not accept it without reservation. A letter to Secretary Crawford at the end of the year reveals how far his suspicion had developed. All European politics after the conference at Troppau, he wrote, revolved around the Neapolitan revolutions and the question of intervention there. What part would England play if the Alliance sent an army into Italy?

That is the question which concerns the United States. Ask her [England's] manufacturers at this juncture, and all the operatives who depend upon them, if they would not like war? most of them would answer yes—if you push them. Ask her merchants, and all who depend upon them? you would not get an answer very different. Ask her army, ask her navy, and all dovetailed in with these great establishments? the answers come by instinct. You have already half the nation; and of those that remain, thousands would join the war chorus.

What would be the result of these pressures upon English policy? Rush concluded:

> She will remain neutral for awhile, draw up an able state paper or two, full of generalities against war, such as all state papers contain; but be getting ready, (though she is always ready,) to take a hand in it. The vocation of a prophet is dangerous; but were I to prophesy at all, it would be much after the above fashion—should war really break out from the present revolutionary materials in Italy and Spain.

Financially England could bear the burdens of another conflict, for, with all its "general havoc," war was apt to "open the way to new profits and monopolies to Britain, from her sway on the ocean, and her insular situation, which keeps war from her own borders."

In domestic politics there was hardly more to trust or admire:

> The Whigs have lost their strong ground, the Reformers having taken it from under them. They are a party of leaders, with no rank and file, fine accomplished men, but as aristocratic as the tories; the descendants of the party which converted parliaments from three years into seven; in fact, the party more inclined at present, openly to impeach popular principles, at least those of our government, than the tories, lest they should be suspected of republicanism. The Tories, having no such fear, can afford to treat us better. Besides, the King does not wish a change of Ministers, as is well understood. If he consulted the public voice out of doors, it would be hard to say where he could get ministers more popular than those he has; unless he went among the Reformers. There is no King of England will ever do this, voluntarily. Popular government suits us for a thousand reasons, but might prove a very different thing in England.

American policy, meanwhile, was moving ahead of British. Recognition sentiment whipped up by Henry Clay was gaining wide support. Monroe sent consular agents to Chile, and finally responded to pressure in March 1822 by recommending recognition of Chile, Colombia, Mexico, and Buenos Aires. Congress overwhelmingly voted this recognition. Thus the United States fulfilled some of her obligations as "Mother of the Republics" in spite of the hesitant political leadership and extensive economic competition of England. This step still further detached the American Minister at London from British sympathies.

Regarding commercial rivalry, Rush had two general causes for complaint against Britain. He repeatedly protested that tonnage and port duties operated against American interests, "at a time when an extension of the wharehousing system with a view to making England a centre of trade for the rest of the world was becoming . . . more than ever a favorite object of her commercial policy." And he was forced to reconsider the old West Indies colonial trade question. Parliament passed an act (June 24, 1822) ostensibly opening the trade, but Rush was not slow, in examining "the true nature" of this act, to point out that the reservations Britain had made were entirely unsatisfactory to America, imposing unequal burdens upon our ships. Thus both America's separate policy and observation of England's withdrawal from the Alliance contributed to the suspicious attitude that was developing in Rush.

Such was his confidence in Castlereagh, however, and his admiration for that statesman's apparently sincere desire to perpetuate peace through liberal and forbearing methods, that he still viewed diplomatic problems in the international frame of reference he associated with Castlereagh's policies. His personal relations with the Foreign Minister remained a controlling factor in his thinking.

No one could have foreseen the tragedy that would end this part of the story. The parliamentary session of 1822 had been exceptionally difficult for the Foreign Secretary—now through inheritance the Marquis of Londonderry—and his fatigue, coupled with the demands upon him in planning the Congress of Verona, sapped his physical energies, and plunged him into a profound mental depression. On the morning of August 12 at Cray Cottage, he seized a small knife and cut his throat.

Castlereagh's death left a vacancy which only one man in English politics could fill, a man long a personal rival of Castlereagh, whom few British politicians really wanted to see in power, but who succeeded in spite of the distrust and fear that surrounded him, simply because there was none other available. This was George Canning, who in September 1822 donned the fading mantle of Pitt.

From Rush's point of view the change was significant. Though few understood fully Canning's complicated intellect and highly subtilized political system, certainly it was clear to the American Minister that the candid, direct, matter-of-fact Castlereagh had been replaced by a much more colorful but much more wily man, of whom it was said that he could hardly take his tea without a stratagem. Professor Temperley describes the difference in these terms:

> The peculiar middle position held by Canning suggested to Tories that he would abandon, and to Whigs that he would maintain, the principles of his predecessor. For he was so unlike him—he was egoistic where Castlereagh was modest, volatile where he was solid, communicative where he was restrained, irritable where he was calm, dominating where he was persuasive.

The actual degree of difference between Castlereagh and Canning on foreign policy appears now to have been much less than their contemporaries thought it, but so great was the difference in personality that the whole emphasis seemed to shift. Energetic, caustic, enthusiastic, Canning raised the government to concert pitch, injected an enlivened spirit into foreign relations. However he actually refined issues or reconciled inconsistencies in his own mind, he caused others to deem him a robust, impetuous nationalist, equally opposed to democracy and to absolutism, to "the excesses of unbridled freedom and of unbridled power." His view of foreign affairs appeared simpler than his predecessor's, for he was regarded as the insular, forthright champion of national interest, of separatism from Europe, of positive aggressive policy. None but the most obtuse could fail to realize that in Canning's eyes, as never in Castlereagh's, America would be put on the defensive in any common undertaking or any discussion of issues affecting them both.

Rush knew Canning intimately, as he had Castlereagh. They were often together socially, in small informal company. But in spite of sincere enjoyment of Canning's scintillating personality, appreciation of his wit and savor of his brilliance, Rush was on his guard. The motives of the new Foreign Secretary were rarely discernible, his statements rarely lacking in guile. If suspicion had been ripening before, now it bloomed full. For Canning was, in the eyes of the New-World republican, "a Briton, through and through;—British in his feelings, British in his aims, British in all his policy and projects."

One more ingredient had been added to the novel receipt of American foreign policy.

II

The American example of democracy at work was both a threat and to some degree an insult to European theories of power. Metternich accused the United States of setting "altar against altar," of casting "blame and scorn on the institutions of Europe most worthy of respect, on the principles of its greatest sovereigns, on the whole of those measures which a sacred duty no less than an evident necessity has forced our governments to adopt to frustrate plans most criminal." He resented "the flood of evil doctrines and pernicious examples," by which America fostered revolutions wherever they occurred, regretted those that failed, and aided those that prospered. This tended to "lend new strength to the apostles of sedition, and reanimate the courage of every conspirator." It would eventually undermine religious, political, and moral institutions, even "that conservative system which has saved Europe from complete dissolution."

The very existence of America accomplished these things, but if in policy she separated from Europe, to what extent was it for the purpose of attacking the old order? Just how far toward an aggressive policy did her rôle as Mother of the Republics carry her?

Rush had occasion to consider this question in February 1823. A certain Andreas Luriottis, agent of the revolutionaries in Greece, called upon him with letters of introduction from General Dearborn, then in Madrid. Rush was aware of the sympathy in America for the Greek cause. He received Luriottis cordially, assuring him

... that the fortunes of his country were dear to the people of the United States, who, cherishing the freedom which they themselves inherited and enjoyed, looked with the warmest sympathy upon the struggle of the Greeks for their national liberties, and that the Government of the United States participated in this feeling.

Through Rush, Luriottis petitioned the American government for substantial help. Adams, replying through Rush, placed his refusal on important considerations of national policy. Neutrality toward revolutionary Greece and the principle it implied became a sort of corollary to American separatism. While promising recognition if the revolt was successful, Adams nevertheless pointed out that constitutional powers to aid were not possessed by the President. Even if they were, he intimated, from reasons of policy they would not be exercised.

The policy of the United States with reference to foreign nations has always been founded upon the moral principle of natural law—*peace* with all mankind. From whatever cause war between other nations, whether foreign or domestic, has arisen, the unvarying law of the United States has been *peace* with both belligerents. From the first war of the French Revolution to the recent invasion of Spain, there has been a succession of wars, national and civil, in almost every one of which *one* of the parties was contending for liberty or independence. To the first revolutionary war a strong impulse of feeling urged the people of the United States to take side with the party which, at its commencement, was contending, apparently at least, for both. Had the policy of the United States not been essentially pacific, a stronger case to claim their interference could scarcely have been presented. They nevertheless declared themselves neutral, and the principle then settled has been invariably adhered to ever since.

Delivering this unqualified statement of policy, Rush had the opportunity to see the full implications of American isolationism as it was developing. In spite of the enthusiasm for aid to Greece, led by such American papers as Niles' *Weekly Register* and the *North American Review*, the government was maturing an actual separation from European affairs, not just a dissent from British or continental policy.

All the factors of his position, these characteristic ones mentioned as well as the host of other social and official preoccupations that were his daily pabulum, had fallen by 1823 into a complicated but precise pattern, so that Rush could feel the full effect of our many-sided policy in all its applications. The pattern was to be crystallized at the end of that year by the Monroe Doctrine, but all its elements had already presented themselves, and since Rush was to play a conspicuous part in the beginnings of the celebrated declaration, it is well to realize that, having already done what he had, it was impossible for him to do otherwise than he was about to. That he should treat Canning's overtures with suspicion, emphasizing the differences between England and America that Canning seemed so willing to disregard, was by that time inevitable.

Years later he himself remarked, "The policy of the United States on the great question of Spanish American independence could not have been different. They owed it to the actual position of the colonies; to their future destinies; to the cause of human liberty in the new hemisphere." Britain's obligations lay elsewhere, he well knew. In the midst of negotiations in 1823 he wrote a revealing paragraph that indicates his sensitivity to the situation:

I am bound to own, that I shall not be able to avoid, at bottom, some distrust of the motives of all such advances to me, whether directly or indirectly, by this government, at this particular juncture of the world. . . . The estimate which I have formed of the genius of this government, as well as of the characters who direct, or who influence, all its operations, would lead me to fear that we are not as yet likely to witness any very material changes in the part which Britain has acted in the world for the past fifty years, when the cause of freedom has been at stake; the part which she acted in 1774 in America, which she has since acted in Europe, and is now acting in Ireland. I shall therefore find it hard to keep from my mind the suspicion that the approaches of her ministers to me at this portentous juncture for a concert of policy which they have not heretofore courted with the United States, are bottomed on their own calculations.

The juncture was portentous indeed. There were three distinct problems in the crisis of 1823 over American affairs: they were Russia's claims in Oregon, Spain's attempts to hold her empire together, and French ambitions in the Caribbean and in South America. Though each required separate treatment, all were related; though partial answers might be achieved by joint Anglo-American action, it was certain a whole answer would lie in American assertion of independence. The principles of this independence—non-colonization, non-intervention, hemispheric separation—had all been stated. Now they were to be codified and strengthened by application.

This is one issue of 1823—the definition of America's independent policy. It became intermixed with another—the adjustment of Anglo-American difficulties. The two developed together, interdependently. The latter appeared first on Rush's agenda, incidentally connected itself with the former, and finally failed of solution because of the strength of the forces of separatism and independence set in motion by the December message.

In the history of foreign policy there are always present such issues among nations as arise from movement in the political world. These are the crisis situations, and in terms of them for the most part we form our historical judgments of men and issues. But there are always present other issues as well, which result not from movement but from more or less stable conditions, the contiguity of two peoples, the share of a common boundary, established patterns of commercial competition. These two levels of diplomacy may have little relationship with each other, as when a commercial convention is arranged quite independent of the larger political scene. But they may come together, thus linking commercial and political interests, and adding to them the vast corpus of emotional, intellectual, and social aspirations that make up the national interest. So it was in 1823. Whether or not America pulled away in isolation from European policy, there still remained unsettled points between her and England that might well be solved. The two hemispheres were joined as well as separated by the ocean; the two nations had to live together in the same world.

To these problems, quite apart from the Spanish American crisis, John Quincy Adams turned his fertile pen in the summer of 1823. During July and August Rush received from him nine long dispatches, characteristically minute, detailed, and careful, dealing separately with the points of issue: West Indies trade, the slave trade, the Northeast boundary, the fisheries question, the Russian pretensions to Oregon, and the international law of the sea. On these Rush was to open negotiations with England, with full powers to conclude a treaty or convention.

Thus for the second time the opportunity came to him to reëstablish the whole basis of Anglo-American relationship. Despite impressment and colonial trade failures, his success in 1818 had been notable. If he could repeat it, he would have every cause for gratification. Yet it had not been easy then, and now it was many times more difficult. He was, he wrote Adams, sensible of the confidence reposed in him, yet he felt also the heavy responsibility it created. There were many signs that the two countries had already grown so far apart they could not easily meet on common ground.

Still, the scope and importance of the negotiation proposed were so great that he could not even read over the dispatches without feeling the immense potentialities for important positive statesmanship in them. On August 16, having mastered the contents, he presented himself before Canning to initiate the discussions.

He developed the outline of the proposals of the United States, and gave Canning an informal memorandum of the various subjects. Then occurred the famous episode that was to have such incalculable results. It was like a powerful reagent poured into the confused chemical solution of Anglo-American relations. Rush, having completed his business, "transiently," that is, incidentally and quite without instructions, raised with Canning the question of French intervention in Spain.

> Pursuing the topic I said, that should France ultimately effect her purpose of overthrowing the constitutional government in Spain, there was at least the consolation left, that Great Britain would not allow her to go further and stop the progress of emancipation in the colonies.

In this Rush was only throwing out a feeler to discern Britain's attitude. He hoped for an elaboration of a note Canning had sent to the British Ambassador in Paris on March 31, in effect acknowledging that the colonies had won their independence from Spain, and asserting that England had no territorial ambitions in the New World, but would not remain passive if France attempted to acquire any part of the Spanish dominion.

Canning answered, not by discussing the note, but by the blunt question, What did Rush think his government would say to going hand in hand with England in the policy described?

> He did not think that concert of action would become necessary, fully believing that the simple fact of our two countries being known to hold the same opinions, would, by its moral effect, put down the intention on the part of France, if she entertained it. This belief was founded, he said, upon the large share of the maritime power of the world which Great Britain and the United States held, and the consequent influence which the knowledge of their common policy, on a question involving such important maritime interests, present and future, could not fail to produce every where.

This was no offhand or casual remark, as previous developments both at Washington and in Whitehall indicated, and as the zeal with which Canning followed it up proved. Nor did Rush treat it as such. He could not answer for his government, though he promised to report the suggestion "in the same informal manner in which he had thrown it before me." He did, however, penetrate to the heart of the matter at once by asking the question that was crucial, for it was symptomatic of the fundamental and principal difference between America and England on the Spanish American question: Would England recognize the new countries of South America?

Canning replied that he considered all America lost to the political dominion of the Old World, but it was not impossible that the present revolutions might end in some compromise by which Spain could retain, for example, commercial advantages. Recognition by England would prevent this, and could therefore not be given at this time.

Rush asked if any steps at all were being taken or contemplated toward recognition. Canning answered that a preparatory step, which would not commit England one way or another, was about to be taken, that of sending a committee of inquiry to Mexico. Though this was obviously an insignificant move, far from revealing a similarity of attitude sufficient to foster a joint action, Rush made no comment.

Canning concluded by repeating his original suggestions for a common declaration. Rush "expressed no opinion in favor of them, yet abstained as carefully from saying any thing against them . . ." The matter was kept entirely open.

At this point in describing the Canning conversations in his memoirs Rush interrupted his narrative to insert a curious account of an entertainment he and Canning had shared one evening several weeks previously. They had played the ridiculously absorbing game of Twenty Questions, which he describes intricately. Since this is obviously a juxtaposition of the dated entries in his diary, the question may be asked, What was he seeking to convey? It may be that he was hoping by this to indicate to his readers how intimate the relations were between himself and Canning. It is rather an ineffective device; indeed it is a little hard to understand just why the *Memoranda of a Residence at the Court of London* of 1845 is not more full on the developments of these conversations. The times required no secrecy; but Rush seemed to feel a delicate reluctance to divulge more than the public already knew.

In June 1845, he wrote a letter concerning his book, in which he said:

I publish enough about Mr Monroes celebrated declarations to make that remarkable point in the history of our foreign policy, intelligible I hope; yet I hold back more than I publish, and always shall. I had many communications from Mr Monroe, directly and indirectly. The channel of the latter was chiefly Alexander McCrea [*sic*], once Lieutenant governor of Virginia, who was sent off suddenly to Europe, as secret, confidential, agent soon after the arrival in Washington of my dispatches making known Mr Cannings overtures to me on the great Spanish American question, for great it then loomed. Mr McCrea was instructed to report himself to me in London, where he first arrived, and he was put in part under my directions. From Mr. Monroe himself, I had various letters. One now before me says "With the part you acted, we were highly gratified. I add, that it laid the foundation of an answer which was given to a communication from the Russian Minister which had expressed strong disapprobation, by the Emperor, of all revolutionary movements, and a disposition to aid Spain against the new states; as it also did, by the compromitment of the British government, of the message which I shortly afterwards presented to Congress" &c &c.

The reasons for his suppression of information, as he gives them, are not satisfying. It is to be hoped that when the great collection of his papers is opened and published, the wealth of material on the years 1823 and 1824 will throw much light into dark corners.

Scarcely had he sent off a dispatch recounting Canning's remarks, than he received a note from the Foreign Secretary, then about to go to the country, "bringing before me in a more distinct, but still in an unofficial and confidential shape," the question of joint action. The note was dated August 20, and read in part thus:

> Is not the moment come when our governments might understand each other as to the Spanish-American Colonies? And if we can arrive at such an understanding, would it not be expedient for ourselves and beneficial for all the world that the principles of it should be clearly settled and plainly avowed?
> 1. For ourselves we have no disguise. We conceive the recovery of the Colonies by Spain to be hopeless.
> 2. We conceive the question of the recognition of them as independent states to be one of time and circumstances.
> 3. We are, however, by no means disposed to throw any impediment in the way of an arrangement between them and the mother country by amicable negotiation.
> 4. We aim not at the possession of any portion of them ourselves.
> 5. We could not see any portion of them transferred to any other Power with indifference.
>
> If these opinions and feelings are, as I firmly believe them to be, common to your government with ours, why should we hesitate mutually to confide them to each other, and to declare them in the face of the world?
>
> If there be any European Power which cherishes other projects which look to a forcible enterprise for reducing the Colonies to subjugation on the behalf or in the name of Spain, or which meditates the acquisition of any part of them to itself by cession or conquest, such a declaration on the part of your government and ours would be at once the most effectual and the least offensive mode of intimating our joint disapprobation of such projects. It would at the same time put an end to all the jealousies of Spain with respect to her remaining Colonies, and to the agitation which prevails in those Colonies, an agitation which it would be but humane to allay, being determined (as we are) not to profit by encouraging it.
>
> Do you conceive that under the power which you have recently received you are authorised to enter into negotiation and to sign any convention upon this subject? Do you conceive, if that be not within your competence, you could exchange with me ministerial notes upon it?
>
> Nothing could be more gratifying to me than to join with you in such a work, and I am persuaded there has seldom in the

history of the world occurred an opportunity when so small an effort of two friendly governments might produce so unequivocal a good and prevent such extensive calamities.

Clearly Canning was taking his overture very seriously. Rush's answer acknowledged that America was in substantial agreement with all Canning's five points except the second. He pointed out that we had recognized the new independent countries, and desired similar recognition on the part of Europe and Britain to secure the happiness and stability of the new continent. He wrote Adams (August 23) that he had tried to reciprocate Canning's earnestness and cordiality, but was governed by two considerations: the danger of implicating the United States in "the federative system of Europe," and that of offending France. Yet, he added, the very earnestness of Canning's letter suggested larger designs, perhaps by the Alliance as well as France, against colonial independence.

An urgent note was introduced by the information that Spain hoped on the conclusion of her civil war to have a European conference dealing with the colonial question. This was, Canning advised the American Minister (August 23), an additional motive for prompt mutual understanding. Rush responded (August 27) that a conference affecting the new nations would be regarded by his government "as a measure uncalled for, and indicative of a policy highly unfriendly to the tranquillity of the world." He fully agreed with Canning as to the urgency of the matter, and went much farther toward joint action than he he had gone hitherto. "I further said, that if he supposed any of these sentiments, or those expressed in my first note, might be moulded by me into a form promising to accomplish the object he proposed, I would be happy to receive and take into consideration whatever suggestions he would favor me with to that end . . ." And he added, that if England would recognize South American independence, it would accelerate the steps at Washington, and "would naturally place *me* in a new position, in my further course with him on the whole subject."

Even before he received this encouragement, Canning had

assumed an air of optimism. He spoke publicly on the twenty-fifth of the friendship between England and America, declaring that "the daughter and the mother stand together against the world." Rush, in his turn, was quite ready to act. He informed Adams on the twenty-eighth that he was urging recognition by Britain, and should Canning ask him whether on such recognition he was prepared "to make a declaration, in the name of my Government, that it will not remain inactive under an attack upon the independence of those States by the Holy Alliance, the present determination of my judgement is, that I *will* make such a declaration explicitly, and avow it before the world."

This was a bold resolution, which might jeopardize Rush's position and his whole career. Aware of this, he analyzed his reasons for Adams. First, British recognition, could he achieve it, would be "an immediate and positive good to those rising States in our hemisphere." Second, a joint declaration by England and America would probably ward off attack by France or the continental powers. Third, even if it did not, and real danger threatened the United States, the government could repudiate his declaration as manifestly without warrant. "I would take to myself all the reproach, consoled under the desire that had animated me to render benefits of great magnitude to the cause of Spanish American Independence at a point of time which, if lost, was not to be recalled." Finally, he relied upon the President to see in his action proofs of good intention, at least, and concern for American welfare. "The result of my reasoning in a word then is, that I find myself placed suddenly in a situation in which by deciding and acting promptly, I may do much public good, whilst public mischief may be arrested by the controlling hand of my Government, should my conduct be likely to draw down any mischief."

Only Canning's espousal of recognition was necessary to precipitate this joint policy into reality. But it was too big a hurdle for Britain to take, for cabinet and King would certainly balk at it. Canning knew this; Rush apparently did not. The affair was really never so imminent as he thought it on August

28. On September 7 Rush received a note (written August 31) in which Canning backed down. Obviously unwilling to meet the condition of recognition, he even declared the whole matter was to be considered, not an offer made by England, but only evidence of one which would be discussed if and when Rush received full powers, as he had on other subjects.

Yet this did not end the matter. Though Rush's distrust of British motives had matured by September 15, when he expressed it to Monroe, and though he had clearly stated to Canning that recognition was an equivalent England would have to grant if she and America were to enter as equals in any measure, the Foreign Secretary nevertheless renewed in an interview on the eighteenth the suggestion that "notwithstanding the footing upon which this subject appeared to be placed at the close of our recent correspondence," Rush might still see his way "towards a substantial acquiescence" in his proposals.

In this interview Rush, as was his wont, developed the general principles and abstract goals of American policy, including the refusal to intermix in European political connections of which our attitude toward Greece was an example, while Canning, never at home among general ideas, stressed the increasing urgency of the crisis and the specific novelties of the case. He offered every persuasion he could for joint action without recognition, even asserting that if a congress of powers was held on the colonial issues he would insist on the United States being represented by Rush, as Minister to England.

"Words so remarkable could not fail to make a distinct impression upon me," the American noted. He had the deeper motives in view: "I cannot be unaware," he told Adams, "that in this whole transaction the British cabinet are striving for their own ends"; but even these ends, if encouraged while watched, might foster the safety and independence of Spanish America.

England it is true has given her countenance, and still does, to all the evils with which the holy Alliance have afflicted Europe, but if she at length has determined to stay the career of their former and despotick ambition in the other hemisphere, the

United States seem to owe it to all the policy and all the principles of their system, to hail the effects whatever may be the motives of her conduct.

As he interpreted the British attitude, the one step necessary to assure him that collaboration would not mean sanctioning British schemes of power was recognition. Therefore he replied to Canning that "the complication of the subject" might be cured at once by his unequivocal acknowledgment of the independence of the new states. Canning asked if recognition would make any difference to Rush's conduct. The greatest difference, Rush responded. If Canning would agree to recognition, he as Minister Plenipotentiary would join in the proposed declaration in the name of his government "under all the sanctions, and with all the present validity" he could impart to it.

Canning then recounted his objections to immediate recognition, which Rush dismissed by reference to the known facts. Spanish American independence was, he declared, an established reality, a question forever settled, the inevitable basis of all just and practical negotiation, in fine the "new political element of modern times" which would "henceforth pervade the political arrangements of both worlds."

Rush found Canning surprised at his readiness to go as far with him as he himself had proposed, if recognition were granted, but he perceived how reluctantly the Foreign Secretary approached that step. The next week (September 26) Canning informed Rush that Daniel Sheldon, American chargé at Paris, had told Sir Charles Stuart that America knew of and disapproved French ambitions regarding the colonies. If Sheldon had said this following instructions he had received, surely it would authorize Rush to join him in the proposed declaration of policy? But Rush preserved his ground, stating that he had had no new instructions and Sheldon probably hadn't either, but that he would go forward with the declaration if the terms he had stipulated were met.

Canning once again recounted his objections to immediate recognition. Seeking a compromise, he asked whether a promise to recognize in the future would not be enough. Rush replied flatly that it would not.

With this rebuff Canning seemed finally convinced, for his overtures came to "a full and sudden pause." Apparently his armory was exhausted of persuasions. For many weeks Rush was not aware of the reason for so unexpected and brusque a cessation, which was simply that Canning, realizing that he could go no farther without granting recognition, and that even if Rush joined him in a declaration it would now come too late to prevent a European conference, sought to reach the same goal by a different route. He turned to Prince Polignac, French Ambassador, and after several conferences elicited from him a joint statement of France's attitude on the Spanish question.

Until he learned of this negotiation with Polignac, Rush was puzzled by Canning's silence. "The termination of the discussion between us may be thought somewhat sudden, not to say abrupt," he wrote Adams, "considering how zealously as well as spontaneously it was started on his side. As I did not commence it, it is not my intention to revive it. . . ." Summing up the results as he saw them, he added,

> Mr. Canning not having acceded to my proposal, nor I to his, we stand as we were before his first advance to me, with the exception only of the light which the intervening discussion may be supposed to have shed upon the dispositions and policy of England in this important matter. It appears that having ends of her own in view, she has been anxious to facilitate their accomplishment by invoking my auxiliary offices as the minister of the United States at this court; but as to the independence of the new states of America, for their own benefit, that this seems quite another question in her diplomacy. It is France that must not be aggrandized, not South America that must be made free. The former doctrine may fitly enough return upon Britain as part of her permanent political creed; but not having been taught to regard it as also incorporated with the foreign policy of the United States, I have forborne to give it gratuitous succour. I would have brought myself to minister to it incidentally on this occasion, only in return for a boon which it was in the power of Britain herself to have offered; a boon that might

have closed the sufferings and brightened the prospects of those infant Republics emerging from the new world, and seeming to be connected as by a great moral chain with our own destinies.

The bitter and sarcastic tone of this observation was not Rush's usual vein; it is an evidence of the curiosity he felt at Canning's change in attitude, and it is likewise a revealing statement of his own view of the negotiation. The memorandum of the "Polignac Conference," the intent of which was to spike France's guns, he did not learn about until Canning read it to him on November 25. Then he reported its substance to Washington. He readily perceived the immediate effects of the memorandum: that it allayed the fears of England by declaring France's peaceable intentions, that it made unnecessary a joint Anglo-American declaration, for it accomplished in its substance all that could have been achieved, that it was a warning to France and to all Europe to keep their hands off Latin America, that it left Russia isolated in her legitimist policy. He was not aware of the suppressed allusions to the United States, except very generally. But he did perceive by the end of November that all chance of England recognizing the new states and defending them jointly with America had gone by.

Enough of his own writing has been excerpted to reveal how various the course of Rush's thought and feeling was throughout the month and more of his conversations with Canning. He was sometimes enthusiastic, sometimes discouraged; now he appeared confident of good result, now dubious; at one point he seemed to rely on the sincerity of England's intentions, at another he scoffed at them. It was an extremely important decision he had to make, and it is small wonder that he should have known changes of heart. The important fact is that despite all the uncertainties surrounding him he immediately assumed a ground on which he would stand, and maintained it stoutly. Though showing himself perfectly willing to advance from it, even at considerable personal risk, he refused to retreat.

Was it, in the long view, a wise course? Judgment on this question is entirely a matter of taste, which can supply material for interminable and bootless discussion (and indeed has done so). Had he under his general powers as Minister Plenipotentiary accepted Canning's suggestion and acted at once in concert with him, it might have succeeded in the immediate aim; it might also have facilitated the general negotiation, and set Anglo-American relations in a novel pattern. Jefferson and Madison were willing to have this done officially. Monroe and Adams, had they been confronted with a declaration signed by Canning and Rush, as a *fait accompli*, might have accepted it without cavil. There might never have been any talk of our slipping like a cockboat under England's man-of-war.

Those who felt the superiority of Britain's power over ours, who found Canning's offer flattering and thrilling, who cared more for good relations with England than good relations with South America, who saw a chance to tie England's enormous strength to our historical mission of liberation, would have favored joint action. Critics more attentive to English and European than American backgrounds have mentioned the disappointment of Canning, who had done much to assert the maturity and stature of the United States to European chancelleries.

But Rush was seeing English policy with far different eyes in 1823 than he had in 1818. The suspicion that had developed in him, his conviction that Canning had other ends in view than aiding liberalism, democracy, and republicanism, the development of an American policy independent and separate—these were the controlling factors in his decision. Recognition by England would seem to have been little enough of an earnest of agreement with the distinct hypotheses of American diplomacy. This formal step would not have gone very deep. There were currents in British opinion it would not have touched.

That the British cabinet [Rush wrote], and the governing portion of the British nation, will rejoice at heart in the downfal of the constitutional system in Spain, I have never had a doubt and have not now, so long as this catastrophe can be kept from crossing the path of British interests and British ambition. This nation in its collective, corporate, capacity has no more sympathy with popular rights and freedom now, than it had on the plains of Lexington in America; than it showed during the whole progress of the French revolution in Europe, or at the close of its first great act, at Vienna, in 1815; than it exhibited lately at Naples in proclaiming a neutrality in all other events, save that of the safety of the royal family there; or, still more recently, when it stood aloof whilst France and the Holy Alliance avowed their intention of crushing the liberties of unoffending Spain, of crushing them too upon pretexts so wholly unjustifiable and enormous that English ministers, for very shame, were reduced to the dilemma of speculatively protesting against them, whilst they allowed them to go into full action. With a king in the hands of his ministers, with an aristocracy of unbounded opulence and pride, with what is called a house of commons constituted essentially by this aristocracy and always moved by its influence, England can, in reality, never look with complacency upon popular and equal rights, whether abroad or at home. She therefore moves in her natural orbit when she wars, positively or negatively, against them. For their own sakes alone, she will never war in their favor.

No joint declaration on whatever subject could have squared this opinion with dominant thought in America, compounded as it was of democracy, national separatism, and the republican mission. Only by insisting for the meager equivalent of recognition as the condition of his action, could Rush have represented the mind and spirit of the people of his nation. Fortunately for the orderliness of his and our history, at least one member of the cabinet felt the same way. And John Quincy Adams could generate a breeze stout enough to sway a whole flock of Monroes, Wirts, and Southards.

With the receipt of his dispatches in Washington, the debates they occasioned, the ultimate resolution of policy, we are not concerned here. The story is well known. Adams' note to Baron Tuyll, and his response to Rush, stated the independent American principles fully matured; Monroe's message of December 2 gave final and authoritative expression to them, in a manner surprising and not a little enlightening to Europe. When it crossed the ocean, the message was at once upon all tongues in

London, Rush wrote; the press was full of it, Spanish American stocks rose on the exchange, "and the safety of the new States from all European coercion, was considered as no longer doubtful." It was, he told Shaler, "very generally approved of" in England; certainly "the best summary of publick affairs interesting to us both."

The ultimate scope of the Monroe Doctrine was long in developing; it was hardly comprehended in its subsequent remarkable extensions at the time of its promulgation. But in the crisis of 1823–24 it loomed big enough. No one doubted that it introduced a new and important pattern into international relations, that the United States could no longer be ignored, that the western hemisphere had a leadership all its own. For Rush it meant the ponderous negotiation he had initiated was placed on an entirely different footing, one far from auspicious.

The preliminaries looking to the general negotiation had been developing all fall along with the conversations on Spanish America, and although overshadowed in August and September by Canning's important proposals, they were not neglected. Rush received the first group of Adams' dispatches late in July; on August 16 he presented the proposition of a convention to Canning, who accepted it noncommittally, remarking that the number and importance of the subjects, with some of which he was totally unfamiliar, would occasion some delay on his part. It was then he made his first suggestions for joint action on Spanish America. The delay lasted seven weeks, while this other question was discussed; meanwhile the remaining dispatches arrived, giving Rush plenty to study. As he comprehended the magnitude of his task, he asked Adams that a colleague be assigned to join him.

On October 8 Canning informed him that Stratford-Canning (just returned from Washington, with Adams' blessing) and William Huskisson would act as negotiators for England, and that all subjects but one, maritime rights, had been accepted by the British cabinet. The omission of this one problem proved a great disappointment to the Americans, for not only was it a matter by which they set considerable store, but it bore tangentially on the slave trade question. This last difficult issue, Canning decided, would be a separate negotiation which he would handle himself. It was a subject very dear to him, on which he spent a great amount of time and energy. Its distinction was not objectionable to Rush, though he stipulated that as a preliminary England would have to declare the slave trade piracy, as America had done already. Canning assented to this, and an act was actually passed through Parliament.

Throughout the autumn the outlines of the negotiation were developed by frequent conversations, but it was perfectly clear that no such efforts for harmony were being made as had characterized Rush's intercourse with Castlereagh in 1818. On maritime rights of neutrals Canning did seem congenial; Rush recalled a previous occasion on which he had praised Jefferson's state papers on neutrality. But this topic the cabinet had outlawed, and on no other was there much original common ground. The separation of the two countries on Latin American policy, penetrating the whole skein of their relations, was bound to affect the attitudes of the plenipotentiaries. It was Rush, as a matter of fact, who first linked the two questions. In pleading for British recognition, he read Canning an excerpt from Adams' eloquent instructions on maritime rights to exhibit the wisdom of full Anglo-American understanding. But it was Canning who first used the Monroe Doctrine as an argument in the negotiation.

It happened in discussing the Alaska boundary problem, and is a good example of the admixture of issues. The Convention of 1818 had established a zone of joint government in Oregon until the English-American boundary could be adjusted. But in 1821 Czar Alexander had promulgated a ukase granting to the Russian-American Trading Company a monopoly as far south as 51°, a claim that affected both British and American interests, and led to the proposal for a joint negotiation with Russia. Sir Charles Bagot was in Petersburg ready to begin conversations. On December 17 Canning, though in bed with gout, received Rush to hear America's views on this question before sending

Bagot instructions. He found our claim much beyond anything England had anticipated; on further study he was amazed to discover that America seemed to wish to guarantee Russia against British expansion north of 55°, and to assume the line of 51° as the settled and agreed boundary between Britain and the United States. This would confine Britain's Pacific coast to the four degrees between 51° and 55°. Even this narrow strip, with Russia claiming exclusive monopoly down to 51°, and America apparently willing to accept 55° as Russian, 51° as British lines, was in jeopardy.

On December 27 Monroe's message arrived in London, with its announcement of the non-colonization principle; on January 2 (1824) Rush saw Canning again. The Foreign Secretary first objected to the American claim going as far north as 51°; then he turned to the non-colonization principle. What exactly did it mean? Canning had not heard of it before. Suppose new land were discovered by Britain near either American continent, would the United States object to Britain planting a colony there? Rush could offer no answer. They discussed the effects of the message on the pending negotiation at St. Petersburg, Canning declaring that he would prefer not to join with America, for the principle Monroe had proclaimed was one Britain would have to object to. Three days later he made the specific proposal, which Rush accepted, that each country should make its own arrangements separately with Russia. America's independent attitude was entirely too independent for Britain to join her. Rush's reasons for agreeing were defensive. By separate negotiations the non-colonization principle would be spared a premature walloping, the chance of Russia and England uniting against it would be avoided, and he would be left free to consider it a controlling principle in his general negotiation without first having to secure its acceptance from Britain, an acceptance that would never have been granted. But he was aware that by this development the Monroe Doctrine had insinuated itself into his problem, that a point of serious difference, symptomatic of the larger differences so clearly stated by Monroe, had established itself in both himself and Canning before the meetings of the plenipotentiaries commenced. However sincere Canning may have been in his attitude toward America, his preparations for the proposed convention were much less effective than the friendly, encouraging coöperation Castlereagh had offered in 1818. America's willingness to choose alternative grounds was likewise less. It was, therefore, with no high hopes that Rush entered upon his arduous duties.

By the middle of January preliminaries were over. Rush had given up hopes of having a colleague, and though Parliament was about to begin, making heavy demands upon Canning and Huskisson, the first meeting of the negotiators was set for the twenty-third of the month at the office of the Board of Trade.

The sittings that began on January 23 lasted until July 28; in these twenty-six weeks there were twenty-six meetings, each with formal protocol; between meetings there was the labor of preparation and argument to be done. This long duration Rush anticipated. He told Adams after the first session that the character of the subjects, the preoccupations of Parliament, his own distractions in running the Legation, would draw it out. But he promised his "best endeavors" and utmost diligence, two promises he certainly more than kept. The ultimate failure of the negotiation was not due to neglect. All three plenipotentiaries worked assiduously for the six months; the protocols reveal their earnestness, Rush's account of arguments their mastery of the subjects in hand. Nor was it due to any neglect on the part of the governments. Adams' instructions were thorough (they cover page after page of the large quarto *American State Papers*, at nearly 1,500 words a page), Canning's attention never flagged. Nor did Rush have any criticisms of his British collaborators. Stratford-Canning won his complete confidence, and of Huskisson, senior commissioner, President of the Board of Trade and Treasurer of the Navy, he told Adams, "Besides his reputation for talents, which is high, he seems to be no less generally regarded as a man of liberal principles and conciliating temper."

But three men in the Board of Trade's musty old offices could not reverse the direction of the world's political movement. Of this they were quite aware. Huskisson remarked, at the first meeting, that should their labors "unfortunately end without any treaties growing out of them, which however they did not wish or mean to anticipate, the failure would at least not disturb the good understanding subsisting between the two nations"; a sentiment Rush cordially reciprocated, not missing its implications.

Despite this skepticism their work met with an initial success on the Slave Trade Treaty, of all issues the one most valued by Canning. Rush presented a draft of a complete convention Adams had drawn up, which the British accepted as a basis of discussion. Canning gave informal encouragement, coinciding, incidentally, with an interview (February 1) on Spanish American affairs in which he revealed that England's attitude had swung in the direction of recognition. The British negotiators raised several objections to Adams' draft, presented some counterproposals, agreed ultimately to a compromise which in the end reconciled both parties, and on March 13 a convention was signed.

This Convention followed the pattern of those negotiated by England with many other powers, except for the issues of search as it had existed peculiarly between America and England over impressment. Fairly well pleased with it, Rush thought the British had given up most of their objections, while he had yielded nothing important; but when the document reached the Senate, that body split along sectional lines, and refused to ratify it as it stood. Southern leaders insisted on making several alterations which were finally unacceptable to England. This came as a surprise both in London and Washington, particularly since the phrase the Senate principally objected to had been in Adams' own draft originally. Rush was embarrassed in his further negotiation, especially when it was pointed out to him that England had declared slave trading piracy, as stipulated; nor did it help when he assured Canning that the President did not agree with the Senate's reservations, and would have ratified the Convention as it stood. The American constitutional idiosyncrasy by which a treaty made in good faith by one power could be altered or rejected by a branch of the other was not to be overcome by Mr. Monroe's pleasant disposition.

The rejection of the Convention by the Senate was not known in England until late June. In the meantime negotiation on other issues proceeded. Rush allowed himself to be governed entirely by Adams' instructions, with the "great and enlarged views" and "profound sagacity" of which he was deeply impressed. On maritime questions especially, including the proposal to abolish privateering, he thought an opportunity was provided to win "the most signal triumph which civilization in modern times would have had over barbarism."

"Many and anxious were the hours devoted to this negotiation," he wrote. "Its long road was often rugged. The discussions were between two Nations, neither of which, from the characteristics of a common race, is quick to yield. . . . The questions all had reference to the past or future. No actual suffering, no existing irritations of practice, were then upon us, in connexion with any of them. This was favorable to their calm consideration and discussion."

Yet in spite of calm consideration for six months, toward the end of July the plenipotentiaries were forced to give up, "persuaded that they had sufficiently developed the sentiments of their respective Governments on the various subjects," and that no agreement was possible. Rush communicated this disappointing result to Adams in a long dispatch on August 12, on the basis of which the reasons for the failure may be briefly sketched.

The West Indies trade question, copious and familiar as it was to both Rush and the British plenipotentiaries, had changed only slightly in outline since 1818, though there had been legal action on both sides since then. England had passed an act (June 23, 1822) which in her view granted important concessions to America, but Adams and Rush exhibited that its privileges were empty, the reciprocity it purported to grant non-existent. The

President granted a considerable measure of reciprocity, but not what in the British view should have been due; an order in council of July 1823 imposed a duty of four shillings threepence per ton on American vessels going to colonial ports.

Having mastered the whole subject in 1818 and worked with it constantly before him, Rush was expert in it (a distinction scarcely anyone has attained since), and argued with vigor from a wealth of detail. The essence of his argument was fairly simple. He contended that to put American vessels on the footing of *foreign* vessels, such as French or Spanish, was no reciprocity at all, for it still left our ships at a ruinous disadvantage in competing with British or colonial vessels.

British ships were permitted to trade with South Carolina and Massachusetts under the same regulations. We did not subdivide our territory for purposes of commercial advantage or monopoly, but held it out indiscriminately to all as one integral system. Britain, however, made different provisions for trade with England and with the Indies; she put any restrictions she wished on our commerce with her colonies, in order to protect her own competing trade with them. The American principle of reciprocity, developed after 1815, was thus squarely opposed to the principles of the empire that had been codified under Charles II, and were still dominant in the imperial thinking of commercial interests. Britain could see nothing wrong, Rush could see nothing right, with the advantage New Brunswick vessels had over Maine vessels in trading with Antigua, Barbados, or Bermuda. It is hard not to conclude, as most have, that Adams and Rush were requiring a complete revision of the colonial system, and of governing attitudes toward it, without offering that diplomatic *sine qua non*, an equivalent. Since months of discussion could not get the diplomats over this impasse, it need not detain us longer, except for the remark that after all Rush did have a point. It was all very well to preserve your colonial system, he said in effect to the British statesmen, but when your doing so places our ships under heavier burdens than yours, or those of your colonies, don't try to pass it off as reciprocity, or expect the treatment from us that true reciprocity would bring.

Rush wished to link with the colonial trade issue the new question of American navigation of the St. Lawrence River, introduced by Adams into the discussion. As instructed, he represented the existing rights of our nationals on that river to be dependent upon British permission, while he claimed as a right based in natural law the equal use of the river by citizens of both countries, and supplied analogues from diplomatic history. The British plenipotentiaries were taken aback (as well they might be); they indicated that they could only consider it under the head of a concession by England. Rush argued that our people had enjoyed the right before the Revolution, had actually fought in the last French war to help win the river's banks for the Crown; by this we had a strong national equity in its use. This the British rejected, ending by a total denial of our right to equal navigation, and refusing to deal with the subject on that basis.

They did propose dealing with it as part of the whole question of the Northeast boundary, still unsettled under the provisions of the Treaty of Ghent. If the two questions could be linked, and approached "on principles of mutual concession," they contended, the "materials of compromise" would be multiplied, and both powers by surrendering concessions and equivalents could obtain better conditions than those existing. But Rush refused to consider navigation of the St. Lawrence a concession by Britain; consequently not only was the negotiation of the boundary question impossible, but even its arbitration as proposed at Ghent was greatly complicated.

Both sides agreed substantially on the matter of the reception of American consuls in British colonial ports which had been opened to our trade in June 1822; but as the status of this question depended upon the ultimate decision regarding the whole colonial trade, no independent settlement could be made. A more serious problem was that of the Newfoundland Fisheries, which failed entirely of solution. France claimed an exclusive right of fishing in her own territorial waters around her island possessions off Newfoundland. Her ships of war had despoiled American fishers, but had left British alone. Rush presented a thorough statement of the case, asking Britain to vindicate the rights America had been granted by the Convention of 1818. England refused to act, because she had no desire to question the arguments France had urged in support of her claims. As the subject stood, Huskisson and Stratford-Canning announced it would have to be eliminated from the discussions, and handled by direct application from Rush to Canning.

No problem did the Americans regard more seriously than the settlement of maritime rights in wartime: blockade, contraband, rights of neutral carriers, and especially the proposal Adams thoroughly explored of abolishing privateering. This Rush proposed, as a cardinal point of American policy, but he announced at the outset that he would not consider any arrangement that did not include impressment as a principal issue of negotiation. Since he had nothing to offer that America had not offered in 1818 as security against the employment of British seamen in our merchant marine, the British representatives refused to treat this and other maritime questions. They held privateering to belong to the same class of subjects, and cast it out with the others. Counterproposals on their part were unacceptable to Rush unless linked with these issues.

The troubled question of Oregon, last subject of the negotiation, had already been complicated by the decision not to join in adjustment with Russia; now Rush stated—for the first time in any clear way, the British said—the American claims. He proposed the continuance for ten years of the zone of joint occupancy established in 1818, and a guarantee of exclusive settlement to America south of 51°, to Russia north of 55°. This Britain rejected, and categorically refused to accept the noncolonization principle. The whole of the unoccupied parts of America, Stratford-Canning declared, she considered still open as always to her future settlement. This stand unequivocally taken, Rush obviously could not agree to any conclusion which subsumed it, for America had already erected a considerable superstructure on the foundation of non-colonization. He attacked the problem from another angle, by an exhaustive examination of the historical records of discovery, on which our claim was based, an elaborate research which the British brushed aside as irrelevant. They offered a carefully drawn counter-proposal setting the boundary at 49°, with free navigation of the Columbia River, but this Rush was unable to accept. He made an effort to compromise, which came to nothing.

Thus on all the points of the general negotiation American and British agents failed entirely to reach a meeting of minds. Having failed, the whole negotiation became but one more testimony to the widening gap between America and the Old World, while, had it succeeded, such was the importance of the subject matter that it might have been a more important landmark in diplomatic history than the Monroe Doctrine or Canning's recognition of Latin America. The failure was inevitable in the circumstances of 1824, but it remained ever afterwards a source of disappointment and chagrin to Rush.

III

The longer a minister remained abroad, Rush noted, the more obligations of a personal nature he incurred, the more social connections he made. He was deep in many projects bearing on cultural relationships: correspondence between British and American agricultural societies, English patronage of an Academy of Arts and Sciences at New York, collection of drawings of British inventions and machines, international collaboration in humanitarian and philanthropic work. Despite his complex tasks both diplomatic and semi-official, he kept his work up to date. When he left London in May 1825, there were only three small matters still unattended to of the eight years' business he had transacted with the British government.

The conclusion of his service at the expiration of Monroe's term had been expected, and the failure of his work in 1824 hardly multiplied the attractions of the position. Furthermore, he was promised a place in the new administration if Adams should be elected. He knew, even while the general negotiation was going on, that it would be the last important undertaking of his ministry.

Several months earlier he had written Monroe of his intentions:

I have remained here much longer than I ever expected when I came away, and now, with your approbation, it is my intention to stay here until the close of your executive term. . . . Had I left my station even last year, I should have come away in debt, in spite of my economical determinations, and I will add efforts, increasingly made to avoid it; but under plans now before me, I cherish the best-grounded hopes of coming away free from this evil. My family being large, and constantly increasing, has spread much surface to expense, and to affliction, during my residence in England. This has fallen with especial severity upon my wife, dooming a large portion of her time to solitude and gloom. Nevertheless I wish not to utter complaints, not being insensible on the other hand to the privilege of having been allowed to represent my country during so long a period at this post, and having sought my most solid gratification in endeavouring to fulfill faithfully and industriously its duties.

There was a dark and difficult side to Rush's personal life in London. Two daughters had died during the eight years, Catherine's health had not been good, his financial position was always precarious. His four sons, three of them well-grown boys, had to be educated, and he wished them to go to American rather than British schools. The latter were "subdivided," so expensive, and so inefficient, he contended, that they could offer little preparation for life in the New World.

For many reasons, therefore, Rush was ready to return to America. But the election in November failed to decide his destiny just as it failed to decide the presidency. A contest threw the choice into the House of Representatives. Not until February was Adams chosen; not until April did Rush receive news of his appointment to be Secretary of the Treasury in the new cabinet.

He wound up his business, spent many days and nights arranging the Legation files that his successor might find all the decks cleared. Finally he presented his letter of recall to the King, from whom he received the gracious and kindly treatment he was accustomed to, and in another six weeks was on board the New York packet going home.

VII

NATIONAL PLANNING

OFFICIAL Washington in 1825 was very different from that Rush had left in 1817. The easy-going informality of Madison's time was gone; Monroe had established an etiquette like that of a European court, which was becoming even more severe and dignified under the precise manners of Adams. And not only more stately, governmental society was also more tense, infinitely more responsive to the political struggle raging beneath the surface of administrative relationships and polite intercourse. No one who participated in the election of 1824 was ever quite the same afterwards. The quiet "years of good feeling" were suddenly gone; in their place after that February morning when the House of Representatives chose Adams over Jackson came bitter antagonisms that ended the party of Jefferson, that expressed sectional and occupational loyalties which in four years were to crystallize as Whig and Jacksonian Democrat.

The Minister to the Court of St. James's had taken no part in the election, nor had the storm of 1824 cast any but a thin shadow as far as London. His old affections, his old loyalties remained his guiding principles; he was out of touch with new currents of opinion. Inevitably he took his lead from those he knew: Adams, Monroe, and the others.

It was not a bad lead. Historical tradition has not been kind to the Adams administration, for its successes seem on superficial view but a continuation of Monroe's policies, its failures part of the intellectual and social revolution that was Jacksonian democracy. But these four years prove on close examination one of the most creditable chapters in the history of government in America. Able and devoted men, animated with a great comprehensive plan for the development of the nation, the President and his colleagues set an example of faithful, imaginative, vigorous public service which has too rarely been emulated, one which deserves the most respectful attention from American historians. Rush found it extremely hard work, for the pace set by the President was one of relentless diligence. The White House day began at four in summer, five in winter, ended at eleven or twelve at night. The cabinet ministers called almost daily to report to Adams; stated meetings occurred once a week.

The executive family made a fairly distinguished group, among whom were a few old-time acquaintances. William Wirt had been persuaded to retain the Attorney-Generalship in which he had succeeded Rush in 1817; his reputation as a jurist and a man of letters had grown steadily in eight years' time; now he was happily settled with his extensive (and still growing) family in a much-too-small house near the executive mansion. John McLean, Postmaster-General, and Samuel L. Southard, master-politician of New Jersey, now Secretary of the Navy, were likewise continuations from Monroe's administration, though both had been appointed in 1823 and were previously unknown to Rush. Southard performed the duties of the Secretary of the Treasury until Rush's arrival. James Barbour of Virginia, a traditional Jeffersonian, one of the managers of Crawford's 1824 campaign, was Secretary of War, a post which removed him from the politics of the Old Dominion and consequently from the combination of Jackson and Crawford men which Calhoun was engineering.

Adams had chosen his men with slight regard for anything but their abilities. He was quite aware that McLean was openly sympathetic with Jackson, but was willing to tolerate even disaffection in his official family for the sake of a job well done. And to give McLean what credit he deserves he did follow Adams in refusing to make the postal service a spoilsmen's paradise, and was eventually to prove a more than competent if more than irascible Supreme Court justice. Most conspicuous example of Adams' desire to get good service rather than a good machine was, of course, his appointment of Henry Clay as Secretary of State, an act so courageous that in another man it would seem a piece of political bravado, but in Adams, who never in his life was guilty of attitudinizing, it was obviously the choice of the best available man despite political inexpediency or past personal differences. Rush liked Clay personally, but he knew Gallatin's opinion on that subject, and he recalled the stories of the Ghent negotiations of 1815, when Adams, rising in the early morning to begin his laborious writing, would meet Clay going to bed after an all-night session at the card tables. The President was a bigger man than most, however. He could work even with "that gamester in politics" (as he once called Clay) if it would accomplish the public good.

Rush had not been Adams' first choice for the Treasury. Unaware of an insulting interview between Crawford and Monroe early in 1825, and apparently not fully cognizant of the depression and lassitude that accompanied Crawford's apoplectic stroke, the President had asked the Georgia Jeffersonian to continue at the post which he had, after all, discharged with some distinction. But Crawford declined, thereby saving Adams and Monroe both some embarrassment. Next Gallatin was approached, but indicated he would not accept a cabinet position. It was after Gallatin's refusal that Adams sent Rush's name to the Senate, where it was immediately confirmed. DeWitt Clinton was offered the English post Rush vacated, but turned it down, whereupon Adams yielded to the importunities of the Federalists and chose the aged Rufus King, the only sheerly political appointment he made, one which did him no discredit.

Immediately on his arrival (July 1825) Rush plunged into a welter of duties. An extraordinary loan of twelve million dollars had to be floated, routine matters consumed day after day of his time, and a variety of additional problems had to be disposed of before Congress met. He listed some of these last in September:

Forfeiture of Norwegian sloop *Restoration*. Withdrawl of permanent deposits from certain western banks. Commissions for cutter service. Chesapeake and Delaware canal stock. Payment of public debt of 1812. Commissions of Land Office. Collectors of Custom. Testing of an alchohometer [*sic*] by experts. Amortization of government obligations. Light-house keepers, &c &c &c

Busy as he was, he found himself handicapped by a personnel inadequate and incapable. Most of the lesser officials were political appointees of several years back; some, like the Register, Joseph Nourse, an old Federalist whom the elder Adams had put in office, were incapacitated by age but still at their posts. The customs service was filled all over the country with Jackson men who had openly opposed Adams' election; others were incompetent, like old General Steele, the Philadelphia collector, so feeble he could not appear at the Customs House regularly or transact business when he got there. Rush recognized this condition and its seriousness at once, but in attempting to deal with it he ran into one of the strongest opinions Adams held, namely, that the civil service of the government should not be disturbed merely because a new president was in office. The principle of "rotation," the contemporary euphemism for the spoils system, he considered pernicious and degrading. He refused to make the American government a continuous scramble for office. The importunities of Rush and others were unavailing against his sturdy honesty. It was an admirable attitude, but it was to cost him Pennsylvania and Virginia, and ultimately would lead to the defeat of the American System.

In this as in other respects Adams was revealing his vulnerable points. However selfless, however devoted he and his colleagues were to the public good, they lacked an intimacy of touch with popular opinion. While they went one way, half the nation went another. Only Southard had the wisdom to grasp the situation they confronted, and trim his sheets to the winds that blew. The President in his inaugural address had recognized that a minority had chosen him. "Less possessed of your confidence in advance than any of my predecessors," he had told his countrymen, "I am deeply conscious that I shall stand more and oftener in need of your indulgence." But popular indulgence could not substitute for an effective political machine, nor would the people shower gratitude upon leadership, however patriotic, to which they could not emotionally respond.

As Rush must share in this credit, so he must share also in this blame. Adams lacked the adaptability of a great politician; Rush could not supply the lack. Clay, Binns, Southard, those who could, were not permitted to do so. Had the President been a little less unbending, had his colleagues been a little more persuasive, the Adams-Clay faction might in four years have built up an organization comparable to that of the Jackson-Crawford-Calhoun party. Then the twelve per cent majority in 1828 might have gone the other way, the American System might have succeeded in another four years in developing agriculture, manufacturing, and commerce *pari passu*, sectionalism might have been rationalized, the collapse of the federal union averted. But the destiny of Adams was an austere and noble martyrdom. His refusal to play the politicians' game confounded his own schemes, and pulled Rush along with him to defeat.

An Aaron Burr, a DeWitt Clinton, a Martin Van Buren, a Mark Hanna, a James A. Farley was badly needed in 1825. There were plenty available, but the President could not bring himself to look the other way. So while the statesmen of Lafayette Square busied themselves planning a national economic and social system, the country at large enjoyed the unusual spectacle of four years' political campaigning. With a prevision of turbulence, Adams had written in 1824, "Prospects are flattering for the immediate issue, but the fearful condition of them is that success would open to a far severer trial than defeat."

Shortly after he settled in Washington Rush turned out a political tract, *The Election of President in the House of Representatives. To the People of the United States*. It appeared first in the *National Journal,* signed "Fox," and was later reprinted as a pamphlet. In it Rush discussed the constitutional issues of the disputed election, comparing it with the Jefferson-Burr case —"no parallel," he thought it—and expounding the theory of representation on which the power of the House rested: "The faculty of representation is as essential to it [i.e., the House], as the property of reflection is to a mirror. This is the only ligament that connects it with the nation, and gives it, collectively or individually, publick importance."

The piece is remarkable only for its calm tone, unusual in that year on that subject, and for its allusions to the "symmetry," the "beautiful economy," of the American constitutional system. To characterize government as a system, to think of it in terms of a precise order and balanced harmony, was no result of Rush's contact with English liberals; indeed it savors of an opposite point of view, for the free economy of Smith, Say, and Ricardo did not include a comprehensive ordering of a nation's community life in political matters. The nationalists of 1825 were close to eighteenth-century mercantilists in their views of government, for against freedom they opposed authority, against laissez faire, paternalism. It was the peculiar intellectual achievement of the proponents of the American System to reconcile a planned economy with the free institutions of the United States. Basic to Rush's representative interpretations of the dominant philosophy was this concept of poised adjustment among separate but complementary parts in the national government. So familiar is it in American political philosophy that it may easily be overlooked in evaluating his rôle as Secretary of the Treasury.

For Rush looked upon his office as an opportunity to give the most extensive expression to political and economic nationalism. The Treasury was in a way the hub of the administration. Planning for a nation meant largely planning its financial and economic life. As the meeting of Congress approached and the necessity to have his first Annual Report ready pressed upon him, Rush began to state both the philosophy and the application of the national system.

I am here in a most laborious post [he wrote Mathew Carey]. I have formed a high estimate of its great duties. I have brought with me to these duties a set of principles on which I believe to depend the wealth, the power, & the happiness of this country. If my health lasts, it is my purpose to give to these principles a higher support than I have done. My notion of a treasury Report is, that it should embrace something beyond a mere account of receipts & expenditures. If it is to be nothing else than this mere matter of arithmetic, this array of dollars & cents in ruled lines, a clerk in my office ought to make it out. I do not deem thus of the great science of finance:— It is not a business of accounts, & I feel that I at least know how to appretiate the magnitude of its true principles, in their bearing upon a whole nation's prosperity. I have commenced a set of Reports embodying some of these principles, & am not easily driven from them; I will add, not at all.

Under this notion of the significance of his work, he prepared his reports with the greatest care, not only for literary style but also for the support he could give the general principles of the American System. He was writing not for one session of Congress only, but for the future of the nation, expounding the principles on which a sound expansion of national wealth should be planned, outlining a "great scheme of national advancement" under which a "provident Government," improving the natural gifts of territorial size and fertility, should study

To give perfection to the industry of a country rich in the gifts of nature, and blessed in the beneficence of its Government; to draw out its obvious resources, and seek constantly for new ones, ever ready to unfold themselves to diligent inquiry, urged on by adequate motives; to augment the number and variety of occupations for its inhabitants; to hold out to every degree of labor, and to every modification of skill, its appropriate object and inducement. . . . To organize the whole labor of a country . . . so that every particle of ability, every shade of genius, may come into requisition . . . in other words, to lift up the condition of a country, to increase its fiscal energy, to multiply the means and sources of its opulence, to imbue it with the elements of general as well as lasting strength and prosperity.

"A policy short of this belongs not to a free and intelligent people," he asserted.

Such an immense task required all the ingenuity and originality he could command, for the only precedents that existed were unsuited to American experience. But there was plenty of help for him in the publications of American writers in 1825. Enthusiasm for social planning was shared by a large part of the literary public of the country. Inspired by a vigorous nationalism which found its counterpart in European nations after the Congress of Vienna, it was also enlivened by the conviction that this new land required a set of policies and analytical tools entirely different from those employed by the speculative economists of the Old World. Daniel Raymond in his *Thoughts on Political Economy* published at Baltimore in 1820 had tried, he said, "to break loose from the fetters of foreign authority; from foreign theories and systems of political economy, which from dissimilarity in the nature of their governments, render them altogether unsuited to our country." The German economist List, when he first arrived in America, rejoiced in this emancipation from the theoretical reflections of the philosophers:

> The best book on Political Economy which one can read in that modern land is actual life. There one may see the wilderness grow into rich and mighty states; progress which requires centuries in Europe goes on before one's eyes. That book of actual life I have earnestly and diligently studied and compared with the results of my previous studies, experience and reflections . . . and the result has been (as I hope) the preparing of a system which . . . is not founded on bottomless cosmopolitanism but on the nature of things, the lessons of history, and the requirements of nations.

Rush felt somewhat like Professor List. He was returning to a land much changed in eight years, with observations of British opulence behind him as a model for that which America might become. But the realities of American life rather than popular European theories, furnished the rule to be followed. Again and again in his writings on finance he contrasted Smithian doctrines with his own conclusions regarding European prosperity and American promise. "The speculative economists of Europe are in opposition to the experience that surrounds them, and not less frequently to each other and to themselves," he wrote. J. B. Say in particular he criticized, joining in the popular protectionist attack upon him and Adam Smith as inconsistent, misleading, erroneous, and unreal.

This rejection of European economic liberalism was to be

found in all the writers on the American System, but Rush was especially vigorous in urging it. He made the contrast between Old World and New more productive of intellectual departures even than List did. America was, he thought, the lodestar of a new era.

An era has arrived, upon which after ages are to look back as to a point in the commercial destinies of mankind. The colonial system is fast falling to pieces: over immense regions it is totally gone, involving the certainty of changes both in the channels and the objects of trade, as vast as they will be various. The family of nations has been extended; new continents, new oceans, are opened to independent intercourse, to a just and equal participation in the benefits of which the United States cannot but be alive.

To replace the mercantile empires the manufactures of America would spring up, bringing to the people of the independent New World opulence formerly accruing to European imperial powers. New lands, new routes of trade, new markets would stimulate a new productivity in the United States, creating a new economic, though not a political, empire.

His Treasury reports became the authoritative statements of the nationalists, not only because of his protectionist arguments, but also because he emphasized the comprehensive character of the American System. It was not, he constantly insisted, a plan for the benefit of one section or one employment only. All varieties of labor in the country were to be benefited. Industry gave sustenance to both agriculture and commerce, for factories needed raw materials and markets.

It is believed that, as these establishments shall rear themselves up, under adequate encouragement, in augmented numbers, and importance, a corresponding activity in foreign trade will become their concomitant in the same portions of the country; since, besides the trade in exports, to which, after supplying to their full share the home demand, they open the way, and which will not fail to bring its proper returns on the broad scale of exchanges, the very existence of manufactures, as they assume great variety and reach perfection, superinduces the necessity of constantly bringing into the country new varieties of ingredients as subsidiary to them. . . . It is then that the farmer, the artisan, and the merchant, give support to each other, each enlarging the occupations and the gains of each; the State, meanwhile, reaping the fruits in fiscal prosperity and political power.

In this passage, and throughout his writings, Rush expressed a complete understanding of and sympathy with the broadest aspects of contemporary nationalistic philosophy. For this philosophy was by no means confined to the economic policies of the national government. It looked to a thorough development of all phases of community living—political, artistic, literary, industrial, commercial, and agricultural. The American System had become by 1825 an ambitious plan for the supremacy of the Republic in all fields of human endeavor, to be won, so it was said, not by the wasteful and lavish patronage of despotic courts, but by the encouragement of individual development through democratic processes.

Of the leaders who gave spirit and content to this comprehensive scheme of national planning, President Adams was in the most strategic position. His political theory was the core of the system. It was a theory which departed far from the notions of a limited government in a state of free individuals that had become classic after Jefferson. This Adams termed a set of "niggardly doctrines," and he accused Jefferson of seeking the least where the most was at hand. He preached an "enlarged nationalism," in which the national government should take a vigorous directing part. Freedom, in the proper sense, was at the basis of the best society, of course, but freedom should not be allowed to become sterile. "While dwelling with pleasing satisfaction upon the superior excellence of our political institutions," he said, "let us not be unmindful that liberty is power"; and power carried with it a moral obligation to accomplish the happiness of every member of society. The national government, consequently, ought to act affirmatively, to do everything not expressly prohibited by the Constitution effectually to promote "the improvement of agriculture, commerce and manufactures, the cultivation and encouragement of the mechanic and of the elegant arts, the advancement of literature, and the progress of the sciences, ornamental and profound . . ."

To this end he recommended continuing internal improvements—"Roads and canals, by multiplying and facilitating the communications and intercourse between distant regions and multitudes of men, are among the most important means of improvement"—increasing the navy—"the only arm by which the power of this Confederacy can be estimated or felt by foreign nations, and the only standing military force which can never be dangerous to our liberties at home"—creating a naval training school; developing those governmental services, like the Patent Office, which encouraged initiative and inventiveness, building a national university—"Among the first, perhaps the very first, instrument for the improvement of the condition of men is knowledge"—and an astronomical observatory—"on the comparatively small territorial surface of Europe there are existing upward of 130 of these lighthouses of the skies, while throughout the whole American hemisphere there is not one"—extension and enlargement of the executive and judicial branches of the government, and of the army corps of engineers to supervise public works; the fostering of arts, letters, and scientific research. ". . . moral, political, intellectual improvement are duties assigned by the Author of Our Existence to social no less than to individual man," he asserted. "For the fulfillment of those duties governments are invested with power, and to the attainment of the end—the progressive improvement of the condition of the governed—the exercise of delegated power is a duty as sacred and indispensable as the usurpation of powers not granted is criminal and odious."

Adams' nationalism, implying so much more than political development only, found its counterpart in many other expressions of the country's physical, intellectual, and spiritual energies. Industrial activity was everywhere increasing; five hundred inventions were being patented each year. Leaders of thought were heartily rejecting the determinism, the pessimism of European writers, for the very facts of American life seemed to belie Malthusian and Ricardian conclusions. Emerson, Thoreau, Irving, others of less stature were building a national literature; Cooper's *Pioneers* (1823) had been greeted as the production of a flowering of arts and letters not second to anything the Old World could offer. Peter Force was gathering his great collection of national archives, Jonathan Elliott his documents on the ratification of the Constitution, General William Hickey his monumental collection of "American State Papers"; historical and biographical labors were celebrating the glories of the Republic. Foreign travelers were describing remote corners of the nation, as were American travelers too, such as Yale's President Timothy Dwight, whose *Travels in New England and New York* appeared in 1822. Noah Webster's *Dictionary* and James Kent's *Commentaries* were in preparation. The spirit of the times was nationalistic. It fostered the notion of planning for the whole country an integrated, blue-printed future, a notion which received its fullest development in Mathew Carey's *Essays on Political Economy; or, the Most Certain Means of Promoting the Wealth, Power, Resources, and Happiness of Nations: Applied Particularly to the United States,* published in 1822, just three years before Rush returned from England.

This book was partly the outcome of Carey's thinking during the depression of 1819–21, but the principles it elaborated had been for many years the theme of his voluminous writings. The Irish-American printer was a conspicuous figure in Philadelphia, his publishing house one of the most considerable in the country. Before 1800 he had begun to devote himself to national issues, soon forming with Hezekiah Niles the conspicuous duet of literary leadership of the protectionist group. Carey sought the "science of promoting national prosperity and happiness," and before 1816 had found his key in the fostering of manufacturers. He considered America still but a colony of England in an economic sense, because she was exclusively an agrarian country, producing only staples, and therefore at the mercy of her European customers. He wished to diversify the products of the nation, to "naturalize the arts in our country," as Henry Clay put it. He proposed "to develop a system which would free America of the economic subserviency that had laid it open to disaster at the hands of English traders following its two wars." He organized the Philadelphia Society for the Promotion of National Industry in 1819, the first of many protectionist associations and clubs he was to have a hand in forming, and which together with his journalistic performances gave him outlets for his vigorous opinions. Carey was the popular spokesman of the American System, as Adams and Clay were its political spokesmen. Rush, who had known him since boyhood, grew closer to him in his years at the Treasury, keeping up a lively correspondence. "You seem never to tire in the work of doing good," he wrote on the receipt of one tariff tract.

With Hezekiah Niles, the Baltimore editor, Rush seems to have had no personal acquaintance. *Niles' Weekly Register*, which Carey termed "the best periodical work ever published in America," had the largest circulation of any protectionist journal. In its columns could be found the most systematic formulation of the American System, the best logical analysis of its broadest implications. Rush read the *Register* and was quoted in its columns, but he had not the same intimacy with Niles that he enjoyed with Carey.

These two journalists had built up a large following by 1825 from the Hudson to the Potomac, their national program rounding out and moving along with the internal improvements platform of Clay and the West. One other figure gave a cosmopolitan touch to the "school" of national economics. This was the Württemberg exile, Friedrich List, whose enthusiasm for protection and participation in protectionist meetings in Pennsylvania won him an admiring following. List had received several favors from Rush while the latter was in London, and found his reports as Secretary of the Treasury so much to his liking that he paid him an extravagant tribute at a dinner given for him by the Pennsylvania Society for the Encouragement of Manufactures in 1827. President Thomas Cooper of the University of South Carolina had attacked the administration in general and Rush in particular in his free-trade *Lectures on the Elements of Political Economy* (1826), alleging that no government ought to try to direct an individual's free choice of occupation. List rejoined with energy. "What a lamentable sight to behold men, who in former times merited well of their country, instead of resting on their laurels, or of fulfilling their duties of teaching the youth how to promote the growth and prosperity of their country, go abroad to excite the feelings of the people by inflammatory addresses, and assail from their chairs at home the worthiest statesman!" he cried. Dr. Cooper had affected "the school-masterly tone of Mr. Say" to represent

the present Secretary of Treasury as not having learned during his ambassadorship at London, from Mr. Canning and Huskisson, cosmopolitical principles, whilst all those who are friendly to American prosperity, estimate the Finance Report of this gentleman as a worthy counterpart to Hamilton's celebrated work, and congratulate the country on having a statesman at the head of the Treasury, who had opportunity and talent to penetrate the mysteries of the English commercial policy, and who sacrifices not the welfare of his country for the vain glory of following false book wisdom.

List and Rush exchanged some letters, and complimented each other's work in the cause of protection, but they did not become personally acquainted nor did Rush participate in the curious quarrel between List and Niles.

The American System as these leaders developed it had become a program of political, economic, social, and cultural planning. Its popular following was drawn largely from New York, New Jersey, Pennsylvania, Maryland, and those parts of the West which had benefited from internal improvements or which, like New Orleans, were bound by the triangular system of internal trade to the manufacturing centers of the East. Finding its origin in the writings of Hamilton and Tench Coxe before 1800, it had grown as American factories had increased until it represented the manufacturing interest, and the intellectualized interpretation given that interest by its political and literary spokesmen. The influence of the latter was profoundly important. The New York *Evening Post*, a free-trade opposition paper, asserted that there was not in the orations of Henry Clay "a single argument which cannot be traced to the dull pages of Niles' Register, and the interminable essays of Mathew Carey."

The principles of the American System had been evolving through many years. As the Jeffersonian concept of a government narrowly constricted in its scope and duties had faded, the notion of paternalism had gained ground. Each policy seemed based on a national need, and proved efficacious by experience. The Barbary Wars and the War of 1812 had justified the demand for a big navy. Access of political power to the West had given impetus to the program of internal improvements, as it had likewise made necessary the careful reëxamination of the public lands policies. The three successive crises regarding the Bank of the United States, and the need of some mechanism for financing war and internal improvements had established the requirement of a solvent banking system that would be advantageous not to one section only but to the whole of the nation. The revolutions in Latin America and the tangled web woven by the European Alliance had brought popularity to the American nationalistic policy in foreign relations and had emphasized the intellectual separatism of the New World. With the breakdown of the colonial empire of Spain and the opening of rich new opportunities for trade had come also the realization of the need for manufactured goods to be used in trade; thus after the depression of 1819 the emphasis among proponents of the American System had shifted from internal improvements, though these were still a major plank in the platform, to the encouragement of domestic industry by tariff protection. Most of the disputes over policy for the next decade were to surround the protection controversy, though this was in reality but one part of the larger program. With the decline of foreign commerce came the need for diversity in domestic productions; thus the cultivation of new and exotic crops was encouraged, and studies were conducted of the culture of silk and hemp. The remarkable increase in population in the half-century since independence indulged an optimism that contrasted with Malthusian doctrine, and encouraged Americans to look to eventual self-sufficiency and successful competition with populous areas of the Old World. To encourage the increase of people, a higher standard of living and a higher wage scale was necessary, a point stressed especially by Niles; this the tariff would accomplish, while free competition behind tariff walls would keep prices within reasonable bounds. And, though this was not allowed by the opponents of the system, an essential aspect of the picture of the future thus painted was a balance among agriculture, commerce, and manufacturing. These three were the primary employments of the people, and they ought to advance together, with equal advantages and reciprocal intercourse. The government could accomplish all these ends by appropriate encouragement of all interests. Like Adams, who emphasized the duty of the government to act vigorously for these purposes, so Carey expressed the spirit of the nationalists in his maxim, "Free government is not prosperity. It is only the means, but, wisely employed, it is the certain means of insuring prosperity."

To these principles Rush was completely wedded, and made them the basis of his work at the Treasury. His first Annual Report described the inseparable connection between manufactures and the wealth, power, and happiness of the nation. He insisted that agriculture, foreign commerce, the development of natural resources, the habits and morals of the people, the equality of the laws, would all be improved by the encouragement of manufactures. Agriculture was "the first pillar in the State," commerce the third, domestic industry "the great intermediate interest, strengthening and upholding both the others." The country "must be in a false position, lying potentially at the mercy of extrinsic events, when reposing only upon foreign commerce and agriculture." He admitted that "other opinions exist on this subject, claiming the support of distinguished names both at home and abroad," yet he cited the example of England to prove "that nations which have reached the most imposing heights of physical and intellectual power" were those in which maufactures were most numerous, and most encouraged by the government. America had some "natural commodities" in the processing of which her industry could begin; she was far from foreign sources of supply, a powerful motive for discontinuing dependence upon them. These were familiar arguments. He recommended no specific legislative changes, choosing rather to stress the general principle which was to guide his administration of the nation's finances.

Apart from his regular report in December, another occasion presented itself for the development of the principles of the American System. This was a communication required by the House of Representatives on the rebate system in foreign trade. The revenue laws provided that if a merchant exported foreign goods he had previously imported within one year of their first arrival in this country, he would receive as a drawback the import duties he had paid. The proposal had been made to increase the time to two years. Rush endorsed the proposal. He determined first that no decrease in the annual revenue would ensue; indeed the benefit to merchants and domestic manufacturers would probably cause an increase, and the benefit to the commerce and navigation of the United States would be considerable. Ardent protectionist, he began his discussion under this head with the surprising remark, "That commerce flourishes in proportion as it is free is a principle that requires no demonstration." But there was an exception to this rule: "Nations in which . . . essential branches of industry have not yet been successfully reared up are manifestly not upon an equal footing with those contemporaneous nations in which they are seen already to exist and flourish . . ." Therefore a nation had first to establish domestic manufactures before it could compete in international rivalries with other national systems older and better developed; only when industry flourished could the luxury of free commerce be enjoyed. Full national independence would be achieved *after* the nation had, by protective policies, fostered a mature productive system; then she could compete with any other country with advantages equal.

He argued that a policy such as the one proposed would at once aid the trade and navigation of the country and benefit home industry too. Hardly anyone believed him, even the merchants and shipowners who favored the bill doubted this assertion, but he made an earnest plea on that basis. He did have support, however, when he pointed out that the technique of trade would be improved by the longer time given the merchant, for he would have better opportunities to exercise his own judgment as to the best time for reëxport. A Smithian phrase crept into the text:

He will be sure to fix upon the appropriate and judicious moment better than others can do it for him. The maxim of letting individuals alone has, in such case, its proper application. It has generally its proper application under systems that are flourishing and free; whilst to suppose its universal application, subject to no control, to no modification, amidst all the diversified and complicated interests of opulent and populous communities, would be to forget the great purposes for which government and laws are instituted, and especially in States that are the most flourishing and the most free.

The "true principle of commercial empire" lay, he argued, in the fewest restraints imposed upon the flow of foreign and domestic goods *out* of a country, carried by its own ships.

The riches of the world concentrate in such a nation, and its power ascends to a height that is proportionate to its riches. Not agriculture alone, not manufactures alone, not commerce alone, but the union of all, the copious treasures of all, make up its riches and power.

The time was exactly right for such a step, for the United States could supply Mexico and South America with foreign goods, as their ports were sucessively opened to our trade. Free nations in Latin America offered opportunities to the United States of which our strategic position between two oceans enabled us to take peculiar and wonderful advantage:

There are epochs in nations that form great and fundamental divisions in their history, moral, political, and commercial. The discovery of this continent itself was scarcely followed by greater results upon the condition of nations than may be expected to flow in due time from its emancipation from Europe; a reflection with at least a sufficient semblance of truth to heighten our conception of the true tone and character of the commercial measures proper to be put in train by the United States in connexion with a political revolution so awakening, so momentous.

Here the American System became very like the old colonial system of the eighteenth century both in intention and in appearance, if not in vocabulary. America, looking southward and to the orient, was envisioning a colonial system of her own.

Only in one respect did Rush deviate from the principles of the nationalist writers; this was in regard to the public debt. Niles, List, Raymond, the Scotch-Canadian Rae, most of the more systematic popularists, all agreed that internal improvements added to the stock of national wealth, and Niles deplored the "feverish and childish efforts to pay off the national debt" after 1821. Money that might have gone to additional roads, canals, or harbors was thus diverted into an unproductive channel. The Secretary appeared not to agree; he made no recommendation in line with this point of view, but accepted with apparent approval the successive appropriations of the Congress for further reducing the outstanding obligations of the government. With this single exception, Rush had become the official representative of the protectionists, their spearhead of policy, their mirror in the government.

I

In the early summer of 1826 Rush was engaged in some tiresome problems of administration. Collectors had to be removed or appointed, their records scrutinized, some of them reprimanded; frauds upon the revenue had been discovered and required exhaustive investigation; banking facilities were needed in the new western states; all had to be done with an eye to the fall elections. In July he interrupted these labors to perform one infinitely more agreeable to him. Together with Secretary Barbour, and in spite of the President's misgivings, he planned to seize the semicentennial celebration of Independence as an occasion for soliciting subscriptions for a fund to relieve the poverty of Thomas Jefferson.

At nine o'clock on the morning of the fourth he and Barbour called at the White House, where a procession of all the officials of the administration formed and proceeded through crowded streets to the capitol. In the hall of the House of Representatives speeches and prayers commemorated the fiftieth anniversary of the nation, after which Barbour and then Rush delivered addresses relating the need in which Jefferson lived, and urged the assemblage to make up the relief fund. Though he could not know it, at the very moment Rush began his speech, Jefferson at Monticello was sinking quietly into death. At one o'clock he breathed his last. At Quincy, a few hours later, death came likewise to John Adams.

Rush was much affected. Though because of the venerable Adams' increasing debility and Rush's increasing duties, their correspondence had not been as lively recently as it was before he went to London, Rush still thought frequently of his happy hours with the elder statesman. As the President made his preparations to go North, leaving final instructions with each department head, it seemed indeed that the nation had passed an era. Of the signers of the Declaration of 1776, only Charles Carroll remained.

II

By fall the political atmosphere of Washington had become almost unbearably strained, though the social amenities even among the most earnest opponents were preserved. Some of the Jackson-Calhoun men, Adams noted in his diary, "under the courtesies of life, conceal a rancor of heart as corrosive as the rabid foam of Randolph." It was hard for Rush to remain unmoved, for Congress had proved almost entirely indifferent to his carefully conceived proposals; but he followed his natural bent for society in a gracious way, sometimes discharging his cargo of displeasure in letters to Binns but generally exhibiting an amiable disposition to all who saw him. A visitor from home found him "very polite as well as his lady, true Pennsylvanians in manners and deportment."

Personnel problems of the department continued to keep him occupied, and he was engaged also in the preparation of a manual "on the growth and manufacture of silk in different parts of the Union," a cherished project designed to diversify agriculture as well as industry and, freeing us from dependence on the Orient, not only supply domestic markets but furnish in addition a commodity which could be used in trade with South America. Nothing very much came of the scheme, but it was an ambitious undertaking which Rush launched with high hopes.

The preparation of his second Annual Report consumed much of the autumn. It was no very enlivening occupation, when he reflected on the reception that had been accorded his first. "That I had not the least support from a single human being in Congress last winter," he wrote Carey, "is true. But I am not the less confident that I am right, & shall probably reserve other recommendations for a Congress that I hope will at least give them an examination." Despite his gloom he worked hard at the task, and achieved some success. The Report of 1826 was admired by the nationalists above all his other productions. Doubtless this was because he devoted almost all the message to the issue of protection, concentrating on this phase of the American System rather than repeating the more general observations he had permitted himself the year before.

The economic depression in Europe, accompanied by a fall in prices, had resulted in a decreased revenue from importations during 1826, which had a twofold importance in Secretary Rush's thinking during that year. In the first place it forced him to think of America's public economy in terms of a world-wide picture, even more broadly than he had done in previous years.

In the second place, it was always uppermost in his mind that eighty-seven percent or thereabouts of the annual income of the United States came from customs duties, "There being no direct taxes of any kind, duties of excise, or other internal duties in operation . . ." This picture could hardly be changed rapidly without doing violence to the economic structure of society. Consequently whatever was done to encourage domestic industry had to be done in such a way that the import and export trade should continue to increase, for since no direct taxes were contemplated, nor other levies on the factories it was hoped would spring up, the "manufacturing interest" did not promise to produce any direct revenue. Our financial structure was built upon mercantile rather than industrial income. Some of the commercial opposition to the tariff stemmed from the appreciation of the conflict of ends implicit in the encouragement of manufactures which would reduce the variety and value of commodities imported, and reduce thereby the national income, at the very time increased national expenditures were contemplated. This attitude was further strengthened by the unfortunate habit some tariff writers had of using the phrase "self-sufficiency."

The conflict was more apparent than real in Rush's thinking, however it may have been in Carey's or Niles's. For Rush repeated again and again as a fundamental part of the government program the equality that should subsist among agriculture, industry, and commerce, the harmony or balance among the several "interests" of the nation. The alternative argument, after all, would have been to foster manufactures so effectively that, commerce having declined until it was no longer able to support the government, a complete revision of the tax basis would be required, to which there were insuperable constitutional, economic, and political objections.

Protection, therefore, remained for Rush but one part of the comprehensive plan of national progress, woven into a skein of many other problems. Fostering manufactures was not designed to make over the nation's economy, or free America from foreign trade. Rather it proposed to develop neglected opportunities within an economy the outlines of which were already fixed, and thereby add a great number of commodities to the stream of commerce. The end of the program was still to increase trade, after the model of England, the greatest commercial, as she was also the greatest manufacturing, nation.

One problem was the inadequacy of customs records. To correct this Rush instituted a better method of accounting, so that in a few years exact information regarding both home industry and foreign trade might be available, "showing how each, under wise principles adapted to each, may advance co-equally; how the channels and the objects of the latter [i. e., foreign trade] may shift under the advance of the former without any loss, but with gain, in effective national results—results operating upon the most extensive interests and enriching to the greatest mass of numbers; or how, under the growth of the one, the other is at all destined to become disadvantageously and lastingly abridged." The collection of facts and data would, he averred, serve as a guide to wise legislation by which the accumulated products of both agriculture and domestic industry could be made the basis of a great foreign trade. Obviously the Secretary was thinking once again not so much of trade with Europe, but with South America and Asia, where American opportunities for dominance were still greatest, or even with the Black Sea, the Levant, and North African Mediterranean ports where, as he had once assured the Neapolitan Ambassador in London, "all we desired was the opportunity" to compete. To encourage English trade, not manufactures but agriculture would have been fostered. England Rush viewed as our competitor. To equalize competition it was still as necessary as it had been in 1818 to free navigation from all burdensome tolls and duties that gave advantages to ships of one nation. This he continued to stress in season and out. It had become, as the result of his London experience, almost as the signet ring of his public career.

The amount of American manufactured goods that annually entered foreign trade was large enough already to give encouragement to the protectionist view. Experience so far had answered the arguments of the Jeffersonians that high prices and inferior quality would result from the tariff. "Apprehensions of monopoly" in industries protected and fostered had proved groundless, for it was, Rush thought, established as a certainty "that competition at home would bring down prices eventually, if not immediately, whilst it creates and diffuses new wealth at home; labor being the foundation of wealth, and producing and disseminating it more universally, and in higher degrees, in proportion as it exists under diversified forms and in full activity." Sectionalism, already a serious issue in American politics, the Secretary saw as the natural result of geographical characteristics. Those regions not favored by "immense and exhaustless treasures of the soil" would properly turn to manufacturing, whereby an internal trade would develop among complementary parts of the Union, "parts naturally destined to make up one systematic whole, where the plough, the loom, and the ship, will each have its appropriate sphere in raising to a proper elevation the entire fabric of our social and public prosperity; in carrying to the highest attainable pitch our riches, our happiness, our power." Only through the growth of industries could this balance of employments as of sections be attained.

The American Republic was not only an experiment in national wealth, but one in human nature as well. Rush characteristically stressed the moral values of the protection controversy, seizing every opportunity to urge that sort of legislation which would promote temperance, frugality, and skill. Reminiscent of his London observations was his desire for the revival of the tea trade, valuable "from its tendency to encourage more largely the taste for an innocent and wholesome drink" in place of those valuable neither financially nor morally. The well-adjusted commonwealth, it appeared, would be made up of well-adjusted individuals.

Much more serious as a national problem than occasional bibbers or improvident workmen was the growing slave population in the South, and this likewise occupied a large place in Rush's thinking. The American System as Rush understood it had no place for slavery, yet the fact of its existence had to be confronted. A private enterprise with which Rush had been associated both in England and America for more than ten years had confronted it, and prepared a program to present to Congress. This was the American Colonization Society, a nonpartisan, non-sectional organization for settling freed Negroes in an African republic. The magnitude of the problem the Society addressed made its ambitions appear almost entirely futile, and in its long history it did not accomplish much of lasting importance for the settlement of the American slavery question. But its significance lies not in what it accomplished, but in the state of mind it created in its members. Composed of persons of all political and religious persuasions, from all parts of the country, it stood as a vital witness to the possibility of dealing dispassionately and creatively with the slave question. To Rush it presented a means of eliminating sensibly yet effectively an important barrier to the national scheme.

The Society had asked for a government subsidy to help it in its work. Rush and the administration supported this proposal, but the southern members defeated it. In the South, although men of enlightenment and vision welcomed the Colonization Society as a hopeful sign for the future, others viewed it as a threat against their social and political condition. Its activities in the 1820's (in which Rush was a leader) contributed to the antagonism Southerners generally felt toward the nationalistic system as a whole.

Indeed, by the end of 1826, opposition to protection had crystallized in a definitely sectional pattern. The country was divided roughly in three parts. The agrarian South and, for different reasons, commercial New England opposed the tariff and all that went with it; the Middle States, from Rhode Island to Delaware, where manufacturing was becoming an important economic factor, and the West, won by internal improvements, were the regions where the American System flourished. The vote on the tariff of 1824 reflected this sectional divergence, as did the location of the nationalist journals: Niles's in Baltimore, Carey's in Philadelphia, Evans's *Workingman's Advocate*, the first labor paper in the United States, in New York. Rush's Pennsylvania was the stronghold of woolen manufacturers, and stronghold likewise of the Bank, whose president after 1823 was his Philadelphia friend, Nicholas Biddle. The South and commercial New England had less of the industrial interest, and adhered likewise to a completely different economic theory. Their centers of learning were the centers of Smithian-Ricardian thought. Harvard made Say's *Treatise on Political Economy* a required text in 1825, Yale in 1827, while Newman at Bowdoin was preaching the same gospel. In the South, Dr. Cooper's lectures at Charleston were supplemented by Dr. Thomas R. Dew's at William and Mary, and similar free-trade teaching at almost every other academic institution. Though of course there were sizable minorities in each section (free traders lectured at Columbia, Princeton, and Pennsylvania), the general political opposition followed the economic interests and intellectual climate of opinion of each section.

As a result, protection and the whole American System was stigmatized by its opponents as a design not for the whole nation but only for a part. The principle of equality and balance among agriculture, manufacturing, and commerce was lost somewhere in the process, and though Rush continued to evoke its comprehensive quality at all seasons, it seemed theoretical and academic. It never took hold of the popular imagination. Commerce had been too long the way of the North, agriculture of the South. To speak of encouraging manufactures was to antagonize each. No protestations of balance or mutual interdependence could keep the American System from seeming but the intrusion of the loom into the affairs of the plough and the ship.

Throughout 1827 lively activity on both sides increased the sectional and ideological antagonisms. This was the critical year, during which the scales appeared almost evenly balanced between the American System and its opponents. The first tilt was in January, when the Mallary tariff bill failed to pass the

Senate by the deciding vote of Vice-President Calhoun. This bill had been introduced at the insistence of Massachusetts woolen manufacturers, a minority in their own state but associated with Carey's clubs and societies south of the Hudson. Once petitions began, they came in a great flood, every interest memorializing Congress for or against increased duties. The cotton manufacturers who had developed an export trade opposed, the woolen manufacturers favored, revision. The Mallary bill was in line with Rush's recommendations, and though its failure was a victory for the South and free trade, the majority for it in the House, and the equal division in the Senate, spurred protectionists to increase their demands.

They began an enlarged campaign embracing all manufacturing interests, pointing toward a general, comprehensive elevation in duties. In May the Pennsylvania Society for the Promotion of Manufactures and the Mechanical Arts held a great convention in Harrisburg at which thirteen states were represented by two or more delegates. Duties on almost every conceivable product were considered, and an "Address to the People of the United States" was prepared by Niles, of which ten thousand copies were published in October. Of course the opponents of protection were stimulated by such challenges. The autumn saw intense activity on both sides, a crescendo of debate over principle and policy, which the Jackson managers began quietly, insidiously to turn to their own political purposes.

Thus as Rush wrote his report for 1827 he was sailing on a turbulent sea. But he felt none of the despair of the previous year, for there were assurances aplenty of support and agreement with his views outside if not within Congress. The theme of this, the most elaborate of his reports, was again the familiar one of interrelationship among agriculture, commerce, and manufacturing, the truly national character of the protectionist program, the possibility of developing a domestic trade that would follow the growth of manufactures in one section of the country. By this internal trade natural advantages could be exploited to the utmost, no artificial barriers or restrictions would hamper the flow of goods, the industry appropriate to each section could flourish. "A vast home trade resembling foreign trade, as well by intervening distances as by the nature of its exchanges, will be prosecuted . . ."

Such a trade could exist only by "the extensive success of manufactures." Rush tried to answer all objections to manufactures that had been urged. He contended for the military and naval advantages they would bring, the increase in wealth produced, the intellectual, moral, and social improvement they promised. The objection that "grapes could be grown in Scotland" if sufficiently protected he pronounced purely theoretical: "There is little hazard of a community ever forcing manufactures not adopted to its soil, climate, and all its other capabilities. Still less can the hazard exist where the powers of legislation are deposited in the hands of those who are imbued with the collective intelligence of the community."

The principal objection, that tariffs would discourage imports while fostering manufactures, and thus injure foreign trade, he answered with statistics which apparently proved the contrary. Foreign trade had actually increased since the tariff of 1824, both as to imports and exports. Rush admitted that theoretically import duties could be raised so high as to harm commercial interests, but he insisted that the existing duties had not reached that point. Indeed some should be raised still higher, notably those on commodities "which conduce to subsistence, shelter, clothing, and defence." To this end he recommended increases on wool and woolen manufactures, fine cotton goods, bar iron and hemp. Tariff on these articles was not sufficient to cause their production at home, yet the importation, especially of wool and manufactured cotton goods, created a trade relationship with England greatly to our disadvantage; our prosperity would be augmented by freeing us from this situation. He proposed a "complete establishment" of American manufactures of these articles, presenting the familiar arguments in support of his contention.

In this third report Rush touched on more aspects of national life than most protectionist writers or most treasury reports customarily did. It was a vigorously argued document, urgent in its tone and comprehensive in its scope. In many ways it is the best statement of the policies of the American nationalists of the 1820's that anyone produced. Rush discussed such diverse matters as the theory of prices in relation to the tariff, the effect of competition on prices, the effect of encouraging manufactures on the number and quality of immigrants into the country, the relation of expanding industry to the public land policy of the government. He argued that the amount of capital in a nation should be kept on the increase in proportion to the growth of population. With a view to the political importance of the population question he termed the public lands policy a bounty to agriculture which ought to be counterbalanced by a bounty for manufactures. The political implications of the system of internal trade he likewise stressed, citing it as a cement to the Union, and as an earnest of his sincerity in urging a balance among all employments he recommended the development and refinement of the warehousing system as a boon to foreign commerce.

The Congress to which this able report was submitted had no particular disposition to oppose its principles. Jackson was known to be in general a friend to protection; the imminent election was not therefore squarely on the issue of free trade against the tariff. But the South had to be won to Jackson in spite of his views. The best way the opposition could do this, as they quickly perceived, was to discredit and defame the administration. Their policy accordingly was planned solely with this end in view.

The political situation at the beginning of 1828 was without precedent since the adoption of the Constitution, though it has recurred since. The administration had only a minority in both houses. All committees were against them, all key positions went to Jackson men. The leaders accepted many of the principal recommendations of the President, but acted upon them in such a way that credit would go not to Adams but to the Congress.

The President was denounced as a corrupt, self-seeking, greedy monster at the same time he was being entrusted with funds for internal improvements or his treaties were being ratified and his appointments confirmed. Rush suffered similar indignities even from those who accepted the principles he embraced. It was a wretched, scurrilous, debased session, devoted not to the service of the country but to building Jacksonian political fences. The time was not ripe for statesmanship. The administration, unable from policy or temperament to answer its criticasters in their own terms, persevered in its program only to see all its achievements used as weapons against it. To Rush's career three efforts of the Congress were particularly important: the report of the Committee on Ways and Means in answer to his third Report, the tariff of 1828, and the House investigation of the expenditures of the government with a view to retrenchment and reform.

The chairman of the important Committee on Ways and Means was McDuffie of South Carolina, inplacable foe of the tariff, the American System, and John Quincy Adams. From his pen came a long, vigorous answer to Rush's report of December. The tariff of 1824, he averred, had seriously injured foreign commerce, indeed it was his general proposition that any tariff even for revenue had that result. Statistics Rush had used he impeached, and he questioned the constitutional authority of the Secretary to make recommendations in his report of the nature he had.

His free trade arguments were as familiar as the protection arguments Rush had used, but couched in telling language they made a strong appeal to the interest of the consumer, the common people, rather than to an ideal of national prosperity. McDuffie was defending the cotton kingdom, for which English trade was essential. Rush's anticipation of new markets in other parts of the world seemed unreal to him. He forecast the ruin of the cotton growers if the tariff were increased, turning Rush's argument concerning internal trade against him. If one section was ruined, he affirmed, others would be also. Furthermore, he concluded, the policy of protection ultimately looked forward to the substitution of an internal revenue system in place of the present revenue system that depended on foreign commerce. This he thought would defeat not only the economic but also the political purposes of the Union.

There is little reason to choose either Rush's or McDuffie's paper as superior to the other. Both were based upon a priori assumptions stemming from different interests and idea structures, pointing toward different courses of national development. Nor is it possible at this distance to conclude satisfactorily whether Rush was right in his attribution of the growth of manufactures to the tariff, and his contention that the tariff aided foreign commerce; or that McDuffie was right in his assumption that prices were increased to the consumer and that any tariff, even one for revenue only, hindered commerce. The question could not have been settled then by statistical information the most exact, nor can it now. Of more importance was it that McDuffie had the upper hand. He commanded a majority in the Congress which, if the proper arrangements could only be made, might be the means of heaping most disastrous obloquy upon the administration.

The proper arrangements were made. Calhoun, Van Buren, McDuffie, with a few others, conceived the Machiavellian stroke that eventualized in the act American history justly knows as the "Tariff of Abominations," one of the most odious misuses of the power to govern in the history of the nation. The strategic problem of the Jacksonians was to unite the New England and Southern members of their party, but this could hardly be done without resolving their disagreement on the tariff question. An elaborate scheme was concocted by which both could be satisfied, and the administration discredited at the same time. A high tariff bill was to be brought in, drafted so as to be acceptable to the Middle States and the West but obnoxious to New England woolen manufacturers, and of course by definition obnoxious to the South. On final passage the Southerners would vote against it; so would the Adams men, for they would (it was thought) be unable to stomach the hardships it imposed upon manufacturers. Jackson followers from the North, on the other hand, would vote in favor of the bill. Thus the tariff would be defeated, as the Southerners wished, but odium of defeating it would fall upon the administration members, costing them the support of New England, New York, and Pennsylvania, while the Jacksonian Democrats in those states could pose as the supporters of the manufacturing interest.

Politically it was a bold, ingenious, subtle scheme, designed to knock the pins out from under the administration in the regions of its greatest strength. Throughout February and March Washington buzzed with the intriguing of Van Buren. Mallary, the Adams leader in the House, had no weapons with which to combat such finesse; but in spite of this when the test came the plot failed. Through a series of mischances, the bill passed both House and Senate, the latter by the vote of Daniel Webster who had some mighty explaining to do, and was signed by the President, becoming, though no one wished it, a law. "The bill," sneered John Randolph, "referred to manufactures of no sort or kind, except the manufacture of a President of the United States."

By principles of logic the failure of this scheme should have boomeranged to destroy those who had so deviously contrived it, but Jacksonian politics had little logic and less justice. The public knew nothing of what had transpired behind the doors of Van Buren's office; all that appeared on the surface was that an absurd tariff had been passed, and the government that passed it had to bear the blame for it. Passed or not, the political effect of the bill was the same. It was a ridiculous travesty on the protective principle, which Rush had none the less to defend.

Along with this oblique flanking attack the House opposition conducted simultaneously a frontal charge. This was the investigation of government expenditures by a select committee on retrenchment and reform. Begun by a novice in Congress out of sincere regard for good government, this opportunity to blacken the Whigs was not overlooked by the Jacksonian majority. A committee heavily weighted against Adams made a long, detailed report of the increased expenditures of the government, proving nothing really but the inadequacy of the executive staff in all departments. Sergeant of Pennsylvania made a minority report, but the effort might as well have been saved. The fact of increased expenditures could not be denied. Those that pointed it out had a political advantage over those that tried to justify it. Adams had called for still greater increases. It was easy for Ingham, Hamilton, Cambreleng and others to term these unnecessary uses of the public money, for the only defense that could be offered was efficiency in government, and most Americans in the South and West in 1818 preferred cheapness, remoteness, and inactivity to efficiency.

Rush smarted under this unprincipled attack, to which there could be no popular resistance. He felt, as did Adams, the injustice to the people from such a Congress, whose conduct touched a new low in political morality. His own department was subjected to the closest scrutiny. The committee found a multitude of things wrong, some of which Rush had already noted in his messages only to have them ignored by Congress. A sweeping reorganization of the department was recommended, including some administrative changes that might have had some merit had they been freed from the grasp of political machines. The contingent expense fund, already so small as seriously to handicap the department, the committee suggested should be further reduced in spite of Rush's testimony that it could not. The language of the report was carefully considered, so that wrongs and improprieties would be imputed though not stipulated. Rush made a vigorous defense of his department and its administration, but he had no way of retaliating upon the House committee except by stressing the need for an increased budget and asking for more clerks.

Under the political superficialities of this smear campaign there was the substance of an important theoretical conflict, which emphasized how far apart in their ideas on government the Jackson and Adams men really were. The committee put it forward as a principle, to which they doubtless felt attached in general, quite apart from its political immediacy, that to multiply offices and dependencies, to add to the cost of government, was inconsistent with the spirit and ends of a republic. Frugality, and the Jeffersonian maxims of the free man in the free state, were the standards they applied with whatever degree of honesty they found consistent with the party struggle, to their examination of the expenses of government. There was enough of an amalgamation of Jefferson and Jackson already to give a democratic complexion to the opposition. Rush, on the other hand, represented that sort of paternalism which has appeared occasionally in American history, the most sympathetic description of which speaks of government in terms of service. The protection movement, and the American System generally, conceived of the state as one of enlarged activities with an augmented bureaucracy necessary to accomplish national purposes beyond the power of individuals collectively to accomplish without political expression. There was nothing fundamentally undemocratic about this concept, unless by democracy is understood that sublimated ideal of free-acting individuals in an isolated rural community which too often has served as a naïve description of Jefferson's theories. Social well-being was never anathema to democracy, if not defined in hypocritical terms. But against leadership from a national administration opponents have always been able to raise cries of centralization, corruption, wastage, and interest, accusations few governments have been able to withstand sucessfully. Certainly in 1828 the Adams administration was not. Its inability to reach the emotions of the people was a critical failing, for the election was clearly going to turn upon the question of "a free or a prosperous America," an America of balanced employments and a perfected national economy, or of laissez faire, competitive enterprise, manufacturers unprotected and miseries unalleviated. Rush's lot was cast with that side on which the burden of proof rested.

III

It may appear strange to term "liberal" that point of view which encouraged manufactures by protective tariff and opposed everything in the laissez faire school of Smith, Malthus, Ricardo, and Mill that is usually thought of as nineteenth-century liberalism. But Carey, Niles, and Rush called themselves liberals, and to their contemporaries it did not seem incongruous. In England in the 1820's the Tory conservative was one who defended the agricultural interest, the Whig liberal one who welcomed or at least was reconciled to the expansion of commerce and the growth of factories. So in America the southern planter seemed by the English measure a conservative, the defender of the industrial interest a liberal.

A deeper meaning lay in the liberal's attitude toward international relations. The conviction that the old colonial system was disappearing, that in its place would come new nations free and self-sustaining, with institutions of government based on enlightened principles, had called forth in certain statesmen new ways of dealing with international problems. But it seemed in 1827–28 that these liberal world leaders were gone. The Czar Alexander died in 1825; his system was already tottering; our relations with England had reached an impossible position. The new order, liberalism as Rush defined it, was seriously threatened in the international as well as in the domestic field.

The English relation had been strained ever since the failure of the Rush—Stratford-Canning conversations. The aged Rufus King, fatally ill, was unable to improve them. In 1826 Adams prevailed upon Gallatin to accept an appointment as King's successor. There were four questions to be settled: the old boundary line disputes in Maine and Oregon, compliance with Czar Alexander's decision regarding slaves under the Treaty of Ghent, renewal of the Convention of 1818, about to expire, and settlement if possible of the West Indies trade matter. Rush was, of course, deeply interested. He followed Gallatin's negotiations closely, smarting even more than most Americans at the insulting treatment Canning gratuitously meted out to us. Liverpool's death in February 1827 seemed to leave no steadying hand or moderating influence to check Canning's determination to chastise America. England refused entirely to negotiate the West Indies trade and other matters of mutual concern.

Then in August death removed Canning. The amiable Goderich succeeded, and Gallatin concluded a general negotiation, including among other things the indefinite extension of the Convention of 1818.

Rush, on learning of Canning's death, poured all his misgivings over Anglo-American affairs into what proved to be a very popular pamphlet, *Sketch of the Character of Mr. Canning*. He wrote it to dispel the notion that the British premier, even though reputedly warm in support of the Latin American revolutions, was a liberal in the American sense, sympathetic with our aims in international dealings. British insularity, British nationalism alone dictated his policy toward the New World, Rush asserted.

He made it his boast, and it was cause of boast to him, that British policy, British interest, the hope of British sway, were even uppermost in his aspirations and schemes. To secure *these*, he called, as he said, the new States of America into existence. Truly he did, so far as the share that England had in that great work was concerned; it goes to make up a rich portion of his fame; as the earlier forecast of Henry Clay, acting upon an expanded love of human liberty, earns for *him* laurels, still richer, in the same field.

"He suddenly found himself the *champion* of liberalism, certainly without ever having been its child . . ." Rush denounced this pseudo-enlightenment, for no successful international schemes could ever be founded on such complete nationalism. American policy, he pointed out by contrast, was based on an affection for free institutions, the principle of reciprocity in trade relations, and notions of international justice.

The pamphlet went through several printings, attracting a considerable attention. In an oblique, but nevertheless an important way, it was a defense of the administration, for it not only explained the suspension of the West Indies trade in terms of the personal antagonism of Canning, but also presented a favorable view of American policy toward the rest of the world that did credit to the traditions which Adams and Rush, too, had done so much to form and uphold.

Rush needed every resource of his pen in 1828, for the campaign was waxing hot, and after the adjournment of Congress in May it occupied his whole attention. For more than a year the Secretary had been writing anonymous newspaper pieces in behalf of the administration, a discouraging and thankless task. At one time he had despaired entirely of doing any good, and asked Adams for the ministry at London Gallatin was vacating. But Adams had another councilor equally desperate: Barbour was proving as ineffectual in Virginia as Rush in Pennsylvania. He also asked for the English post, and was awarded it. The President was sympathetic. "The majority of the people in their respective States are inveterately opposed to the administration; and there is scarcely any condition so mortifying as that of being a minority at home."

There was some hope still for Pennsylvania, however. The conventions in every state meeting to endorse Adams for re-election had to agree on a running mate for the vice-presidential nomination. The possibilities were not numerous; the Adams party soon fixed on the Quaker State as the one whose electoral vote needed the most wooing. A caucus at Harrisburg proposed the name of Governor Shulze, but he declined to be considered. In his place Rush's name was inserted, not with any particular enthusiasm, but with some hope that, as the top-ranking Pennsylvanian in the government, he might carry a popular following. Rush was pleased to accept, but he had no confidence of success, and such were the political scruples of the time that he thereupon ceased his public campaigning altogether. What chance he had, therefore, of influencing the result was removed by his inaction.

Others were not so passive. From the presses all over the country poured books, pamphlets, resolutions, and testimonials, overpraising one side or damning the other. Adams was reviled as an aristocrat, his father's career reviewed to prove he could not have begotten a true republican, every conceivable means was used to vilify and reproach the administration. Rush was not spared. His abilities were scorned, his London ministry criticized. "Have you, like Lord Chatham, called forth the talent of the country in the service of the country?" demanded the Albany Jacksonians of the President. "Could no diplomatic or cabinet ministers be found of an order of intellect and accomplishments superior to Rush, Barbour, Southard, Middleton, Heman Allen or Ninian Edwards?" Another pamphlet referred vaguely to Dr. Rush: "Your train is swelled by the whole tribe of apostates, from the great family in New-York to the little family in Philadelphia—by all those who wander about the circles of political society without a home—by John Binns and the Secretary of the Hartford Convention!"

Political scribblers on the other side were not outdone. Among burning pages of slander against Jackson some paused to profess confidence in "the talents, patriotism and private character of Richard Rush." The "Great State Convention of Friends of the Administration" at Concord, New Hampshire, took pleasure in recommending the Secretary. "He is descended from one of the purest Revolutionary patriots: he is conspicuous for his talents, and distinguished for his virtues and industry. He has had long and varied experience in high and important posts, and is, in every respect, well qualified for any station to which the votes of his fellow citizens, or future events, may raise him." But for most of the Adams men Rush's importance lay in his support of the American System, while for most Jackson scriveners he only fitted into the picture they were drawing of aristocracy and wealth.

The climax of this exchange of paper blows came (for Rush) in midsummer. John Randolph, whose pen was characteristically as splenetic as his oratory, published an appendix to a new edition of his speech on retrenchment and reform of February 1 in which he attacked the personalities of the cabinet. Though all members received their share of abuse, none was treated with the savagery he meted out to Rush. Not fit, he wrote, to be Comptroller, Madison had made him Attorney-General, Adams had selected him to preside over the Treasury, and now he was candidate for Vice-President. He recalled the battle at Bladensburg, where General Winder had been

... assisted by "The Flying Cabinet," as Wilkinson had the insolence to designate them in his diagram of that famous rout. In this memorable *dis-engagement* the GRAND ROLE was played by Mr. Attorney General, "for that time only," *without his hat.* ... And verily, never did political adventurer make more of his *parts*, than this solemn gentleman has done. Never were abilities so much below mediocrity so well rewarded; no, not when Caligula's *Horse* was made Consul.

A few days ago I stumbled upon the following stanza of an unfinished poem [Randolph continued] on the Glories and Worthies of our Administration:
"And as for R——, his early locks of snow,
  Betray the frozen region that's below.
  Though Jove upon the race bestow'd some fire,
  The gift was all exhausted by the sire.
  A sage consum'd what thousands might well share,
  And ASHES! only, fell upon the heir!"
These lines are the only article of the growth, produce, or manufacture, of the country north of the Patapsco, that I have, knowingly, used since the Tariff bill passed. They are by a witty son of a witty sire—as Burns sings, "a true gude fellow's get."

This was not the first time Randolph had baited Rush. Since 1826 he had brutally assailed him on the floor of the House, ridiculing also the memory of his father. Rush had provocation enough. He determined to answer the Virginian in his own terms. Accordingly he sent to the *National Journal* a long letter signed "Julius" which appeared on July 26 and was immediately reissued in pamphlet form by Peter Force with this title page:

> John Randolph,/ Abroad and at Home./ The Fiend is long, and lean, and lank,/ And

moves upon a spindle-shank. OLD SONG./ By Julius./ Washington . . . 1828.

It is unique among Rush's writings, for never before or afterwards did he indulge so in personalities; but it was not unique among the scurrilous tracts of that year. It was angry, vitriolic, acidulous, and cruel; but President Adams considered it "only severe retaliation."

Rush lampooned Randolph's bizarre, comic appearance and his shrill voice as he moved in London society. "His grotesque aspect, the object of popular stare and scientific speculation; his everlasting attempts at *effect* whether in conduct or conversation; his harrangues, given out in accents so novel . . . his diverting lapses from the observances of the world; his profound obeisance to rank . . . kept showing itself in ways exquisitely ludicrous. . ." He portrayed him as "a sort of wandering whimsiculo" posturing in the clubs and drawing-rooms of London, "who looked only in sneers, and spoke only in sarcasms." "What a ridiculous charlatan I am describing." Thirty years Randolph had been in public life, yet he had achieved nothing. His sterile career had been a combination of Harlequinism and depravity; a "hideous Brazenface" he was, "incorrigible in his foul appetites." Rush concluded his burning pages with a sentence in which there is some justice:

This side of the commission of flagitious crimes that incur the public vengeance of the law, it is probable that a worse individual than John Randolph is hardly to be found; one who, in his life of more than fifty years, has done less good of any kind, public or private, and who has devoted himself more unremittingly to giving pain to others; who has committed more offenses against those good feelings and good manners that are the cement of the social and moral world; whose career has been [more] broadly marked by affectation, mummery and malevolence.

It was a remarkable performance for a customarily temperate and reserved individual. Though it has no value beyond the issues of that year of acrimony, it is probable that Rush more thoroughly enjoyed writing it than anything else he ever did.

His pen was busy every day with other tracts aimed at larger audiences, in which he sought to present the case for the American System, and defend the Adams administration as its proponents. From one pamphlet Rush wrote, his longest and most serious, it can be perceived how important he considered the fate of the protectionist ideas. Published late in 1827, it bore the title page:

Letters/ to the/ People of Pennsylvania,/ upon the Subject/ of the/ Presidential Election./ Originally Published in/ The United States Gazette./ By Simon Snyder,/ A Native of Pennsylvania./ "If we suffer ourselves to be led captive by *Military Glory*, this Republic must/ inevitably share the same fate of all that preceded it."/ Letter, No. XX./ Philadelphia: Printed for the United States Gazette Office/ 1827.

It was reprinted in 1828. Not without significance is it that Rush chose the signature of Simon Snyder, first democratic governor of Pennsylvannia and his own preceptor in public life, under which to appeal to the voters in behalf of manufactures. The custom of anonymity was a familiar one, but Rush came near exceeding its liberties; he described himself as a person with no stake in the election, one never in public life, but a merchant frequently called to Europe on business!

The twenty "letters" in this tract deal with all the principal issues of the campaign, from the House of Representatives election to the "corrupt bargain" between "Blifil and Black George," as Randolph had termed the appointment of Clay to the State Department. The opposition, Rush declared, had blocked internal improvements, had impeded foreign commerce by defeating the West Indies trade bill, and had discouraged domestic industry by defeating the tariff. It had failed to support a large navy by refusing to vote for a naval academy, had opposed the constructive efforts of the Colonization Society, had embarrassed the administration's attempts to make economic and political progress with Latin America at the Panama Congress.

But most important of all was the issue of nationalism opposed by states' rights. This Rush presented as the central issue of the election. The pamphlet being addressed primarily to Pennsylvanians, he had no hesitation in laying all the blame for opposition on the South, where also he found the liveliest anti-national spirit. He pulled out all the stops of sectionalism, ignoring Jacksonian supporters in the North, trying thereby to portray the contest as one of North against South.

States' rights, Rush asserted, had been the bane of our national existence. But for jealous refusal to surrender sovereign powers, the Revolution would have ended two years sooner. Every subsequent national enterprise had been heckled by the lingering spirit of particularism. Now the Southerners would undermine the national system by their construction of the Constitution: "a construction which would render our bond of union a *mere rope of sand*—a construction, which would eventually degrade the general government to the condition of mere commissioners of the State sovereignties." He cited the resolutions recently passed by the Virginia legislature against national tariffs and internal improvements, accompanied by a declaration that Virginia would sustain the general government in its legitimate powers; against the latter ten senators had voted, an act near to treason in its implications. Shall the enemies of the Constitution be elevated to positions of control and administration, he asked?

He argued for the constitutionality of the tariff and internal improvements—"the high power to make a road, to build a bridge, or to dig a ditch"—and of the Panama Congress mission; and ended with strictures against non-voting. Only a fourth of the eligible voters of Pennsylvania had exercised their suffrage in the previous election, a culpable negligence, "Snyder" charged. "To this highly favoured nation is confided the great experiment, whether or not, Man is capable of self-government. If this great experiment fail, the world is destined to experience another long night of barbarism."

"Simon Snyder" scarcely made a stir in the election excitement, even in Pennsylvania. James Buchanan, Jackson manager, appreciated as no one else the possibility of uniting Philadelphia laborers with up-state farmers and miners for the nucleus of his strength, adding to it whatever woolen manufacturers had been seduced by the "abominable" tariff act into believing a vote for Old Hickory was a vote for protection. Not social groups, however, or political traditions or economic interests explained the way the vote went. Party lines were obliterated in the chaos of personalities and recriminations. The Jackson campaign was much the better conceived and better managed of the two. Binns was the Adams manager. He did his best, but he was no match for the bold strokes of Buchanan. His bag of tricks contained nothing new, and in competition with the enthusiasm of the popular side his efforts paled. The best he could contribute was a series of cartoons based on Jackson's execution of six Tennessee militiamen years earlier. Carrying at the top six black coffins, they became known as "Binns' Coffin Hand Bills." So successful were they in attracting attention that Binns published other series lampooning or attacking the General, until he became the most notorious publicist in the election.

He suffered for it. When the results were in, and it was known that Jackson and Calhoun had carried Pennsylvania, a mob intoxicated with victory stormed Binns's house and office. But the publisher was prepared for them with barricades they could not penetrate, and escaped without injury.

Rush wrote a long letter to this staunch friend in the hour he learned definitely of the loss of his own state.

The issue of our elections in Pennsylvania, is, to be sure, matter of regret. I have seen how ardent have [been] your endeavours to prevent such an issue. To have done our duty, so as to look back without reproach, is, at all times, an honorable lot. So let it be with yourself and those around you in Philadelphia on the present occasion. For myself, I have felt it a duty to be perfectly passive in all respects as regards the contest, since I was made a candidate, leaving others to act, and the people to decide.

This was not quite a correct description of his rôle, but there were good reasons for convincing others of the truth of it. "I have seen with sincere concern the personal inconvenience to which yourself and family were put on the night of the election, but trust that there will be no repetition of such scenes."

Concerning the defeat of his own candidacy he expressed no chagrin.

Individually, I never permitted myself to form hopes. I shall therefore not be disappointed. There is evidence enough here, that my candidateship was not of my own seeking, but the contrary; not but that I was heartily willing that my name should be used, if it were thought that it could do the least good; but I never thought it would. It seemed to me an occasion where all personal wishes should be entirely lost sight of, in the principles and cause at stake. It was therefore always my opinion that some citizen ought to have been taken up for the Vice Presidency from a state less doubtful than Pennsylvania, and whose vote might have had a chance of being drawn to the common cause by such a measure.

He was, nevertheless, apprehensive about the future. "We must still hope for the best, and never despair of the Republic," he wrote. But he was filled with forebodings of evil. "I trust in God that General Jackson, if he be elected,[1] will not do the mischief which many of his past actions lead us to fear. Honest we all believe him to be, though of such violent temper and passions." At this point Rush made one of the most egregiously erroneous guesses that was put forward in this entire period, a guess which reveals his ignorance of Jackson's true character:

My own prediction is, that he [Jackson] will resign, and Mr. Calhoun be the President; not, indeed, immediately, but long before his first four years run out. He knows not the immense labors that devolve upon the President. For the labors of the field he may equal any body; but the complicated, diversyfied, everlasting, labors of the cabinet—these he will not, cannot, bear. Wholly untrained as he has been to them, neither his years nor his health, can bear them. Once in the post, his triumph will be complete. Possession will soon satiate. He will remain long enough to put his system in operation, whatever

---

[1] Returns from other states were not yet in.

it is intended to be, thus tasting the sweets of power, if sweets they can be called. He will then close his extraordinary career, consulting at once his ease, and his further fame, by a resignation. Such is my belief.

The results of the election made Rush feel somewhat better. Indeed, though the electoral vote stood 178 to 83,[2] the popular vote was much closer, Adams receiving forty-four per cent of the total; and such was the unequal distribution of the electoral representation that a good case could be made that again as in 1824 the people's will had hardly been expressed. Certainly the methods of the Democrats in Pennsylvania and New York were of a character to cast doubt on the validity of the result. Possibly, as Professor Channing remarked, it was more honorable to have been defeated than elected in 1828.

Many of the administration apparently thought so. Clay, Porter, Wirt came back to Washington rested and refreshed. They seemed to find a challenge in defeat that brought them new strength. The gloom of the previous year only Southard retained. He alone of the cabinet had held his state for Adams and Rush; having tasted victory, defeat was the more bitter.

Rush was of two minds. He dreaded retirement, but he could not contemplate longer service with a Congressional majority against him. He turned to his winter fiscal campaign—"It will, as usual, be severe"—and his last report as relief from the rigors of political crises.

Technically Rush was an able steward of the Treasury. This, combined with the prosperity of the four years of his tenure, produced an accounting that truly was a credit to the administration. The nation was in an opulent financial condition, it was at peace, its fiscal structure was sound. Jackson inherited the results of successful service. Moreover, Rush had expanded the scope of the department, by the establishment of branch banks in the new West, improvement of the revenue service on

---

[2] This was the electoral count for President. For Vice-President Calhoun received 171, Rush 83, Smith of South Carolina 7.

the Great Lakes (this at the behest of his crude but colorful friend, John Jacob Astor), and in many other ways. He had adequate cause to be satisfied with his record.

These reflections sustained him through January and February, and he could contemplate the end of his term with some complacency. Rush alone of the cabinet urged Adams to participate in Jackson's inauguration. He attended the President through all the last hours of the term, finally after dinner on March 3 he handed in his resignation at Adams' new dwelling on Meridian Hill.

But this interlude of peacefulness and adjustment was brought to an abrupt end for Rush by Jackson's inaugural address. There had been a coldness between the General and Adams officialdom, understandable after the scurrilities of the campaign, but it was not expected that he would do anything to preserve these animosities. It was therefore a complete surprise when Jackson spoke of the "task of *reform*" in language that imputed inefficiency, even dishonesty, to his predecessors. This, together with a general comment on fiscal policy, Rush interpreted as a public attack upon him and his colleagues by the new President. His bitterness and resentment, fed by Adams', waxed hot in the spring as he returned to private life.

His brother James seized this inopportune moment to ask Richard to present a request for an office for him to Jackson. When Richard curtly refused his mother joined in importuning his help. A measure of Rush's strong feeling can be gathered from his reply to his mother and brother:

General Jackson has taken away my office, and I am left with a wife and seven children, without a farthing of income; and with but contingent prospects of earning one. I have no complaint against him for this, as no citizen has any claim of right upon the tenure of office. But I must decline becoming even the remote messenger or medium of passing to his hands a letter that looks, eventually, to an official favor at them.

Indeed, as the full extent of the revolution in administrative personnel which Jackson wrought became clear, it seemed to

NATIONAL PLANNING

Rush that a new age had come in the government at Washington. Since 1811 and before, the same group had dominated the national government. Now not only a new president, but a whole new bureaucracy was ushered in. Adams retired not like a defeated but resolved leader of a party; rather he withdrew as a persecuted martyr, leaving the leadership to Clay and others of the nationalists. Rush, having to choose between Clay and Jackson, faced a period of indecision and hesitation. New patterns were in the making, new alignments, a new structure of politics. The American System was still fundamentally sound, but as a popular rallying post it had failed. Niles was giving up, so was Carey; Rush did not surrender his principles, but he had to adjust them to the new conditions of Jacksonian Democracy.

VIII

PRIVATE CALLING AND PUBLIC DUTIES

It was eighteen years after his retirement from the Treasury Department before Rush was again called to public office. This period of his life, from 1829 to 1847, was as long as the period of continuous service which preceded it, and it is an exceedingly interesting one, during which his private concerns as a party leader in Pennsylvania, as a gentleman farmer at the edge of Philadelphia, as a man of letters, and as an agent abroad for various American interests, all brought him rich experiences, that have a significant place in the social changes of the thirties and forties. It deserves careful attention from his biographer, for it reveals him at the most independent period of his life, less dominated by the opinions of others, less susceptible to their leadership, than he had been in his several official positions. But the materials for the study of these two decades lie mostly in private archives which cannot be utilized for this work. When a fuller study of Rush appears, all his manifold activities of these years can be given their due; among other matters the curious history of anti-Masonic politics in Pennsylvania will be much more comprehensively told than has hitherto been possible, and light will be thrown on the Bank issue of Jackson's administration. For the present purposes all that is contemplated is a brief account of those activities that were public in their nature, with no more than a few references to his other employments.

Ruch faced a serious problem of personal finances when he left the Treasury in March 1829. He had built a pleasant home in Washington in which he had lived only a few years, but without a salary he could no longer maintain it; his properties in Philadelphia were not sufficiently remunerative to make it worth while to try to meet the high cost of living there. He did have some land in York County, however, and some property in the town of York. To that little city he removed his family in

March, establishing Catherine and five of their children there. Ben, the eldest, and Richard Henry, were in school, the first in Princeton, the second preparing for West Point. Rush sold his holdings in Philadelphia and rented his Washington house for five hundred and fifty dollars a year, in order to amass a capital fund on which to start private life.

He had some idea of returning to the practice of law, in which York offered an opportunity; but this would be postponed at least a year, for he had arranged before he left the Treasury to perform an errand that would be both remunerative and pleasant. This was an era of canal building. The Erie Canal with the prosperity it was bringing New York had started projects all over the East. Pennsylvania was already honeycombed with waterway connections; Pittsburghers had conceived of linking their city with Philadelphia by a great trunk canal through the seven Allegheny ranges; expenditures for these magnificent ditches were the political footballs of the decade. The Chesapeake cities, viewing with no enthusiasm the diversion of richly laden barges to northern routes, were determined to emulate the Yankees. Commercial interests in Georgetown and Alexandria formed a corporation, which mapped a canal route from the Chesapeake west to the District of Columbia, thence up the Potomac, around the Little and Great Falls, through the mountains to join the Ohio River. Over this waterway, they hoped, would come the agricultural products of the great western country, in exchange for the manufactured goods they would import and sell in the vast markets thus opened. But the project had foundered for lack of funds. The directors of the corporation turned to the best resource left them, a loan from foreign capitalists. They needed an agent to conduct the negotiations abroad, and quite naturally turned to Richard Rush, who had been one of the supporters of their scheme, who knew the history of it as well as any of them, and who had had more experience in foreign countries than anyone else available. Articles of agreement were entered into, and after he settled his family in York Rush left at once for England.

Sailing from New York on the last day of April, he had a miserable, unhappy passage of twenty-two days during which he was horribly torn between seasickness and homesickness. He remained in Liverpool long enough to recover, then proceeded by stage to London. There he stayed eight weeks, calling on all his financial acquaintances, interviewing bankers, and trying vainly to find the capital he needed. Even the support of powerful friends, among them the Duke of Wellington, who was exceedingly kind, could not produce results. Constantly discouraged at the rebuffs he received, he occupied his free time renewing the pleasant relationships of earlier years, visiting the tomb of his two little daughters who had died during his ministry, studying the political crises surrounding Catholic Emancipation and demands for electoral reform. In July, encouraged by his London advisers, he crossed to Holland, his first (and only) visit to the continent of Europe. The beauty of that lovely land enchanted him; he wrote enthusiastic descriptions of it to his family, but he seemed after two months to have got no further with his business.

Returning to London in September, he spent another month in the financial marts of that city. He had a grand time at the theatres, comparing Fanny Kemble's Juliet with his memories of Mrs. Siddons in the same rôle, and with his host of friends in society. But his funds were running low, and he faced by October the unwelcome prospect of having to return empty-handed. Quite unexpectedly he began to receive encouragement in letters from Holland; for a month longer he labored, and on November 20, 1829, jubilantly concluded with the Amsterdam banking house of Cromelines a loan of 3,750,000 French francs. In spite of the dangers he made a hurried winter voyage home.

The importance of the canal issue was dwarfed in this case as in all others by the coming of the railroad, and this chapter in Rush's life was soured for him, not only by the unpleasant separation from his family, but by the ultimate refusal of the corporations that had hired him to pay him in full for his services. It was the source of considerable unpleasantness for him until his death, and even then he left a sizable claim against the city of Washington. "Corporations have no souls, as Sir Edward Coke said a long time ago," he remarked. But the trip had afforded him some pleasant moments. It had been a welcome interlude between public and private life, had refreshed his cherished contacts in England, and had given him new insights into British politics.

There was great interest in America in the change of ministry in England. The accession of the Whigs, representing, as they appeared to, the liberalism of Britain, and traditionally friendly to America since their espousal of the colonial cause in the Revolution, was presented to the public in a great flood of articles as a new era in British politics which promised a more friendly attitude toward the United States. In this propaganda Rush took a hand, publishing a number of letters over the signature "Temple" on *The English Whigs*. He opposed the popular attitude, bringing a great body of evidence to prove that the Grey ministry was no more liberal or republican than the Tory régime of Wellington had been. The true representatives of Whig principles, those who had attacked the principles of the Holy Alliance, like Lord Holland, he pointed out, were not in the government, or if they were they had been relegated to subordinate positions. Rush urged Americans to look for no helpful measures from Lord Grey. Like Huskisson advocating free trade, he would not let his principles operate beyond the interest of England.

The latter was always ready to bring his principles into operation just at the point where English manufactures had the complete ascendancy. So, his lordship will be careful that his meliorations, whether for parliamentary representation or otherwise, do not quite reach the point that would seriously impair the established influence of the English aristocrat, or, in the terrible commotions that are coming on, the great hereditary principles and systems of the European world.

A Whig, he declared, was only less a King's Man than a Tory. Both alike were remote from republicanism, "both alike afraid of taint, from coming too near to the people." He emphasized, as he had so often done before, the peculiar differences between America and the Old World, stressing the fact that a change in ministry could not bridge the great gulf that separated the ideals and the political habits of the two countries. His few months in England had not made him any the less an ardent nationalist, an enthusiastic proponent of the principles of the American System.

But to be an adherent of the American System in Pennsylvania in 1830 was almost the equivalent of being without a political party. The Jackson machine in the state was stronger than it had been in 1828, the Clay machine had just held its own. But there was a great group of persons whose opinions had no political expression in the platforms of either party, who found themselves dissatisfied by the attitudes on leading public questions, particularly the canals within the state, expressed by the Democrats and the National Republicans alike. In this respect Pennsylvania anti-Jackson men were facing the same need for readjustment that all followers of Adams were facing in other regions. But in Pennsylvania the struggle was more bitter and more vocal. In the next few years Rush was to be at the center of it.

In Washington the Jackson administration was being made ridiculous by the vanity of women and the obstinacy of a sentimental old warrior. Winsome Peggy O'Neil had been relieved of her widowhood by the gallantry of General Eaton; the cabinet was crumbling; "Our great men are exhibiting themselves in attitudes," wrote the disgusted Adams, "which seem to require the Talents of a new Painter for the Rotunda." Clay himself was appearing steadfast only in his opposition to the Democrats, willing, it seemed, to compromise the provisions of the program he had so long defended to gain support of disaffected Democrats. The Bank issue was beginning to split the administration. People in southern Pennsylvania especially were saying that the only solution for the financial problems they faced was to oppose the rechartering. The time was ripe for a new political movement. With the suddenness of a crusade it came, in 1830, with the organization all through the southern and western part of the state of local committees of correspondence of the anti-Masonic movement.

In April 1831, newspapers published a public letter from four citizens of York to Richard Rush, asking his opinion of the Masonic Order, and declaring their intention of publishing his reply. Anti-Masonry was flourishing in New York; a certain William Morgan, apostate Mason who had threatened to reveal the secrets of the society, had been kidnapped and apparently murdered. The result was an outburst of indignation against the Masonic order, which very shortly began to express the political unrest of the anti-Jackson Democrats and the anti-Clay Republicans. Rush in his public reply heartily espoused the cause of the new revolt. He placed the arguments on the highest political plane. "I see objections to secret societies, because," he wrote, "pursuing objects not known to the public, through means not known to the public, they act under diminished responsibilities to the public." In America, where "primary principles of politican and social action, are all in the face of day," one could not properly be first a Mason and then an American. Yet the trial of Morgan had revealed all too clearly the willingness of some Masons to place the integrity of their order before the integrity of the laws of the country, even indulging in intimidation. The press, legally and traditionally free, had evidently been bought by the "abandoned fiends of the order." Every free man who cherished the liberties of America should unite to suppress such treacherous, mysterious, unprincipled attacks upon the birthright of the citizens.

The question quickly passed beyond that of the Morgan trial and Masonic activities. This was only the lighting of a fuse. It gave that which the American System had always lacked during the Adams administration, namely, the grounds for a popular attack upon the Jacksonian party. In Pennsylvania the next three years were taken up with the attempt of the National Republicans and the anti-Masons to unite together against Jackson, for both espoused the principle of protection. The anti-Masonic convention of May 1831 contained only those who were "friendly to a system of national internal improvement, and who have no connection with, but on the contrary, are opposed to the Masonic combination." The movement seemed to offer to Rush his best opportunity to continue advocacy of the policies he had for four years as Secretary of the Treasury defined and propagated. In its largest aspects it was the successor to the Protectionist societies Carey had formed which had used all the surplus political energies of the state in the twenties.

Rush wrote voluminously for the anti-Masonic movement. Through his efforts York became one of the centers of agitation. But as Jackson's policies on the Bank reached their fruition, he discovered he was veering more and more toward the administration. Both Clay and Jackson were Masons, but Clay had not the same record of patronage of the order that Jackson had. In the 1832 state election the attempt of the majority of anti-Masons to unite with the National Republicans was defeated by the publication of one of Rush's letters at a strategic moment. One anti-Masonic paper noted that "the bitterness displayed by Richard Rush in his occasional effusions was calculated to disgust the friends of Mr. Clay wherever they have been circulated." The leading anti-Masonic order in Boston was hot against Rush: "In the city of Philadelphia the letter was disregarded, but in York County—the residence of Mr. Rush, and elsewhere—the National Republicans were equally enraged and disgusted at the letter, and in York they refused to vote at all, or in the moment of indignation, threw their votes for Jackson."

Though this account was exaggerated, it is true that Rush's tone had antagonized many Clay men who might have voted for the anti-Masonic candidate for governor. But he was determined to prevent such a combination until the Bank war in which he was fighting could be settled. Though as Secretary of the Treasury he had been one of the leading supporters of the Bank of the United States and had devoted much of his last Annual Report to praising its work, he now joined in the campaign against it. The reasons which persuaded him thus to reverse himself arose from the local situation in Pennsylvania, where many were convinced that the Bank had hampered the commercial interests by its policies in relation to state banks. Rush was attacked throughout the state by the National Republicans, and subjected to a barrage of abuse of dimensions he had never before experienced. Biddle, of course, was deeply affronted, as were many other Philadelphia friends; his membership in the American Philosophical Society was revoked during one of the most remarkable transports in which the board of that venerable institution ever indulged itself. His attitude on the Bank cost him the senatorship in December 1832. The legislature was considering him, Jonathan Sergeant, and William McKean, the son of Thomas McKean with whom Rush had nearly fought a duel in 1809. The Clay supporters in the legislature tried to combine with the anti-Masons behind Sergeant, but the Rush managers blocked this move; then, his letter approving Jackson's removal of the deposits appearing just at this time, the anti-Masons deserted Rush, and McKean was chosen.

Firmly and notoriously supporting the administration on the Bank issue, Rush now emerged as a Democrat attempting to bring the anti-Masons into the Democratic ranks. This strange amalgamation would have been disastrous from the point of view of the movement itself, but it would have prevented the combination which did take place between Clay's managers in the state and Thaddeus Stevens, the messiah of anti-Masonism in its waning years. The disgruntled element among the German Democrats nominated Henry Muhlenburg for governor in 1832, thus splitting the Democratic party; Rush tried to lead the German anti-Masons also behind Muhlenburg, and some did go with him, but the traditional spectacle of the Germans marching to the polls to vote, regardless of previous commitment, for "Sheneral Shackson," defeated his attempt, as it had all previous ones. The only result of his maneuver was to rend asunder the Pennsylvania Democrats and assure the election of a National Republican anti-Masonic candidate. This combination by the mid-thirties came to be known as the Whig party; by the time it achieved political stability Rush was in the camp of the opposition.

His political efforts were not apparently leading Rush anywhere but into a maze during the thirties; yet the complex streams of thought that characterized the Jacksonian era all flowed into the one great stream of a renewal of democratic enthusiasm, to which the crusade of Anti-Masonism lent a tone of high morality. As he stressed the distinctions between America and the Old World, and as he defended free institutions against secret societies, Rush experienced a sort of revival of his principles. In his writing in these years he turned more often than ever before to the fundamental problems of political relationships. He re-read some of the great Renaissance and eighteenth-century classics of politics, infusing something of their spirit into his work.

In nothing does Rush appear to better advantage than his writing. Not only was he a pleasant stylist, but he seemed also imbued with a sense of the importance of his subjects, giving his pages at once a gravity and a charm. His many tracts on anti-Masonism and the Bank have little of permanent interest, for the issues they dealt with died in the depression of 1837; but in 1833 he published a book which may still be read with profit and delight. It was the first installment of the journals he had kept while Minister in London, carefully edited and emended to do something to improve the relations between the two countries.

Fearful as he was that a general European war was about to break out, in which we would inevitably be involved, and convinced also that our best policy was an understanding with England along the lines he had tried to draw while in London, Rush easily reconciled this point of view with his deep conviction of the separatism of America in spirit and in policy from all European ambitions. Oregon, the fisheries, the Canadian relation, and the Northeastern boundary questions were still persisting, but Secretary Van Buren was having considerable success with

Charles Vaughan, the British Minister. Our relations with France, however, were clouded by a quarrel over spoliation claims. It was a strategic moment to take advantage of the good feeling with England to improve it.

Rush's intention was made very clear in his preface. He hoped, he said, to educate the people of both countries, unhappily ignorant as they were of the questions that existed between them, and of the point of view of the other side. He made arrangements for simultaneous publication of the book in London and Philadelphia, though with a slight difference in title which has been confusing to bibliographers ever since. The Philadelphia edition issued as *Memoranda of a Residence at the Court of London;* the English edition omitted the first two words. It proved necessary to bring out a second edition within a month at Philadelphia, oddly enough from different plates by a different publisher. Most copies in the United States today are the London edition, and pagination usually refers to it.

It was a delightful work, full of scintillating description and amusing incident, as well as serious discussion of diplomatic questions. Rush had carefully excised all unpleasantness and all his resentment of English arrogance or journalistic criticism which he had confided to his diaries when they were written. Adams was not deceived by the amiable impression the book gave, but he approved of the deception; "Blessed are the Peacemakers," he wrote Rush. His English friends were fulsome in their compliments. Vaughan found it helpful in his labors. "It does honor to your taste & to your discrimination," he declared, "& it will do a great deal of service in carrying on that improvement in the feelings of the two countries towards each other, which has been for some time in progress to my great satisfaction . . . . the precis you have given of the questions under discussion between the two Gov[ts] & not finally settled, will be an excellent text Book for the next American Minister who may be appointed to reside at the Court of London."

I

As he gravitated toward the Democratic party, Rush found himself more and more out of sympathy with political leaders in York, who were strong in the Whig union of anti-Masonry with National Republicanism. This, together with some personal matters, caused him to leave York and settle on a farm he owned a short drive out of Philadelphia. Here in a handsome little cottage a century old he built up a small estate, which he called Sydenham, combining farming with a modest law practice that access to the city made possible. His reunion with many old friends was a stimulation and joy to him. Sydenham became a familiar rendezvous for the leading members of the Democratic party in Philadelphia; Rush was once more in the political swing of things.

Not unnaturally he was singled out for some public services, for he had earned the gratitude of the party by his defense of Jackson's Bank policy in the state where that issue had been most warmly disputed. The first sign of favor came in 1835 when Jackson appointed Rush and Benjamin Howard of Baltimore joint commissioners to settle a boundary controversy between Michigan and Ohio. A second came in July 1836, when John Forsyth, Secretary of State, notified Rush that the President had chosen him to act as the agent of the United States at London to secure the Smithson bequest. His salary was to be three thousand dollars a year, his expense fund two thousand dollars, and a letter of credit for ten thousand dollars drawn to M. de Rothschild was to cover legal expenses. He would be required to post a bond of a hundred thousand dollars, and to leave at once.

This came as no surprise to Rush, for he had been influential in persuading Congress to make the necessary appropriation for the mission. A curious and rather wonderful story lay behind it. James Smithson had been a scientist of some ability during the first quarter of the century. Born the bastard son of the Duke of Northumberland and Elizabeth Hungerford Keate, a woman twice married and twice widowed, he had started life as Lewis Macie, studied at Pembroke College, Oxford, won fame as an analytical chemist and mineralogist, visited Paris in 1791 and become converted to the republican doctrines of the Revolution. Friend of Sir Joseph Banks, Sir Humphry Davy, Humboldt, Arago, and others of the scientific world, he represented the liberal social philosophy which was one of the vitalizing elements of scientific research at that period. A gambler, a bachelor, something of an eccentric, restless and wayward, he lived entirely on the continent after he began his chemical work. He inherited the fortunes of his mother's families, the Hungerfords and Keates, and those also of her two husbands, Dickinson and Macie. Consequently when he died at Genoa in 1829 he left a substantial estate, which he had surprisingly willed to the United States of America for the purpose of creating "an establishment for the increase and diffusion of knowledge among men." Why he did so no other reason than his affection for republican principles can explain, and this, of course, was hardly enough for other claimants to his fortune, among whom was the British Crown. After several suits had failed the Crown notified the President that the estate was in the safekeeping of the Court of Chancery. This was in 1835. Congress at first opposed the acceptance of the gift, but the pressure of learned societies and scholarly persons overcame their reluctance, and in 1836 the appropriation of ten thousand dollars was made for the expenses of securing the bequest.

Rush posted his enormous bond with the help of his brother-in-law General Mason and Benjamin Howard of Baltimore. With his son Ben, and with Peggy O'Neal Eaton, blushing in her new dignity as wife of the American Minister to Spain, for a shipmate, he sailed from New York to Liverpool, where he arrived on August 31, 1836. Reaching London, he instituted suit in Chancery in the name of the President, claiming the right of the United States to the estate. Then began an interminable succession of days and weeks in which nothing was done. There were arrears of more than eight hundred cases on the Chancery docket. Nothing could hurry the Court's majestic processes. A member of Parliament warned that "a chancery suit was a thing that might begin with a man's life and its termination be his epitaph." Four months elapsed as fall passed into winter before the first hearing was held; then winter passed into spring and spring to summer as the Master in Chancery studied the case. Prospects seemed encouraging for the United States, for both Crown and executors put up very little fight, but legal details were tedious and expensive. "It seems that something is to be paid for every step taken," Rush complained, "every line written, and almost every word spoken by counsel, senior and junior, solicitors, clerks, and everybody connected with the courts, and officers attached to them." But he persisted. "I follow up the Smithsonian Legacy in a way that I hope may induce the Chancery lawyers to make an end of the business the sooner, if only to get rid of my teasing," he wrote his wife.

Advertisement for heirs produced none, but did turn up vexatious small claims against the estate and revealed some extraordinary things about Smithson's life on the continent. This occupied the latter half of 1837, causing delays which vexed Rush sorely.

But London was offering its usual diversions. During "the first interval in my little Smithsonian steps" he went to the dockyards at Greenwich, where he observed "the alarming advances made in naval preparation, above all, war steam-ships, and totally new marine artillery," which England could boast. With troubles in Canada, especially with rumors of England's arming the Indians on our western frontiers, he was exceedingly apprehensive of these naval preparations. He wrote Joel Poinsett, the new Secretary of War, careful accounts of what he saw, urging effective defense armament in America. England had, he thought, greater military strength than he had ever seen, greater sources of revenue than ever before; he warned Poinsett that no outcry about debt or taxes would prevent her going into war.

Uprisings in Canada had occasioned great debates in Parliament on the bill to reorganize that province. Durham, who Rush heard was *"perhaps the most choleric man in Europe,"* was going to Quebec as "dictator." Excitement was so high that "government steamers have been sent out from Falmouth to cruise for our New York packets kept back by easterly winds, that their letters and papers may be obtained if fallen in with." The atmosphere was charged with emotion and anxiety. "We live," he remarked in another letter to Poinsett, "in an age in which the world is moving forward and we are not the nation to lag behind. On the contrary, it is a paramount advantage we have, it is in fact an element of power with us, that, having existing establishments that fetter us less, and minds more ready for new investigations, than is generally seen in older nations, we adopt improvements sooner and more effectually."

Entertainments at the country homes of the Earl of Clarendon, Lord Lyttleton, Mr. Coke's wonderful "Holkham," and many others helped pass pleasant week-ends; the death of King William, the accession of the young Queen and plans for her coronation were absorbing topics for Rush's letters home. But the legacy business was still paramount. At the beginning of 1838 he restated the position of the United States and made certain concessions, in order to expedite matters. The Master's report, ready in March, was made and confirmed, and finally on the ninth of May Chancellor Lyndhurst solemnly pronounced the decree adjudging the Smithson bequest to the United States.

Two years was excellent time in which to complete a Chancery suit in those days of *Jarndyce* vs *Jarndyce*. It was a tribute to Rush's conscientiousness and energy that the matter had not dragged out much longer, and he flattered himself that he had put through the business "sooner than Congress and the executive expected." But it was still necessary to collect the bequest. Most of it was in three percent annuities, which he decided to convert into gold and bring home as bullion. Selling a hundred thousand pounds worth of annuities was not a simple matter. Rush and Colonel Aspinwall, our able consul at London, proceeded very cautiously, lest they flood the market and depress the price. Aspinwall acted as commission agent at a nominal percentage, and the sales proceeded throughout June. Rush was pleased at the way things went, though he was constantly anxious for its finish. Once a peculiar worry struck him:

The little Queen I have always understood is a great eater, and every newspaper tells us she is a great frolicker. Now, if the little thing should chance to be taken sick in these junketing times of the coronation, only think how the stocks would come down. People would have the Duke of Cumberland before their imaginations and what not besides—so, as we are now at the close of the week, I think we had better get to work again on Monday or Tuesday in earnest, not waiting for a rise lest, peradventure, a fall should plump upon us instead . . .

On June 26 the sale was successfully over, the prices obtained satisfactorily high. Aspinwall arranged for insurance, and late in July Rush stepped aboard the New York packet *Mediator* with 104,500 pounds in gold sovereigns packed in boxes in his custody.

The crossing was stormy and rough. A very tired man landed at New York on August 28, where he met two messengers of the Bank of the United States who accompanied him to the Mint at Philadelphia. There he deposited his burden with the Treasurer, receiving receipts in the name of the United States of America. On September 15 he rendered a full account of his expenses to Washington.

Of all his public services the founding of the Smithsonian Institution was the one in which Rush took the most pride. It was an achievement that seemed to fulfill all those cultural ambitions of the "enlarged nationalism" he had embraced. But the recovery of the estate was not the end of the job. Congress seemed anything but enthusiastic, while President Van Buren, struggling almost in isolation with the problems of a disintegrating party, refused to exert himself on a side issue. The country to which Rush returned was in the midst of an economic depression; half a million dollars for arts and letters was hardly a popular cause.

The first step was taken in January 1838, when Secretary

Forsyth invited the leaders of the American intellectual world to make suggestions for the use of the money. Rush's letter contained so many proposals that were later adopted that it may properly be called the blueprint of the institution as it eventually developed. He recurred to a suggestion Peter DuPonceau had made to him many years before, that American diplomatic and consular officers abroad should be authorized to collect objects of art and natural curiosities from all parts of the world; he added that army and navy officers could furnish information about the geography, the flora and fauna, the Indian aborigines of our own country. He opposed the notion of a teaching institution. Rather he recommended a building in Washington, a learned journal, and a lecture program. Such an institution could enable the United States to become an intellectual leader among the states of the world. It would be "a new power in the Republic."

But Congress, lacking the leadership of the President, did nothing with the grant. Jackson wrote letters of praise from the Hermitage, executive officers congratulated Rush, individual congressmen seemed friendly enough, yet years passed and no organization was set up. Rush kept writing to every one of his acquaintances in high position, and he published several letters on the uses that might be made of the fund, but to no avail. The change of administration in 1841 discouraged him, for he had vigorously opposed Harrison, and was reluctant to see the General in a position to run off with "the first merit of such a recommendation," but the Whigs revealed no more friendly disposition to the fund than Van Buren had. In 1841 Rush complained to the sympathetic but powerless Poinsett that it might "lag for 27 years, as Girard College is doing under the Philadelphia Common Council." There was a personal motive in his importunacy. He had left an unexpended balance of 750 pounds with Rothschild's when he left London, a balance which he confidently expected from Forsyth's and Jackson's representations would come to him as a bonus. He had preferred a claim for it to the Secretary of State, but Forsyth turned him over to the President. Van Buren, "frightened at every thing pending his second election," had said he must go to Congress. This Rush at first refused to do, but by 1842 he had such need of the money and such support from friends that he agreed to present a claim. "I am independent of banks, I thank god, and of the world," he wrote a confidant; "but this sum which I am about to demand of the government, which I would neither ask nor take unless I believed myself to have earned it justly, would be acceptable to me just now, I will own to you, with a family of some size coming into life, and much of my property reduced in its present value by the rascality of our banks." Colonel Aspinwall was very helpful, writing a letter for Rush to use in pushing his claim. ". . . you effected [the Smithson suit] with an unexampled despatch, entangled as the business happened to be in the meshes of Chancery. . . ."

With the help of Ingersoll and Webster, Rush got his bonus. But the Institution still waited presidential leadership to take tangible form. When the Democrats returned to office in 1845 Rush renewed his letter-writing, in the hopes that Polk, by "taking this Smithson fund under his marked patronage, would contribute an item, and not an inconsiderable one, now and hereafter, to his just fame." He wrote George Bancroft, Secretary of the Navy, that only presidential sponsorship was needed for success. Men of science and letters throughout the country would be pleased, Polk would stand in contrast to his feckless predecessors, the important work of the bequest could begin. Though the President did not act officially, he had a way of getting things done. Activity began in Congress, and on August 10, 1846, Polk signed the bill establishing the Institution. Many persons had had a hand in it; in the House John Quincy Adams had made it a special concern of his own; but it had been Rush who after securing the bequest had kept the subject alive, made plans for the organization, and over eight years assaulted the apathy of indifferent politicians until they were forced to take a needlessly long postponed action. He deserves a place beside James Smithson as the one who gave his concept substance and reality, who cajoled a republic into being worthy of the confidence of an idealist, who founded the most significant public institution for the encouragement of science that America can boast.

On September 7, 1846, the regents, of whom Rush was one, held their first meeting, on the eighth they organized committees, on the ninth they rode through Washington with the President and his cabinet to choose a site for the building. The next May, with elaborate ceremonies in which, ironically enough, the Masonic Order played the most conspicuous part, the cornerstone of the first building was laid by the grand master of the Masons of Washington, the Vice-President, *ex officio* chancellor of the new institution, gave a speech, as Polk with Rush at his side looked on. Until his death Rush was to regard this consummation as the most gratifying achievement of his career, and was continually to fight in Regents' meetings for the strictest performance of the services to humanity envisioned by the dimly remembered English scientist who had glimpsed in the New World the social freedom that might foster the intellectual independence of science.

IX

REPUBLICANISM AND NATIONALISM

The depression produced a characteristic political reaction in 1840 in the defeat of Van Buren and the triumph of the Whig ticket with "Old Tippecanoe" at its head. Rush had worked hard in behalf of Van Buren and was "struck down with chagrin at our defeat." ". . . who could have supposed that a country like this would have been carried away by the foolishness we have witnessed?" he wrote Poinsett. "I confess I did not. . . . The nation has been drunk in electing General Harrison President, and repentance must come when the drunken fit passes off."

He had no intention, however, of allowing the defeat to disorganize the Pennsylvania Democratic party. It was, he thought, a duty "that we should rally, and rally soon, if we would preserve our government and our Union." As soon as the inaugural was over and the cabinet appointments announced he published a long letter signed "Anthony Wayne" in the Philadelphia Democratic organ, *The Spirit of the Times*. Appearing on March 13, 1841, it was addressed "To the Democratic Party of Pennsylvania on the next Presidential election", and urged that the Pennsylvania Democrats all unite in a four-year campaign to put Commodore Charles Stewart in the White House in 1845. This attempt to exalt the fellow Pennsylvanian who had commanded the frigate *Franklin* that took him to England back in 1817 came to nothing, but Rush continued to write publicly and privately for the Democratic cause throughout the troubled Whig term. He used many pen names; one of his favorites was "John Dickinson"; he circulated his pieces throughout his extensive acquaintance.

"Re-annexation of Texas," "re-occupation of Oregon," "54°-40' or fight" carried James Knox Polk to victory by a narrow margin in 1844. Rush had published a pamphlet and some letters in support of Polk, but he was far from happy in the new party tone of expansion, enthusiasm, and conquest. The excited spirit of the country belonged to young men and Westerners; he was too old now to be stirred by dreams of military glory. Fitfully busy with his "rural pursuits," he had no contacts with the lustiness of the West, whose preachers of "Manifest Destiny" were inspired, James Russell Lowell remarked, half by religion and half by rum. He remained cautious regarding expansion, and became alarmed when both the Oregon and Texas issues, generalized symbols of revival, seemed to be leading us to the brink of a conflict with England. Sydenham was the meeting place of Philadelphia Democrats who favored arbitration rather than war. Mr. Peter, the British consul, was among the guests at one dinner when "we had Oregon on table—as one of the courses."

Just how Rush could best serve his party in the Oregon-Mexican crisis was a question over which he and his friends puzzled. He was suggested for this post and that, but none came to him. His correspondence was filled with public affairs, his party's and the nation's. What seemed lacking above all, he thought, was a calming voice, a plea for reason.

Shortly after the new year he decided to undertake a task for which he alone was fitted, one which offered an excellent chance to influence public opinion. This was the writing of a historical account of the questions outstanding between England and America, in the form of a second series of his London journals. If done at all it must be quickly done, so during the first months of 1845 Rush worked furiously. He arranged with Lea and Blanchard of Philadelphia for printing in America, and by April had put forward plans with the help of Colonel Aspinwall for simultaneous publication by Richard Bentley in London.

"It is my humble but most anxious aim, in publishing the work," he wrote Aspinwall, "to contribute a mite towards warding off an 'Oregon' war; of which I fear there is some danger, unless there be great prudence on both sides." He sought "to heal, not inflame," for "The English think too badly of us, and we of them just now. . . . There are enlightened thousands in England wholly ignorant of the present and past questions between the two countries; who do not, for instance, imagine, that we have any more claim to Oregon, than to land in the Moon; and who, if they knew that *we* (half civilized, and entirely rapacious, as they think us,) had endeavoured, more than 20 years ago, to induce *them* to give up the practices of the buccaneers, would be utterly astonished." It was largely to these "enlightened thousands" of England that Rush wrote, for he conceived the issue of war really rested with them.

Memoranda of a Residence at the Court of London, Comprising Incidents, Official and Personal, from 1819 to 1825: Amongst the Former, Negotiations on the Oregon Territory, and Other Unsettled Questions Between the United States and Great Britain came from the new steam presses of Lea and Blanchard late in June 1845, and nearly on the same day in London. The first American copy went to the President, the first English to the Queen. Its success was everything Rush could wish. It was a work of great charm, revealing himself probably more than he knew, continuing the pattern of his earlier volume. Congratulatory letters poured in from both countries. Buchanan wrote appreciatively from Washington, from Montpelier Dolly Madison sent "devoted affection"; Mr. Adams seemed pleased. Messages came from Lady Lyttleton, now governess to the royal children, Lord Ashburton, Sir George Staunton, "Miss Edgeworth, the celebrated authoress," Dr. Holland, Sir Robert Inglis, American Minister Everett, and a hundred more. Rush felt he had done some good. Though he had suppressed parts of the story, particularly material dealing with the Monroe Doctrine negotiations, he believed he had given a clearer picture of the problems of Anglo-American relations than had been available before, one calculated to produce a more temperate disposition on both sides.

Meanwhile Polk was playing his dangerous game of bluff, to the discomfiture of Buchanan and Rush as well. In his first Annual Message in December 1845, he demanded all of Oregon, and step by step throughout January, February, and March of 1846 he pushed on his defiance of England, finally in May giving notification that the joint-occupancy agreement Rush had negotiated in 1818 was to be terminated.

The effect in England might have been disastrous had not a group of public men with large investments in America been working all this time for arbitration. Ashburton, whose long-time association with American statesmen and ownership of half a million dollars of Pennsylvania bonds predisposed him against war, realized that if peace overtures were to be made they had to come from England, for the American President had gone too far to retreat. He exerted his considerable influence at Whitehall for peaceable adjustment, and in February sent Rush a letter proposing his services as mediator. Rush forwarded the letter to Buchanan recommending the acceptance of its offer. Throughout the winter and spring these two private citizens, one in London, the other in Philadelphia, labored tirelessly for conciliation.

Complicating their task was the crisis in our troubled relations with Mexico. Since the annexation of Texas a year before, war had been threatening; finally in January Polk ordered General Taylor to cross the Nueces into disputed territory. This, coinciding with the defiance of England, seemed likely in Rush's view to commit us to a double war, against Mexico on the southwest and Britain in the northwest and on the Atlantic. The difficulties ahead, he wrote Buchanan (who profoundly agreed), "scarcely appear to have had a parallel since :76. We are to be born anew under some great aspects of nationality; and may like wisdom virtue and firmness as in those days, carry us through with success and glory."

War with Mexico had another effect which concerned Rush. This was the change it wrought in our connections with France. As he had contemplated the probability of an "Oregon war," he had believed there was some chance of aid from France. There were always Frenchmen anxious to despoil Britain, and certainly neither Louis Philippe nor the ministry of Guizot was strong enough to resist a popular demand for war. Thiers needed a "cause," Palmerston was always aggressive. These two—"the pepper pots of Europe," Rush called them—were fanning whatever flames of bellicosity they could find, so that Anglo-French trouble was not inconceivable. The American chargé at Paris, returned from his post in January, had dined with Rush, informing him that France would be in the field with America within six months if we declared war on England.

But the Mexican war changed this picture. Though the King and Guizot might not have been able to prevent French aid to America over Oregon, our Mexican crisis gave them the opportunity to unite with England in stopping the war, or in aiding Mexico, making common cause for the collection of long-standing debts owed by Mexicans to European creditors. Rush was apprehensive of this possibility; it seemed here was the case for "the balancing principle we have long been threatened with," and France, before January, a potential ally, after the beginning of the war on the Rio Grande became a menace not only to immediate success but to the tenets of the Monroe Doctrine as well.

Happily, as the Mexican crisis grew more serious, the English crisis passed away. By May 1846, when Polk notified Britain of the termination of the convention of 1818, Ashburton's work had borne fruit in England. The ministry was ready to conciliate, negotiations were commenced, and on the fifteenth of June a new treaty was signed. With this treaty a cloud of gloom lifted from Rush's mind. Though the President was being attacked all through the West for giving up more than had been expected, the East was fairly satisfied, Rush himself pleased. "On the whole," he told Buchanan, "I think you made a wise settlement of that long-pending difficulty. My own impression was ever very strong, that England was ready to appeal to the sword, unless she got territory and advantages south of 49; and I will candidly own to you, that she took up with *fewer* at last, than I supposed she would have done. This I ascribe to the energy, and whole course, of our government, since Mr. Polk came in, at which I was a little startled at first, but it came out nobly. . ."

The adjustment of the Oregon question seemed to mark a period to a negotiation in which Rush had been long concerned, "a great epoch in our annals—one not unlike, under some parallels that might be drawn, the war of 1812 in its acceleration of our national character." He was moved to contemplate a third book, tracing the whole history of the one issue which in the perspective of his career seemed finally to have reached a termination. But he had written much, and there was the deterring consideration that to reopen the subject might add to the antagonisms so rife in the West. "Whether I shall venture upon another volume or not, I am quite undetermined. Sometimes I feel half inclined; then again the other side of the scale kicks the beam. . . . If I live as long as my mother, who was out here this week at 86, in good health, I shall have time to make up my mind." He never did publish the book, though part of it was to come out in occasional publications a few years later, the rest after his death.

Shortly after the New Year, on January 19, 1847, Rush was in Washington on Smithsonian business, and called on the President. "He is an exceedingly intelligent gentleman, and I had a very interesting conversation with him about public affairs," the President noted in his diary. Among the many subjects that Polk was particularly interested in was Rush's account of the officiousness of General Scott, who was then the cause of no little consternation and distress to the President. He had likewise been an annoyance to President Adams, and Polk found himself listening to the story of a previous occasion when a cabinet had been split nearly to the breaking point by the bumptious General.

Rush was pleased with the President, though he was not greatly impressed with him as a successor to Madison, Monroe, and Adams. These were great memories. But he wished to be fair, and he recognized the truth of Polk's distrait remark, that the President was the "hardest-working man in this country."

This meeting, together with the Smithsonian business, brought

Rush within Polk's consciousness, and since he was striving to spread his patronage throughout the North as much as possible to counteract the Whig charge that his was a Southern, slave-power administration, he marked Rush down for preferment. It came sooner than expected. Late in 1846 Polk had nominated Charles J. Ingersoll to be Minister to France, after that gentleman had used every possible means of solicitation for the position. The Senate, however, refused to confirm him. Polk then turned (probably at Buchanan's urging) to Rush. Early in March 1847, he sent his name to the Senate, where it was immediately confirmed and on March 3 the commission was issued. It came as a complete surprise to Rush, and caused him some embarrassment at first, for Polk and Ingersoll were having a bitter quarrel following the Senate's action, the President concluding Ingersoll was "a base and unprincipled man." Rush was inclined to take his friend's part, but Ingersoll urged him to accept the appointment, as did Buchanan, and with this encouragement he agreed to do so. He was, as a matter of fact, thoroughly delighted with the prospect of going abroad once more. Retirement, even as busy a retirement as his had been, was galling. He welcomed the opportunity for service, particularly such service as he was competent to perform.

His friends shared his pleasure. Congratulations poured in from all over the country, and for ten weeks preparations included testimonials and farewell dinners in Philadelphia. Departure was delayed until June, both because of the illness of Mrs. Rush, which finally prevented her from accompanying him, and to await the course of the campaign in Mexico.

On the Mexican War also depended his instructions, which were of a general character, dealing with two classes of subjects, the first a series of commercial questions to settle with France including duties against American tobacco, the second a reflection of Polk's rugged assertion of the complete independence of America from foreign interference in her Mexican War. This issue, which had been relieved by the settlement of the Oregon matter, now turned on whether England would consent to the annexation of California, with the command of the Pacific which it would give the American Union, and whether she could draw France with her in effective measures, even war, to prevent it.

But the most serious aspect of his mission was the relation of America to a Europe seething with discontent, a French government tottering unsteadily on very weak foundations. "You come at a most critical moment in public affairs of Europe," George Bancroft wrote from London; "and your curiosity will be almost as much stimulated, as was your father's eighty years ago, when he found Paris in a ferment, & the Farmer's Letters the great subject of conversation; then the sympathy for America was free from apprehension, now, perhaps, the existence & the prosperity of America are regarded with terror by European conservatives; for the success of our system is destined to revolutionize Europe."

The possibility of an overturn in the French government Rush, like all well-informed persons in America, had anticipated, and had taken into consideration when contemplating the probability of a war with Britain over Oregon; but before he arrived in France he had not estimated the chances of immediate revolution. His first preoccupation was to study this matter.

Louis Philippe, *roi bourgeois*, was seventy-four years old in 1847, in the seventeenth year of his troubled reign. He was a prudent, hard-working, much-traveled man, who had spent many years in exile, some of them in America. Kind and pacific, laboring diligently for peace at home and abroad, he was in Rush's opinion thoughtful, careful, considerate, simple and well-intentioned. His ministers had been men of considerable intellect, respected by foreign nations; Guizot, the present premier, was eminent in the world of letters. France was prosperous, her public works progressing, her press free and her intellectual leaders productive. One would have thought her a nation peacefully growing into opulence and power.

But rarely was a government more reviled or a king more disliked. Most Frenchmen found the King if not sinister at least boring. Lamartine expressed the emotion of many of his class: *La France, s'ennuie;* and Guizot smarted under the charge that the ministry did nothing. Indeed, the Orleans monarchy had known scarcely a day of peace or security since it began. Opposed by Legitimists, Bonapartists, Republican Reformists, Socialists, attacked by a host of left-wing doctrinaires, Louis Philippe represented not a united nation, but only one social class within it; in 1847 this class, the bourgeois, was split between Conservatives and Reformists, so that even what support the King could command was ineffectual. He offered no glory, no adventure, no color to catch the loyalty of the people. His very simplicity, his affectation of bourgeois dress and style of living, his pleasure in his large family, his thrift, his unkingliness, produced in his subjects no particular admiration or affection, only lassitude and indifference in the well-disposed, distrust and suspicion in the disaffected.

Rush perceived the unpopularity of King and monarchy as soon as he landed at Havre in mid-July (1847). When he reached Paris it bore in upon him like a smothering blanket.

The press was pouring forth its daily fire upon all public measures. One paper, and only one of any account that I could at first hear of, gave the ministers support. . . . The general fault-finding appeared to be coupled with distrust of the King. He was accused of being selfish, hypocritical, crafty; forgetting his promises, forgetting his duties to the nation, in exclusive devotedness to the interests of his family, and perpetuation of his dynasty. The Republicans said he had deceived them, and the Legitimists continued to be his foes. The Bonapartists had no sympathies with him. . . . All combined their voices to render Louis Philippe unpopular, and draw down upon him suspicion and hatred.

Rush sought in vain for the causes of such discontent. Had it been a movement of the industrial classes, exploited and without privileges in the political life of France, he could have understood it; yet the threat to the monarchy came not from this group, but from the middle class, whose reflection the monarchy was. For this opposition there seemed no good reason.

Was France going down? was her prosperity undermined? was taxation weighing ruinously or heavily upon her? had her poor increased? where was I to look for signs of depression and misery? Or was the King a tyrant, or trained in a school of idleness or vice, or goaded on by a guilty ambition because looking to the continuance of his dynasty? Were laws neglected, or the people tongue-tied? On the contrary, the King and his Ministers were governing through the laws. The press was abundantly free, as witnessed by the unsparing attacks upon the King, his Ministers, and measures. If I looked to the country, instead of the newspapers, or speeches at political banquets, I should have thought I had come to a country abounding in prosperity of every kind and full of contentment. France appeared as well off as could be expected of any country where opulence, prosperity, and power, existing on a large scale, must have drawbacks.

Her agriculture had improved, her manufactures were flourishing, her foreign commerce had increased in these two decades more rapidly than in the fifty years preceding. Her army was as large as necessary but no larger; taxes were heavy, but the public works were adding to the riches, strength, and security of the nation. Paris had been beautified, her streets widened, slums destroyed, and the population of the city had increased. The electoral law was disgraceful, two hundred thousand voters choosing the representatives for all France; this was a mockery on representation, Rush acknowledged, but he pointed out how long England had taken to achieve her reform, and how short a time comparatively the agitation had run in France. As for the King's dynastic ambitions, these did not appear very serious or improper to Rush.

If Louis Philippe desires to perpetuate his dynasty, what King would not? What did Napoleon do for his family? or rather what was it that he did not do for all of them? And if Louis Philippe aims at continuing one of his sons on the throne, by striving to make the country prosperous by a pacific policy, after the exhausting wars France has gone through, is that wrong? His sons are not drones. They have been well educated, are said to be intelligent, and known to be brave.

The antagonism aroused by the recent marriage of one of his sons to a Spanish princess Rush thought entirely misplaced.

In spite of all his achievements the King was clearly beset with dangers. "This must be the case with any King of France," Rush observed. "It is difficult to be king and republican on the same throne."

Because of the unpopularity of the government, there was very little done. Guizot's patriotism and statesmanship were unquestioned, but he devoted himself mostly to the distribution of patronage and manipulation of elections by which he kept himself in power; Rush found him personally brilliant, officially amiable, but aloof almost to the point of apathy when American concerns were discussed. Often referring to Washington or the *Federalist Papers* in his speeches in the Chamber, Guizot appeared to have almost no interest in contemporary relations with the United States. On the tobacco monopoly, or on the Mexican question, Rush could get nothing out of him.

The King seemed to be taking the lead in these matters personally. Several times he opened conversations with Rush on the Mexican War, expressing strong opinions on the advisability of peace. Rush gave him an account of the differences which had led to the war, but "The King still dwelt upon peace. It was the topic constantly coming back to him." Gradually the reports of military victories seemed to impress Louis Philippe. He had not at first believed America would really be able to defeat the Mexicans; when he was convinced he still discussed with Rush over cigars in the gardens at St. Cloud or at Neuilly Palace in Paris the terms of peace. Moderation, he lectured the Minister, was the wisest rule for all nations in the improving state of the world. Louis Philippe could no more understand or appreciate the ebullient American nationalism than Rush could accept the criticism of Mr. Polk's war. As for the tariff on tobacco, the King several times expounded the benefits of free trade, but would not discuss the specific issue.

Under these conditions Rush found himself in the fall of 1847 bored with Paris, bored with his mission, exasperated with the government. The work he had been sent to do he could not get on with: it seemed to flounder in a welter of ministerial indecision and kingly disinterest. Though the court was attended by the greatest minds of France, the atmosphere was one of conventionality and repose. Paris was neither intellectually exciting, nor beautiful, nor politically important; it was only expensive, for an American minister excessively expensive, more so even than London had ever been. The King might lay aside the great state of the Bourbons, sport his "sentimental umbrella" and dress like a shopkeeper, but in "this artificial and opulent capital" the diplomatic corps maintained establishments as elaborate as they had in the London of Castlereagh and George IV.

There were some moments of animation, of course, sometimes when Rush was moved to the delight he had experienced in London. He renewed his acquaintance with Baron Humboldt, "the philosopher, the man of genius, the votary of science; possessing knowledge so universal, with worth and modesty so great, that all respect him," whom he had met many years before at his father's table in Philadelphia; Bancroft came over from London to work on his history, which gave Rush some rare evenings with Guizot or Thiers in company (but, of course, never at the same time); he met de Tocqueville, whom he was to know better; he talked long and often with Robert Walsh, the able American consul at Paris.

In addition, he derived a great deal of surreptitious amusement from the attitude of Americans toward the court. One of his most constant annoyances was the duty of presenting gifts sent by American citizens to the King. Some he refused entirely to deal with. He sent a list to Buchanan of presents that had been rejected. These included

1. A set of false teeth
2. Six barrels of flour
3. A Cotton Mattress
4. A Picture

5. A drag for a carriage wheel.
6. A written proposition to exchange natural curiosities with his Majesty.
7. Sundry propositions and inventions to be submitted to the Prince de Joinville
8. Several claims upon the King for services or expenses rendered or incurred in his behalf when travelling in the United States.

It was an embarrassing but an amusing spectacle. "O, ye powers! I have received a book for donation to the Queen, yes, truly, with her name in golden letters on its elegant binding outside, accompanied by a letter to her Majesty, and another to the Princess of Joinville, to be presented with the book, which said book (ye powers once more!) contains pictures so downright and monstrous in all particulars that I do assure you, in soberness," he wrote Buchanan, "if exposed at the window of any bookstore in our good city of Philadelphia or Lancaster, would forthwith lead to an indictment for an offence contra bonos mores. Yet Dr Beach, of New York, the author of the book, may perchance think that because I do not present it, I lack zeal for science, as he treats of obstetrics! I will bear his thunders sooner than present his book to any decent woman in Christendom."

If Americans were eccentric in their choice of gifts, they were even more so in their avidity to be presented at court. For the reception announced for the first week in January, literally hundreds of applications had poured into the Legation before Christmas.

Our numbers will probably be greater I am told, than from all other countries put together—if England be excepted. I cannot help wishing the desire to go to court here, was less vehement with our good people; for although Louis Philippe knows how to respect our national power, and I trust rights, I have a notion that to fraternize with republicans is not much to his taste,—at least in this numerous way; besides that we are not supposed to be especial lovers of Kings ourselves.

The situation was so ludicrous it was being ridiculed in Paris; Rush reflected on the old maxim, "Beware of the inquisition in Spain, the stilletto in Italy, the mob in London, and *ridicule* in Paris."

In spite of the great electoral reform banquets and rising Socialist agitation, Rush perceived no danger of an immediate change in government. Two days after Christmas he attended the King's opening of Parliament, and listened with interest unmixed, apparently, with cynicism as Louis Philippe, at the close of the year 1847, told the deputies that France possessed in her constitutional monarchy the means of surmounting all obstacles and satisfying all the material and moral interests of her people.

The evening of February 22, 1848, had been set by the Reformists for the climax of their series of popular banquets. There was to be a public procession, and the largest demonstration they had yet staged. In the drawing rooms of the official circle the banquet began to replace the grisly Praslin murder scandals as the chief topic of conversation.

But there was not much serious apprehension. Late in January Rush advised Buchanan that the ministry was strong enough to resist the Republicans, and though a fortnight later Mr. Walsh warned him of the danger, he found Guizot reassuring. The King was calm, insisting the government had taken every precaution and order would be maintained. On February 20, Thiers gave a reception where, far from observing a revolutionist on the eve of his triumph the American Minister recorded only his pleasure in the conversation of "this remarkable Deputy, Financier, Parliamentary debater, and Historian." The night before the banquet the company at the Duchess de Rochefoucault's spoke of it with no unease, and at a gaudy ball given by the Belgian Ambassador it was said that the ministry expected no disorder.

In the face of this unanimous opinion that nothing serious was afoot, Rush went to bed on the twenty-second with confidence and security. He awoke the next morning in the midst of civil war.

"A Revolution has come like a thunder-clap," he wrote in his journal. "All Paris in consternation; barricades, troops, cannon, mobs, cavalry in quick movement, some in full gallop, wheeling into one street and issuing from another; numerous heads looking out from upper windows in amazement."

For the next two days fighting continued. All was "rumor and uncertainty. People seemed stunned." Going to the Legation across the river he learned that the government had forbidden the banquet at the last moment on the twenty-second, a sudden blow to the hopes of the crowds that had gathered in the streets, and that rioting had begun almost at once.

On Friday, the twenty-fifth, it became known that the King had fled.

The belief seems to be that a complete Revolution has been effected, the people having the upper hand everywhere, and none of the troops or national guards any longer acting against them. They are in possession of the Tuileries, made a bonfire of the King's carriages, the King, Queen and Royal Family escaping through the gardens. I go to Quai d'Orsay, in front of my house; see the people looking out of the Palace windows; see them throwing furniture out of the windows; see them pass by the place where I stood. They shout out, with guns and sabres in their hands; they display trophies brought from the Palace, such as patés, cooked meats, bread, and other eatables. Also caps, artificial flowers, and other finery. Soldiers mix in with the people and shout too. Some of the soldiers stick loaves of bread on the points of their bayonets, holding them up exultingly. Anxious to know how things are at the Legation, I leave my stand at Quai d'Orsay and attempt to go there by the bridge of the Invalides, it being impossible to cross any other. I go on foot. Arriving at this bridge, I see an immense crowd on the other side, women as well as men, all hallooing, singing, dancing, and shouting. Some are rolling empty wine-casks along the ground—so says my servant George, who is with me. Others hold them over their heads with uplifted arms, sending forth louder shouts and playing off antics, as if inflamed with drink. I do not cross the bridge. On this side, broken squads of the municipal guard are to be seen riding here and there, and detachments of horse artillery hurrying, I know not where. All is wild disorganization. I return to my house, after being baffled in this attempt to reach the office, fatigued and glad to get home.

The amount of bloodshed was ghastly. Americans in Paris flocked to the Minister's home to exchange notes and to join in mutual protection. One lady from Boston brought an American flag she had made; Rush had never flown one, and refused now to hide behind its protection. "No outrages on private property had as yet been committed, that I had heard of, much less on the houses of Foreign Ministers, during the raging of this tempest. On the contrary, it was stated that some of the fighting bands among the people, on hearing that thieves had broken into a shop to rob it, shot them on the spot."

By the evening of the twenty-fifth the monarchy was gone, in its place a provisional republican government proclaimed, its membership a rollcall of the minority party in the Chamber of Deputies. For Rush, events had moved faster than he could keep up with.

I almost ask myself, Can this be a reality? Only on the night of the twentieth I was at the Tuileries, the King, Queen and Royal family feeling secure in fancied strength. Everything brilliant around them; ladies to have graced the highest, or any spheres; functionaries of state, and military officers; all the patronage, all the honors, of a great monarchy in their hands,—its army in their service. So it was a week ago. Now the King and Queen are outcasts; destitute for the present, and uncertain of their fate. The others, all scattered and gone.

Paris was certainly boring no longer.

I

The Provisional Government worked fast. It secured the allegiance of the army and navy, occupied all government offices, established connections with Baron Rothschild. Rush characterized the leaders for Buchanan: the historian Lamartine, the astronomer Arago, men of letters and of science, famous representatives of French intellectuals; Dupont de l'Eure (President of the Council), "an old sterling friend of constitutional monarchy, and companion of Lafayette, respected by every one, and now *republican* because constitutional monarchy has been found wanting." Ledru Rollin, an "unscrupulous, violent, dangerous man," a lawyer, leader of the extremists, radical editor, boisterous, heavily in debt; Cremieux, a Jewish barrister recently turned Republican; Marie, a lawyer and republican, Garnier Pages, Mayor of Paris; these formed the executive council. Among them Lamartine, "a noble fellow, the saving angel of France," already stood out. He had shown great courage in appearing on the balcony of the Hotel de Ville before an enormous crowd armed with muskets and demanding the red flag as the symbol of the new Republic. This, Lamartine cried, they could not have, but rather the tricolor, "which had made the tour of the World with glory, while the red flag had only made the tour of the Champs de Mars, trailed through torrents of blood."

The first question which arose for Rush was of course the attitude he should take toward this new government, as yet without official standing among nations. Though there were precedents in America's recognizing the South American revolutionary governments, the experience of making the decision himself was new to Rush, and his action obviously of considerable importance, not only to his career and to the policy of the United States but also to the new government.

Before he had time to think the problem through he was called upon by an army engineer, Major Poussin, who had been many years in the United States in his professional capacity and was a naturalized American citizen. Poussin urged him to take on his own initiative the step of recognizing the government, pointing out that such a move would add immediate strength from abroad to France, would be a significant gesture of aid to the cause of republicanism, and would establish the United States once again as the sympathetic supporter of self-government in France.

The suggestion was not unattractive to Rush, but it was a heavy responsibility, one which he hesitated to assume without consulting his colleagues in the diplomatic corps and without considering carefully his position as his country's official representative, accredited to an overturned government. From the point of view of America's national interests, there were many reasons in favor of recognition. A friendly relation with a stable French government, established by such an act, would go a long way toward giving America a powerful ally in her diplomatic contests with Britain. Had there been clear-cut and explicit understandings between France and America during the Oregon dispute, Britain would have been more easily circumvented. Then, too, the Minister was not called upon to question the sovereignty of a government. His obligation, based on United States policy expressly stated and previously applied, was to acknowledge every new government abroad, when it was seen to exist *de facto*, regardless of its origin or its form. The Provisional Government was clearly the *de facto* government of France, though it had been in existence less than twenty-four hours. Would it be right or expedient to wait a month or more before instructions could come from Washington? "Was it for me to be backward, when France appeared to be looking to us?"

Moreover (Rush argued to himself in his journal) this was the nation so warmly associated with America in the Revolution, so traditional a friend in American distresses, now for the second time emerging as a powerful colleague in republicanism, the only great nation in Europe to represent the American way of life. "Thoughts like these decided me to act, not instantly, but promptly." Rush informed Major Poussin that, as soon as he had official notification of the existence of the Provisional Government, and of Lamartine as its Foreign Minister, he would recognize the Republic.

The next day, a Sunday, the Legation staff and the consul, Walsh, gave their support to Rush in his projected move, and there only remained consultation with others of the diplomatic corps. This was not easy; "All were astounded," he told Buchanan. "Not half of them were even to be found during the first shocks; and, moreover by as much as I was able to learn, all were plump and decided against doing anything."

Unfortunately Rush first approached Lord Normanby, the British Ambassador, who discouragingly hoped to defer action. Did the American Minister, he asked, wish to separate himself from others of the corps in this manner? Rush pointed out the peculiarity of his situation, his being so far from his government that ratification would come so late as to make recognition after instructions had arrived a meaningless formality.

He assured Normanby that he would do nothing until he received official and formal notification from the government of its existence, and of the officer appointed to deal with foreign affairs. He returned to the Legation, where he found the South American ministers were prepared to follow his example if he moved at once; later in the day the official notification from Lamartine arrived.

On Monday, his resolution strengthened by Latin American support, Rush donned his diplomatic dress, took the Legation secretary and Major Poussin with him to the Hotel de Ville, where he was at once conducted to the Provisional Government. In a brief address he presumed to offer the congratulations of the American people to the new régime, mentioning the ancient friendship of the two nations, their mutual adventure in republicanism, that form of government which united social order with public liberty, and hoped that, as General Washington had once remarked to a French envoy, the "friendship of the two Republics might be commensurate with their existence." M. Arago replied in a short address for the Provisional Council, and the President, Dupont de l'Eure, approached Rush, greeted him warmly, expressed his gratitude and that of the French nation.

As the Minister left the Hotel de Ville, the guard presented arms, the crowd burst into cheers, shouts of *Vive la République des États Unis!* were heard. He went as quickly as possible to see Lord Normanby, that he might apprise him of what he had done before it got into the newspapers. Normanby, he found, was "still under more or less amazement, and there the subject has ended with us."

Two days later the Papal Nuncio published a letter to Lamartine which was tantamount to recognition. This greatly strengthened the American position, and made it easier for Rush to write his account to his government. He did so in full, both to the President and in a personal letter to Buchanan explaining the whole transaction in more informal terms. "I must humbly hope that my course will be approved by the President, yourself and the cabinet," he wrote.

The South American representatives followed Rush in acknowledging the Executive Council, as he had advised them. Lamartine was particularly grateful for his activities. As soon as he received Rush's notification, he remarked, "Two good things have quickly happened for the Provisional Government: the Nuncio's letter, and Recognition by the American Minister, the one representing the head of the Church, the other the head of Republicanism in the World."

"I need not remark," Rush wrote in a letter to Buchanan, "how greatly the revolution adds to the interest of this mission."

As he watched the progress of the new government through the winter and spring he became more and more its apologist among the foreign representatives. He discounted the exaggerated stories in the antagonistic English press of violence in Paris; the city, since the twenty-fourth of February when the fighting ceased, had in all truth "witnessed less disturbance of the public order than Philadelphia under the reign of the fire companies," he declared. "I am sorry to say so, for the sake of our good city, but I think it true."

Indeed, the English press was misrepresenting everything that happened in republican France, with the same injustice, Rush growled, that America had received at those hands for fifty years, especially since the Mexican War. He constructed his official dispatches with great care, so that their publication in America would counteract the influence of British anti-republican propaganda.

Constantly interrupted by "French gentlemen calling for information about our constitution—&c &c," he found such a lively interest in the American governmental system that he began to assume a curious and to him most welcome position, that of interpreter of republicanism to the committee preparing a draft of a new constitution. The American precedent was obvious, curiosity concerning it was great. Rush tried to explain the system of checks and balances, the differences between Senate and House, the principles of federalism, to a nation accustomed for centuries to centralization, bureaucracy, and absolutism.

Among his frequent callers was de Tocqueville, with whom Rush pleaded for a double branch of the legislature. Lamartine was showing himself in favor of a single house, and de Tocqueville, in spite of his notorious admiration of the American system, seemed to agree. Rush spoke strongly against it, declaring the only precedent of a unicameral government in America—the Pennsylvania Constitution of 1776—had been a failure. He found some of the moderate Republicans, men like Dupin and George Lafayette (son of the Marquis), with him, but the leaders of the Council publicly declared for one house and a plural executive. George Bancroft came over from London to participate in the discussions. He, Rush, and de Tocqueville sat many long hours together comparing the American and the French nations, the possibility of a federative principle among the departments, the nature of the executive and the legislature. Buchanan, infected as was so much of America with enthusiasm for this new French revolution, sent Rush a carefully prepared brief on the American doctrine "that our State Constitutions were the only sure pillars of the Constitution of the United States, which works by its own inherent force in some things, and through the States in others; the latter instrumentality exemplifying the federative principle, the former the national principle; and the combination of the two giving to our Union its efficiency, and securing thus far its duration." He pointed out the differences among the Dutch, Swiss, and American constitutions, proposing the application of federalistic principles to the French situation.

Rush was convinced by the end of April that the new government could not be federal. The French, he advised the Secretary of State, "are very prone to centralization, and fear that they could never construct on the basis of their parliaments in the departments, any thing like our State Sovereignties. Their habits, all their preconceived opinions not to say prejudices at present, their position in Europe, and towards Europe, externally, &c &c seem to forbid it—say some of the most eminent of them with whom I have as yet conversed." But, he added, the French were "a 'wonderful people' as Washington said, and wonderfully improved, since he said it. Even in working out things their own way, let us hope that they may work them out right at last."

As the meeting of the National Assembly set for the fourth of May drew near, it became obvious that the Republicans did not have a majority. The broad extension of the franchise had produced a true sampling of the wishes of the nation unprecedented in France, whose people, unused to innovations, voted more against the radical theories of the Socialists than in favor of the Republicans. The complications this introduced into the task of constructing a government were both serious and confusing. Rush feared that no constitution could be acceptable unless it reproduced some of the features of a monarchy, thus appealing to the spirit of the people; but he took comfort in the remark of one delegate, who told him, "We set up a Republic without Republicans, but give us time and we will have both."

The temper of the Assembly was surprisingly moderate, even avowed Monarchists being anxious to support a republican establishment, ratify the liberal edicts of the Provisional Government, and most of all suppress the radicalism of the Paris Socialists. But difficulties were accumulating rapidly, particularly financial troubles as the result of the disappearance of money; combined with this was the distrust of the bourgeois Assembly by radicals who had expected better fortune at the election. The latter climaxed on the fifteenth of May, when a mob stormed the Assembly, drove them out of the Chamber, and proclaimed a new régime. The riot was suppressed by the National Guard, three hundred malcontents arrested, and order restored; but Rush was alarmed. If so much could be done so easily, what would be the effect of a second, better organized attempt?

While the Committee of Eighteen appointed to draft the new constitution were at their labors, the weakness of the Republic was revealed by the Assembly's vote to admit Louis Napoleon to the seat for which he had been elected. Although Napoleon sensed that the occasion was premature and resigned by letter from England, the debates on his pretensions were so fierce, the opinion of the majority so vigorous in his favor, that Rush considered it a defeat for the government.

At this inauspicious moment the Committee of Eighteen reported their constitution, a long and careful document written in high hopes and great faith, modeled on the American plan but without American federalism to support it. A single executive limited to one term of four years, a single house in the legislature, universal suffrage and popular sovereignty gave it the appearance of true democracy, but Rush thought it awkward and ponderous. The theoreticians and academicans who wrote it had looked to the frame and not the substance of the American government; they had borrowed principles to engraft upon the French nation that had no correspondence to reality.

How little effect it had was made immediately evident by the outbreak of a great insurrection in June. Like that of May 15 it began in riots among the city's poor, but it grew to such proportions that it dwarfed the Revolution of February. Alarms rang through the night of June 23, by the twenty-fifth the whole city was a battlefield, the Assembly voted supreme dictatorial powers to General Cavaignac, the Executive Council ceased to exist. Casualties were enormous. They included the Archbishop of Paris, who had made a remarkable but futile attempt to stop the fighting; and though prompt, efficient action by Cavaignac had suppressed the insurgents by the twenty-eighth, Paris remained an armed camp, a place of hatred and despair. Fifty thousand troops were still quartered within the city in July, the press was bridled with restrictions, political clubs were suspended.

From freedom under monarchy France had passed in less than a year to subjection and terror under a republic. "Anticipations of what is to come baffle all, and the remark I now hear most frequently is, though it may look like a paradox, that nothing is certain except the uncertainty that hangs over the political future of France."

The spectacle of bold republicanism collapsing, to be succeeded by internal chaos, demoralization, and dictatorship—even the dictatorship of the able Cavaignac—was a sore disillusionment to Rush. His position was no longer that of republican advocate, but rather that of a witness to the failure of revolution. The summer revealed the changes in men's minds. Thiers and Louis Napoleon were both elected to the Assembly amid great excitement. Some satisfaction came from other capitals of Europe, where the inspiration of French republicanism was calling forth a lively new spirit of reform and revolt. Andrew Jackson Donelson, American Minister at Berlin and Frankfort, wrote frequently to Paris of the revolutionary movement in Germany, which with Hungarian nationalism was attracting as much attention as the French among American intellectuals. Calhoun and Webster in Washington were extolling the liberated mind of Europe; hundreds of American visitors came to the Paris Legation en route to Budapest, Frankfort, or Berlin.

Rush would have found this more encouraging had it not caused such a serious drain on his finances. French postage was excessively high, and the custom of sending American official correspondence in the English postbags he had discontinued when the Revolution began, "not thinking it discreet in times like these, (and never having liked that kind of unpaid favor from a foreign government)." He was forced to confide his dispatches to private citizens whenever he found them traveling homewards. Persons from all over America were sending mail to the Paris Legation to be distributed all over Europe, as far away as Constantinople; even speeches of members of Congress were sent for the Minister to pay postage on. "I am trying to think of some remedy for it all; & under your good auspices and support," Rush told Buchanan, "am even meditating a sort of *revolution* to shake off the *old abuses* in this matter of our good people saddling the government with postage."

Mortified by this difficulty, Rush was also distressed during the summer of 1848 by the impossibility of dealing with the demoralized government on the business of his mission. The tobacco tax and the whole problem of free trade ought soon to be solved, but General Cavaignac could not, the Assembly would not, act. As August approached, Rush became reconciled to this inaction, for it was but one more disillusionment in the whole picture of collapse the republican movement now presented. The Austrian invasion of Italy split the Republicans on the issue of war, and as the first elections under the new constitution approached the confusion increased.

Indecision, disunity, and lack of imagination were causing the Republic to fall apart, but within France herself was emerging a new leader, no *littérateur* to sit with Arago or Lamartine, nor general to vie with Cavaignac, but a swarthy, ugly little man who bore a magic name. The sun of the Republic set as the new star of Louis Napoleon glitteringly rose; Rush mourned the passing, but he mourned even more a people inadequate for self-government.

Louis Napoleon, bête noire of the radical Republicans, took his seat in the Assembly on September 26, his campaign for the presidency already well started. By mid-October Rush was hearing everywhere that he could win the election if he would only hold his tongue. A fortnight later, trying to make the complex situation clear for Buchanan, Rush reluctantly concluded, "Louis Bonaparte has the best chance of being the first President of the Republic; so the most shrewd all think at present." So many of Louis Philippe's old ministers were coming back to the Assembly, even Guizot trying for a seat, that republican enthusiasm languished. Rush could not "easily yield my assent to any encouraging prospects of its durability."

The election on Sunday, December 10, was an overwhelming victory for Prince Louis. No one was surprised; the ineffable wizardry of a name that stood for order and glory neither the savior Cavaignac nor the brilliant Lamartine could resist. A cycle had completed itself: from boredom in liberty under an Orleans king, to brave republicanism in February, to chaos in the spring, to dictatorship in the summer, to the Prince-President at the end of the year. For Rush the real interest in his mission had ceased. Though he watched and reported meticulously each step of the new government in domestic affairs and in the Italian relation, he found Louis Napoleon as adept in stalling on free trade and tobacco imposts as Louis Philippe had been, or Guizot or Lamartine or the Assembly. Personally he did not like the Prince, politically he resented him. Republicanism had failed, liberty was gone, the American interest was sidetracked; the year's events as far as Rush was concerned seemed to have made no real difference except to deprive the French people of a free press and political clubs.

Another election had taken place, even more important to Rush's future. In November Zachary Taylor had defeated Lewis Cass for the American presidency by a margin of a hundred and fifty thousand votes, and on the fourth of March Buchanan retired to "Wheatlands," his home near Lancaster. At first, relying on preëlection promises, Rush thought his tenure secure until he had completed three years, that is, until 1850, but the ways of Whig politics were devious, and not long after the inauguration Taylor wrote Rush that he was appointing William Rives to succeed him.

Surprised at this move, Rush was both humiliated and angry, his discomfort increasing as a long delay intervened before formal notification was sent to the French government. His Democratic party loyalty caused him to resent Taylor's removals, not only of himself but of Bancroft and others. Even Robert Walsh, long consul at Paris, was to go. The new President was "the Great Pledge-Breaker," Rush's son Benjamin wrote; the new appointments were "shameless."

In July Rush poured out his distress to Buchanan. He did not want to end his mission by resignation, for two reasons. The first was a public concern: after "the extraordinary events" he had witnessed "a natural desire" that the new administration should approve his actions, so that it might be seen that the whole country, not just one party, sanctioned his course. "Had I been left here until next spring, this approbation would necessarily have been implied, and then I should have carried it home with me—asking for my recall in the spring."

The second reason involved his recognition of the Provisional Government, a step which had been taken in the midst of revolution, "displeasing to the whole diplomatic corps of Europe, assembled at this great central point of Europe." In this Rush felt that his action had been so unusual and so representative of the American spirit in international relations that the country would "lose face" if the new government did not endorse him.

The United States as here represented, was the only great power that took the step. I was, in fact, the only representative of *any* power that took it instanter. The new American states, (and what are they, all together?) looked up to me, and naturally waited my lead. England, the only power that France really looks up to, respects, and I had almost said *fears*, did not recognize. . . . My recall, among the very first of our foreign ministers, by the new administration, now operates, constructively at least, in the eyes of the diplomatic corps here, as an unfavorable commentary upon my course.

Obviously he was exaggerating the importance of the matter, for Taylor and John Clayton, the new Secretary of State, far from thinking one way or another about the recognition problem, were busy with the esoteric employments of the spoils system. But Rush's understandable desire for approbation, his uncertainty of the future, his actual embarrassment in his equivocal position, made the summer of 1849 a most unhappy one for him.

For six months no official notice of his release came, though he was packed and ready to leave. Mr. Rives, he heard, intended sailing on the first of August, but did not come till long afterward. Rush spent the time in routine business, in following Napoleon's course in Italy, or in commiseration with Walsh and others. News of Polk's death, so soon after his retirement, added the appropriate touch of the tragic to his gloom.

Finally in October, formalities completed, his successor near at hand, he paid his last respects to the Prince-President, talked long and sorrowfully with de Tocqueville, and left for Havre on his way home.

He had been away twenty-seven months, had lived through a revolution, had served his country's interests as best he could, had taught the gospel of republicanism to a proud nation which had proved an intractable pupil. It had all ended in Louis Napoleon's Bonapartism in France, Zachary Taylor's Whiggery in America. He did not want office any longer. Private objects and interests, he decided, were more precious to him; he turned his eyes once again to the rural quiet of Sydenham.

X

LAST YEARS

A PUBLIC career so long and diverse as Rush's deserved a climax, a fanfare, and then a conspicuous retirement in the classical tradition of Washington, Adams, Jefferson, and Madison. It is one of the shortcomings of this story that it cannot conform to the pleasant pattern, for the climaxes in Rush's career never came at the right time. The London mission had stretched out beyond its notable successes to end with a failure; the enlarged nationalism of the American System had been postponed too long after the ebullient war spirit subsided, and had had perforce to compete with Jacksonian Democracy; the attempts to find a political niche during the thirties and forties had been futile; and now the savor of the French mission had been ruined by political chicanery. Rush went into retirement quietly. It was an anticlimax. His son Ben suggested that he appeal to the people when he returned, for election to the Senate would be the perfect justification. But this was asking too much. "No, No, No, No, No, No, No, No, No, No, No, No; 12 noes to make it *sure*," Rush replied. He had never fared well at the people's hands, and now, when they were exercised over new issues, unresponsive to leadership of the sort he could give, there would be no point in taxing his strength or trying his patience.

The peace Sydenham offered was too enticing to be resisted. The lovely, low-walled cottage, shaded by its towering old trees, with the banister from Milton's house that Bentham had given him, with its furnishings from two worlds, with its books, many of them inscribed from old friends in three countries, was a haven of repose well known to much-loved friends. Here he gratefully withdrew, with such of his family as was still with him. Mrs. Rush was now seriously ill; Rush found her frighteningly changed after two years' absence. He devoted many hours of each day to her, the rest of his time to correspondence on public affairs. He had remarkable memories to draw on; the fifty years of his mature life had seen changes almost incredible in the American people. He knew what Ashburton felt when that genial old gentleman had come to America in 1842: "People here stare when I tell them that I listened to the debates in Congress on Mr. Jay's treaty in 1795, and seem to think that some antediluvian has come amongst them out of the grave."

There was a maxim of Chesterfield that Rush was fond of repeating: Every man ought to do something worth writing of, or write something worth reading. Over a long span of years he had done both. Benjamin Ogle Taylor paid a tribute to his record: "From your personal associations and intimacy with the illustrious men of your times, connected too as you have been with some great events of our country, I can not but hope that we shall have something more from your pen, that will be read with deep interest on both sides of the Atlantic."

But it was not easy to think of public problems in the terms current among most Americans. Even in the two years he had been away crucial changes had taken place. Abolitionism had become a mania in the North. To Rush it seemed the worst aspect of the slavery question. It, rather than slavery itself, was the real threat to the Union. As "a citizen of the Middle States" he had, he declared, always tried to view "this angry question" calmly, to avoid the biases of North and South alike, and find "national ground" on which to stand. He could not condone the enthusiasts of his own section. "The Northern madmen have treated you shockingly—horribly," he acknowledged to Poinsett of South Carolina; "but I trust we shall get the better of them all yet. . . . Thousands of our people go as strongly for southern rights, as any southern men could or need do. This is my case and long has been."

The more he studied the problem the more it seemed clear that, to save the country, radical antislavery agitation would have to be quieted. The Compromise of 1850, with its despised Fugitive Slave Law, offered a basis on which understanding could be built, but it would have to be built by Northern men. In a public letter he published in November Rush urged his fellow Pennsylvanians to look to the nation rather than the section. The Compromise Act was not enough in itself, he declared, to cure "the bitter dissentions and menacing aspects" of the slavery question. It would have to be followed by good conduct, by mutual conciliation and forbearance, "above all, by the faithful performance of constitutional obligations" enjoined by the Act.

"The historian of the downfall of this republic," he wrote, "if our fatuity has predestinated its downfall, will point to the emancipation by England of her West India slaves, as the epoch when our northern hostility to slavery assumed its furor and inveteracy." The abolitionist tracts of American radicals were read abroad, and spread misunderstanding of our problems there. Europeans could not realize how unsatisfactory abolition would be as a solution. But they criticized in their ignorance, and Americans, revealing little independence of mind, smarted under their strictures. "Thus abolitionism and modern free soilism, by fortifying Europe in its denunciations of our slavery, are helping Europe to undermine our democracy." Having originally forced slavery upon us, Europe was now reproaching us for immorality and barbarism. Let America turn away from these fruitless foreign agitations, he pleaded, and find her own ways of handling the problem; they would be far better than any Europe could suggest. Let Northern statesmen recognize the altruism of those enlightened Southerners who were leaders in the Colonization Society, and work with them rather than against them for a peaceful consummation of their common aims. Otherwise "our magnificent Union is to be dashed to pieces by sectional short-sightedness and unscrupulous fanaticism."

Rush's position was bound to be ignored between extremes of both sides. It was, nevertheless, a tenable and a reasonable ground. It was shared by his friend Buchanan, and reached its culmination in that statesman's nomination for the presidency in 1856. This, Rush congratulated Buchanan, offered "the best hopes of saving the Constitution and the Union in the present distracted state of our country."

As he engaged in "the pursuits which his library afforded,"

Rush brought his thinking on foreign relations to a fruition far different from his conclusions on domestic issues. It was Union sentiment that persuaded him to support the Compromise of 1850, and it was nationalism also that led him to abandon his lifetime adherence to the principle of American isolation. In his last publication on international problems, Rush advanced far ahead of most of his generation, accepting a point of view that was a decided contrast to the policy John Quincy Adams had labored with all his soul to develop, and Rush himself had always championed hitherto.

The occasion was the appearance of a pamphlet by William Henry Trescott of South Carolina on the "Foreign Policy of the United States." In two long letters Rush responded to questions Trescott asked, and was prevailed upon to let his letters be printed.

He agreed, he said, with the division Trescott made of diplomatic history into three periods, from the Peace of Westphalia to the Treaty of Utrecht, from Utrecht to the Treaty of Paris in 1763, and from 1763 to the present day. The last period was the most important and stirring: "It comprises the most startling revolutions among nations, revolutions in which Goddesses of Reason were enthroned in place of other gods, and kings toppled down." In these years America emerged as the champion of human liberties, and in international law as the defender of the concept of neutral rights. The state papers of this country from the beginning of the wars of the French Revolution formed, he thought, the best code of international law regarding neutrality in existence. It was our distinctive national contribution to the cause of world peace.

But even more significant to present politics was the change which Rush thought he saw developing in American relations to Great Britain. When we were a new and weak nation, we had been uneasy in the presence of England's great power. Anxious and brooding in our inferiority, we had competed with her on the sea, and sought to emulate her path to opulence and world dominion. Now, however, conscious of our strength, with nothing more to fear from Britain, the sense of our own power was blinding us to hers.

Of all the nations of the world, Britain and the United States had the largest number of interests in common. They ought to recognize the identity of their aims, and join in an alliance beneficial to both peoples.

New developments among nations, and new geographical relations opening between oceans and continents, are not simply extraordinary, but must become in many respects revolutionizing upon the intercourse, interests and opinions of mankind. Vast changes at hand must necessarily affect some of the rules of our political conduct. Sooner or later, we shall have to review former opinions.

Then follows a statement which, as it is impressive in its present-day interest, so likewise seems to sum up that international extension of democracy to which all of Rush's career had pointed:

We are part and parcel of Christendom, and it is no longer possible that a great nation like this can be wholly detached from its movements, lest we should get into "entangling alliances." This was a wise rule when we would have been the weaker part, perfectly wise. Then, concerted movements of any description might have become entangling to us. Amidst the agitations of the present and uncertainties of the future in Europe, where else can we so well look as to England for national characteristics intermediate between arbitrary systems of government on the one side, and communism or socialism seeking to ally itself with power on the other? What other nation is so near to us in the great attributes of national and individual freedom, or runs so parallel with us in the prosperity resulting from both? Certainly no other.

Thus the Minister who had declined Canning's overtures for an Anglo-American understanding which would have been but the agency for attaining English ambitions, had by his seventieth year concluded that an alliance would offer the best and most permanent security for both peoples, equally strong and equally free, defending together the liberal doctrines of a free government which were their common heritage. But by 1851 it was too late for Rush to do more than theorize.

As he was proposing this remarkable alteration in the traditional structure of our political relations with other countries, our affairs with England were not prospering. The old question of the fisheries had flared up again; England had placed a new interpretation on the Convention of 1818, by which she closed all large bays of Newfoundland to Americans, drawing a line "from headland to headland" within which New Englanders were not to be permitted. William L. Marcy, Secretary of State in Pierce's cabinet, wrote Rush as the only surviving negotiator of 1818 to ask his opinion. Rush responded with a long account of the negotiation compiled from his diaries, defending the Treaty and supporting the American construction. His letter was published to furnish Marcy ammunition for his contention, and became the authoritative statement of the American view of the troublesome clause.

While rummaging through his papers in this research Rush ran across some letters of General Washington that had come to him in a curious way. They were friendly, intimate letters addressed to Tobias Lear, the last personal secretary Washington had employed; they revealed the patriot off his pedestal, immersed in his domestic concerns at Mount Vernon. Lear, after a few years in consular service on the Barbary Coast, had taken his own life, leaving his widow, a niece of Martha Washington, in desperate circumstances. Rush had relieved her poverty and made it possible for her to live the rest of her life in comfort. She had committed the Washington letters to his care in the 1840's, and he had written a little book around them, but had never published it. In 1856 Mrs. Lear died, and the next year Rush had Lippincott's print his manuscript in a handsome format for private circulation. He dedicated the work to Charles Ingersoll, a tribute to a friendship that had begun more than sixty years earlier at Princeton. Ingersoll was pleasantly surprised. "I cannot but be flattered by a dedication which is to circulate me as a sort of avant coureur to anecdotes of Washingtons appearance in undress," he wrote. *Washington in Domestic Life* was sent privately to a host of people, and Rush received many appreciative letters in return. A modest performance, but a pleasant one, it gave the writer much satisfaction to end his literary career with a monument to the *Pater Patriae*.

By 1857 Rush was ready to close his long stint of writing. He had produced a trunkful of books, pamphlets, and articles, most of them on issues long forgotten; few of them indeed seemed worth preserving. He went through the whole lot, burning the majority of them, saving only those which he thought might interest his family. Other trunks that contained an enormous accumulation of correspondence and official documents he also opened, but these materials he could not destroy. Instead he began to go through them systematically, arranging and cataloguing each in his precise, methodical fashion. He had never thrown away a letter or a document, not even an invitation he had received; consequently here was the whole of his life in review. Hundreds of letters from his family, from Adams father and son, from Gallatin, Madison, Monroe, Crawford, Clay, Calhoun, Webster, Story, Johnson, Jackson, Taney, Castlereagh, Bathurst, Ashburton, Canning, Erskine, de Tocqueville, Lamartine, Bancroft, Princess Lieven, Pozzo di Borgo, and countless others. It was a precious treasure, the spoor of a fascinating journey through a fascinating age. He read them over, tied them in neat little bundles, and wrote notes on the outside recalling the incidents with which they dealt. Then he laid them carefully back in their trunks, where they could wait until the curious eyes of another age might find them out.

His life was in the past. Of the eleven children that had been born to him and Catherine, he had buried six; Catherine herself slipped quietly away in the fullness of years. Of his close associates in public adventures only Ingersoll and Buchanan were left. Adams, Clay, Story, Calhoun, Webster, all the others of that glittering generation that had turned the dark night of 1812 into a glorious morning were gone. The second generation of independent Americans, his generation, had already given way to young men, new names in the political firmament, some of them from those "geographical expressions" beyond the Alleghenies, as Randolph of fantastic memory had called the western states. These young men had a rich heritage, if they could face the terrible tasks ahead of them. "A great country is to be in their hands," Rush wrote in a passage which may serve as his valedictory. "Its institutions, its freedom, its past and prospective renown, open a magnificent future. But not if subordinate men with cunning minds bear sway. This, in the end, would undermine it for all that is highest, purest, and most lasting; for all that is truly great in nations. And this would happen, though our fields might continue to produce their crops, our workshops their fabrics, our seaports their ships and steamers, our mines gold, and our population indefinitely to increase."

In the summer of 1859, not at his beloved Sydenham but at his brother's home in the city which he used more and more after Catherine's death, he was stricken with a serious illness. His hold on life grew feebler as the days passed, and during the afternoon of the thirtieth of July he expired. He was within a month of the end of his eightieth year.

BIBLIOGRAPHICAL NOTE

The writer's interest in Richard Rush was awakened when, through the agency of Mr. Julian P. Boyd, he was permitted to examine the enormous collection of letters and documents carefully arranged by Rush himself, now preserved in the family home in Chester County, Pennsylvania. This collection is so extensive and so interesting that when it is finally made available to the scholarly community it will form a major source both of information and color for American history during the period 1809–59. In accordance with the wishes of the owners, none of that material was used in the foregoing pages; but here I may acknowledge the courtesies and kindnesses of Mr. and Mrs. Benjamin Rush during a delightful spring in their home.

In the Historical Society of Pennsylvania are several hundred Richard Rush letters, some as yet uncatalogued. Many to John Adams, John Quincy Adams, Madison, Monroe, Peter DuPonceau, John Binns, and others are in the Simon Gratz Autograph Collection. Those to William Shaler (American consul at Algiers while Rush was in London) in the Shaler Papers were called to my attention by the competent staff of W.P.A. cataloguers. The Poinsett Papers and the Buchanan Papers contain sources of letters of the Mexican War and the French Ministry period. The Society Autograph Collection, the Conarroe Autograph Collection, the Dreer Autograph Collection, and the Peters Papers yielded some treasure. The permission of the Society to reproduce or quote from these materials is gratefully acknowledged.

Since the Ridgway Library of the Library Company of Philadelphia was originally a Rush family establishment, the largest collection of family papers outside the private archives is here. The letters quoted in the text from Rush to his father and mother, his brothers, his wife and children, as well as some of those to Binns, are from this collection. They are quoted by permission. My thanks are due to Mr. Austin Gray and his staff for efficient service and coöperation.

The New York Historical Society collections contain over a hundred letters to and from Rush; Lord Ashburton, Colonel Aspinwall, John Trumbull, Monroe, and Gallatin are the principal correspondents. Mr. Alexander Wall made them available to me and has given me permission to use them.

There is not sufficient space here to enumerate the books,

pamphlets, and articles Rush published during his long, active career. Since they formed a primary source for the narrative of his life, the most important of them were analyzed or at least mentioned in the proper place in the text. A separate bibliography is being prepared and will sometime be issued independently. But it may not be amiss to attempt to straighten out the confusion that has surrounded his *Residence at the Court of London*, references to which have so frequently appeared inaccurate as to paging or volume.

Rush originally had a vaguely formulated plan of issuing his journals, edited and supplemented with material from his official dispatches and private letters, in a series of volumes that would cover the whole period of his ministry. He never got around to doing this, but twice—once in 1833, and again in 1845—when relations between America and Britain were seriously strained, he did issue parts of his contemplated work in order to elucidate the diplomatic questions at issue, placing them in their historical perspective. A third edition, with a few new items, was published posthumously under the editorship of his son, styled by him the fourth edition. The titles in each case were similar. The 1833 volume dealt only with the first year of his London Mission, 1817–18, and related the negotiation of the Commercial Convention of 1818. The second series, published in 1845, began where the first had left off, the first entry being February 12, 1819, and continued until April 1825, but there is a two-year gap, between July 1821, and July 1823. This gap is marked in one printing of the English edition of 1845 by a division into two volumes, but the American edition is continuous, the hiatus occurring at pages 390–91.

Following is a list of the editions, with the variations in title:

Memoranda of a Residence at the Court of London. By Richard Rush, Envoy Extraordinary and Minister Plenipotentiary from the United States of America, from 1817 to 1825. Philadelphia: Carey, Lea & Blanchard, 1833. (First American edition, first series, dealing with the year 1818.)

A Residence at the Court of London. By Richard Rush . . . London: Richard Bentley & Son, 1833. (First English edition, first series, paging and title page different from American.)

Memoranda of a Residence at the Court of London. By Richard Rush . . . Second edition, revised and enlarged. Philadelphia: Key & Biddle, 23 Minor Street. 1833. (Dedication to James Madison and preface to the second edition, new in this printing. Text unchanged. This is the second American edition, first series.)

Memoranda of a Residence at the Court of London, Comprising incidents official and personal, From 1819 to 1825. Including Negotiations on the Oregon Question, and other unsettled Questions Between the United States and Great Britain. By Richard Rush, Envoy Extraordinary and Minister Plenipotentiary from the United States, from 1817 to 1825. Philadelphia: Lea & Blanchard, 1845. (First American edition, second series.)

A Residence at the Court of London, Comprising Incidents, Official and Personal, from 1819 to 1825: Amongst the Former, Negotiations on the Oregon Territory, and Other Unsettled Questions Between the United States and Great Britain. By Richard Rush . . . London: R. Bentley, 1845. (First English edition, second series, paging and title page different from American. Bound either in one or two volumes, some of the latter paged continuously, some by volume.)

The Court of London from 1819 to 1825: With Subsequent Occasional Productions, now first Published in Europe, By Richard Rush, Minister from the United States from 1817 to 1825. Edited, with Occasional Notes, by his Son, Benjamin Rush, U.S. Secretary of Legation at London from 1837 to 1841. With an Alphabetical Index. London: R. Bentley & Son. 1873. (This styled "fourth edition" by Benjamin Rush.) 536 pp.

The "Subsequent Occasional Productions" referred to in this "fourth edition" are some miscellaneous papers published by Rush from time to time, including his journal during the French Mission. They were gathered together after his death and issued as

Occasional Productions, Political, Diplomatic, and Miscellaneous. Including, among others, a Glance at the Court and Government of Louis Philippe and the French Revolution of 1848, while the Author Resided as Envoy Extraordinary and Minister Plenipotentiary From the United States at Paris. By the Late Richard Rush. Edited by his Executors. With a copious index. Philadelphia: J. B. Lippincott & Co. 1860.

Only a word needs to be said regarding secondary works. The great corpus of historical literature dealing with domestic history in Rush's period scarcely mentions him, in spite of the frequency with which he appears in the correspondence and memoirs of his contemporaries. With all who study the diplomacy of the post-Napoleonic era, I share a large debt to Dexter Perkins, C. K. Webster, and H. W. V. Temperley, whose critical writings are classics of their type. It is no criticism of their works or their points of view to observe that our understanding of this period will be infinitely enriched when America's relation to the Old World, the Orient, and Latin America is studied as intensively in other respects as it has been in the political. The enlivened national spirit and the development of the democratic hypothesis characteristic of this portion of our history received part of its impulse from the intellectual and emotional currents of union with human endeavor elsewhere. Some of the story is known, part of it has been written, but it has not yet been put together in its single and continuous coherency. For this we await a master hand.

INDEX

Abolitionism, 273 ff.
Academy of Arts and Sciences, New York, 176
Academy of Fine Arts, Philadelphia, 8
Adams, John, 2, 6, 9 f., 17, 28, 31-33, 37 f., 41-43, 45-50, 53 f., 67 f., 71, 75 f., 182, 198, 216, 272, 278
Adams, John Quincy, 3-5, 32, 37, 47, 76 f., 79 f., 86, 96, 104 ff., 107, 110 ff., 113, 115, 119 f., 123, 125 f., 133, 140 f., 144, 151, 154 ff., 159 ff., 166, 170 ff., 177, 179-182, 188 ff., 191, 194, 197 f., 207 f., 210 ff., 215-218, 221-225, 230, 235, 242, 246, 249, 275, 278
Agriculture, and national planning, 194 ff.
Agricultural societies, 134, 136, 176
Aix-la-Chapelle, Congress of, 108, 117 ff., 126 f., 135 f., 141
Alaska, see Oregon
Alexander I, Tsar of Russia, 130, 168 f., 213
Algiers, 78, 137
American Colonization Society, 203, 219, 274
American Jurisprudence, 69 ff.
American law, 48 ff., 68 f.
American nationalism, 51 f., 69 ff., 138 f., 179 ff., 187 ff., 219 f.
American navy, 95, 189, 238
American Philosophical Society, 233
American separatism, see Isolationism
"American System," 182-185, 188-196, 202-209, 212, 216, 225, 230, 231
"Anthony Wayne," pen name used by Rush, 244
Anti-Masonic party, 231 ff.
Arago, Dominique F. J., 237, 260
Arbuthnot-Ambrister affair, 126-129, 130, 136
Armstrong, John, 53, 54-66
Art, British, 96 ff.
Ashburton, Alexander Baring, Lord, 101, 134, 246-248, 273

Ashford vs. *Thornton,* 99
Aspinwall, Colonel Thomas, 107, 239 ff., 245 f.
Astor, John Jacob, 45, 224
Astronomical observatory, national, 189
Bagot, Sir Charles, 2, 77 f., 127, 168-169
Balance of employments, national policy regarding, 204 ff.
Bancroft, George, 242, 251, 255, 264
Bank of U.S., 22, 24, 28, 193, 232, 234, 266
Banks, Sir Joseph, 237
Barbary Wars, 193
Barbour, James, 180, 198, 215 f.
Baring, Alexander, see Ashburton
Barney, Commodore Joshua, 58-66
Bathurst, Henry, Earl, 94, 123, 128
Bayard, James A., 47, 68
Bentham, Jeremy, 88, 100 f., 272
Berlin-Milan decrees, 12
Bexley, Nicholas Vansittart, Lord, see Vansittart
Biddle, Nicholas, 204, 233
Binns, John, 7, 9, 20, 26, 28, 29, 40, 43, 44, 52, 183, 199, 216, 221
Black Sea trade, America and, 93
Bladensburg, battle of, 54-66, 217
Blockades, 114, 125 f., 175
Board of Health, Philadelphia, 8
Boston Patriot, letter to, 52, 72
Boundary controversies, international, 106, 110 f., 112-114, 154 ff.
Boundary controversy, Michigan and Ohio, 3, 236
Brazil, 137
Brougham, Henry, Baron, 98 f.
Browne's Civil and Admiralty Law, 68
Bryan, George, Jr., 10, 17
Buenos Aires, 148
Buchanan, James, 220 f., 246 f., 255 ff., 263-269, 274, 278
Bureaucracy, 180 ff., 212

California, 251
Calhoun, John C., 16, 198, 205, 209, 221 f.

Campbell, George W., 48, 60 f., 130
Canada, relations with, 1, 9, 44 ff., 53, 112 ff., 121, 123, 134, 238 f.
Canals, 227 ff.
Canning, George, 1, 140, 149 ff., 152-176, 192, 214 f., 276
Canning, Stratford-, see Stratford de Redcliffe
Carey, Mathew, 52, 184 f., 190 f., 193-200, 204 f., 213, 225, 232
Carroll, Charles, 198
Cass, Lewis, 41, 269
Castlereagh, Robert Stewart, Viscount (later Marquis of Londonderry), 47, 84, 93, 104, 107, 108-120, 123-129, 131-138, 141-150, 168, 170
"Cato Street Conspiracy," 131
Cavaignac, General Louis Eugene, 266 ff.
Chancery, Court of, 237 ff.
Chase, Samuel, 14, 72
Chauncey, Commodore Charles, 80
Chesapeake, U.S.S., 7
Chesapeake and Delaware canal, 181
Chesapeake and Ohio canal, 3, 227 ff.
Chile, 148
Clay, Henry, 16, 24, 27, 31, 76, 147, 180, 181, 183, 191, 193, 219, 225, 230
Clayton, John, 270
Clinton, De Witt, 181, 183
Clinton, George, 22, 28, 29, 30
Cochrane, Admiral Sir Alexander, 57, 137
Cockburn, Admiral Sir George, 54, 65
Coke, Thomas W., Earl of Leicester, 239
Collectors of revenue, 22, 197, 210
Colombia, 148
Colonial System, British, 113, 116, 117, 123, 148
Columbia river, boundary at, 113, 116, 121, 175 f.
Commercial Convention of 1815, 106, 110 f., 112, 117, 121
Commercial Convention of 1818, 2, 3, 110 ff., 118-126, 130, 131, 136, 138, 168, 213 f., 247, 277
Commissioners of loans, 22, 28, 30
Committee of Eighteen, 266 ff.

Common law indictments in American courts, 71, 73
Compromise of 1850, 273 ff.
Congress, European, 135 f.
Consuls, American, in British colonial ports, 174
Contraband, law of, 114, 119, 125, 175
Conversations of 1824, 3, 134, 140, 154 ff., 167 ff.
Cooper, James Fenimore, 190
Cooper, Thomas, 192, 204
Coöperation, international, 100, 134, 136, 176
Correa, Abbé de, 18, 75
Court of St. James's, ceremonies of, 89 f.
Coxe, Tench, 192
Cranch, Judge William, 74
Crawford, William H., 21, 76, 81, 146, 180, 181
Cray cottage, 109, 118, 149
Crowninshield, Benjamin W., 66, 77
Cuba, 143 f.
Cumberland, Duke of, 93, 240
Customs records, 201
Cuthbert, Mary Rush, 56, 67, 84

Dallas, Alexander J., 66, 75, 76
Davy, Sir Humphrey, 82, 100, 103, 237
Dearborn, General Henry, 27
Democratic Press, 7, 26, 40, and see Binns, John
Dexter, Samuel, 50, 75
Dew, Thomas R., 204
Discriminating duties, 68, 112
Duane, William, 7, 8, 9, 31
Du Ponceau, Peter, 241
Dupont de l' Eure, Jacques C., 260
Durham, John Lambton, Earl of, 238 f.
Duval, Gabriel, 14, 15, 19, 21, 48, 50
Dwight, Timothy, 190

Election of 1812, 41; of 1824, 177, 179; of 1828, 212 ff., 215-225; of 1840, 224; of 1844, 244 f.
Ellenborough, Edward Law, Lord, 99
Elliott, Jonathan, 190

Emancipation, 274
Embargo, 1812, 24, 29
Emerson, Ralph Waldo, 190
Emigration, English, to America, 89
English Whigs, The, 229
Erie, Lake, battle of, 45
Erskine, Thomas, Baron, 98
Erskine Agreement, 12
Eustis, William, 39
Evans, George Henry, 204

Federalism, in France, 1848, 264 ff.
Federalists, 13, 39, 40
Ferdinand VII of Spain, 127 f., 143-145
Fisheries dispute, 4, 106, 110-116, 120 f., 154 ff., 174 f., 234, 277
Florida, 78, 93, 110, 126-129, 134, 140 ff., and *see* Transcontinental Treaty, Arbuthnot-Ambrister, Spain
Force, Peter, 190
Foreign Bible Society, British, 91
Foreign trade, national policy and, 196 ff., 201 f., 205 f., 219
Forsyth, John, 144, 241
"Fox," pen name used by Rush, 183
France, Rush's ministry to, 3, 250-271; and European Alliance, 134, 139, 163 f.; and Spanish colonies, 152 ff., 155; and our Mexican War, 247 ff., parties and public opinion in, 251 ff.; Revolution of 1848 in, 3, 250-271
Franklin, Benjamin, 43, 82, 97
Franklin, U.S.S., 80, 81, 82
Free-port bill, in Parliament, 116
Free trade, 203-204, 208-209
Fugitive slave law, 273 ff.

Gallatin, Albert, 4, 12 f., 15 f., 21 f., 25-28, 34, 39, 47 f., 65, 68, 84, 101, 104 f., 116-126, 130, 135, 140, 141, 144, 181, 213
Gallatin, James, 105, 117
George III, 93 f., 132
George, Prince Regent, later George IV, 47, 76, 84, 89, 109, 132, 139, 161, 166, 178
Gerry, Elbridge, 24
Ghent, Treaty of, 65, 67, 106, 110-113, 119, 138, 181

Gibbon, Edward, 68 f.
Gibraltar, American-British fracas at, 134
Giles, William Branch, 12
Gloucester, Duke of, 94
Goderich, Viscount, *see* Robinson, Frederick
Goulburn, Henry, 117, 120
Granger, Gideon, 66
Great Britain, Rush's ministry to, 79-178; agriculture, 97; American relations with, 22 f., 36 f., 110 et seq., 136, 148; aristocracy, 90-96, 166; art, 96 ff.; clubs, 102 ff.; commercial relations with, 68, 85 ff., 118-126; laboring classes, 87, 131; law, 70 ff., 96, 97 f.; liberalism, 96 ff.; navy, 94 ff., 238 ff.; press and public opinion, 102, 126, 128 f., 130; public finance, 96 ff.; reform, 96 ff., 100, 101; science, 100; and European Alliance, 115, 135 ff., 139, 145 ff., 148; and Spanish colonies, 141 ff., 152-176; and French Revolution of 1848, 263 f.
Great Lakes, 44, 77
Greece, revolution in, 140, 150 ff.
Guardians of the Poor, Philadelphia, 8
Guizot, François Pierre, 247 ff., 269 f.

Hamilton, Alexander, 2, 292
Hamilton, Paul, 39
Hardwicke, Earl of, 88
Harrison, William Henry, 241, 244
Harrowby, Dudley Ryden, Earl of, 94
Hartford Convention, 71
Hickey, General William, 190
Holy Alliance, 130 ff., 133, 135, 139 ff., 145 ff., 166
Howard, Benjamin, 236 f.
Humboldt, Alexander, Baron von, 237, 255
Huskisson, William, 112, 117, 167 ff., 175, 192, 229

Impressment, 29, 36, 53, 106, 110, 114-119, 123-125, 154 ff., 175

Indians, American, 9, 22, 126-129, 134, 238
Industry, domestic, national policy and, 194 ff.
Ingersoll, Charles, 9, 40 f., 242, 250, 278
Intercourse with enemy, 52, 71 ff.
Internal commerce, 194 f., 205 f., 219
Internal improvements, 189, 219, 220
Intervention, in Spain, 115 f., 135; in Latin America, 115, 135, 136, 142; in Italy, 1820, 146 f., 268
Irving, Washington, 130, 190
Isolationism, American, 130 ff., 138, 145 ff., 148, 152 ff., 275

Jackson, Andrew, 3 f., 127 f., 140 ff., 179-182, 198, 205, 207, 209, 212, 216, 220, 221-224, 230, 236, 241
Jackson, Francis James, 12
Jefferson, Thomas, 2, 6, 14, 19, 28, 31, 42, 72, 75, 92, 165, 168, 179, 188, 198, 202, 212, 272
"John Dickinson," pen name used by Rush, 244
Johnson, Samuel, 6-7
Johnson, Justice William, 74
Jones, William, 48, 53, 61 f., 64, 66

Kent, James, 71, 190
King, Rufus, 181, 213

Lamartine, Alphonse de, 252, 259 ff., 269
Lansdowne, Henry Fitzmaurice, Marquess of, 128, 131
Latin America, independence of, 4, 68, 78, 79, 106, 115, 126, 135-138, 140 ff., 152 ff., 161 ff., 171, 193; commerce with, 196 ff.
Laws of the United States, 2, 51 f., 69
Lear, Mrs. Tobias, 277 ff.
Ledru-Rollin, Alexandre Auguste, 260
Leib, Michael, 9, 12, 31
Leipzig, battle of, 47
Leopard, H.M.S., 7
Letters to the People of Pennsylvania, 219 ff.

Lewis, William, 6
Liberalism, 130, 180 ff., 213 f.
Liberia, 203
List, Friedrich, 186 f., 191-192, 197
Liverpool, Robert Jenkinson, Earl of, 109, 128, 132, 145, 214
Loans, 1811-1812, 22 f., 29 f., 45
London, description of, 84-103
Londonderry, *see* Castlereagh
Louis Philippe, 247-258, 269
Luriottis, Andreas, 151 f.

McDuffie, George, 208 f.
McKean, Thomas, 7-9, 31
McKean, William, 8, 233
McLean, John, 180
Madison, Dolly, 64, 66, 246
Madison, James, 2, 4, 6, 11-13, 16, 22, 25 f., 29, 31, 38-42, 45, 47, 53-66, 68, 75, 165, 179, 217, 249, 272
Malthus, Robert, 190, 194, 213
Manufactures, American, 194, 195, 200
Marcy, William L., 277
Maritime law, 4, 110, 114 f., 125, 154 ff., 167, 175
Marshall, John, 50, 70 f.
Maryland machine, 12-16
Mason, John T., 14, 64, 65, 237
Masonic order, 231 ff., 242
Memoranda of a Residence at the Court of London, 157, 235, 385
Metternich system, 94, 130, 135, 150
Mexico, 148, 245 ff., 254 f., 264 ff.
Mill, John Stuart, 213
Monroe, James, 2, 4, 16, 27, 38, 55-58, 62 f., 63, 65 f., 75-79, 105, 119, 131, 133, 141, 144 f., 148, 161, 165, 171 f., 176-181, 249
Monroe Doctrine, 1, 13 f., 16, 27, 139 f., 152 ff., 157 f., 166 f., 169, 176
Morals, private, national policy and, 202
Muhlenburg, Henry, 233
Murray, Catherine, *see* Rush, Catherine Murray
Murray, William Vans, 8

Naples, revolution in, 1820, 146, 166
Napoleon, 12, 31, 47, 52 f., 67 f., 125
Napoleon III, 252, 266 ff., 271

INDEX

National Assembly, French, 1848, 265 ff.
National Intelligencer, 26, 50
Neutrality, 110, 114 f., 119, 175, 275
Niles, Hezekiah, 152, 191, 193 f., 197, 200, 204 f., 213, 225
Non-colonization principle, 169 f.
Normanby, Constantine Henry Phipps, Marquess of, 262 f.
North American Review, 152
Northeast boundary, 154 ff., 174, 213 f.
Northwest boundary, 113, 116
Nourse, Joseph, 182

O'Neil, Peggy, 80, 230, 237
Onis, Don Luis de, 141, 143
Oregon, 152 ff., 168, 175 f., 213 f., 234 f., 244-249

Paine, Tom, 131
Panama Congress, 219, 220
Paris, Treaty of, 1783, 120
Patent Office, 19, 189
Passamaquoddy islands dispute, 116
Pennsylvania, politics of, 6 f., 9, 15 f., 28, 30, 40, 220 f.
Pennsylvania Society for the Encouragement of Manufactures, 191 f.; convention of 1827, 205
Pensacola, 93
Philadelphia, political parties in, 23, 39 f.
Philadelphia Society for the Promotion of National Industry, 191
Pierce, Franklin, 277
Pinkney, William, 14, 16, 27, 39, 48 ff., 72, 74
Planta, Joseph, 107
Poinsett, Joel R., 238 f., 244
Polignac, Prince Jules de, 134, 163 f.
Polk, James Knox, 3 f., 242-250, 263, 271
Portfolio, 7
Portugal, 78
Postage, foreign, 267 f.
Pothier on Contracts, 68
Princeton University, 6
Private claims, 106 ff.
Protectionism, 53, 199 ff., 204-207, 212, 232

Public lands policies, 207
Public works, 189

Quadruple Alliance, 133, 139, 140, 148

Randolph, John, 13, 27, 31, 37, 198, 210, 216 ff., 279
Raymond, Daniel, 186, 197
Reciprocity, 68, 110, 112, 116, 121-123, 148, 173
Recognition, of Latin America, 140 ff., 147 f., 156 ff.; of French Republic, 260-263, 270 f.
Reformists, French, 250 ff.
Republicanism, French, 264 ff.
Retrenchment and reform, 210 ff.
Revolution of 1848, 3, 250-271
Ricardo, David, 184, 190, 213
Ripon, Earl of, *see* Robinson
Rives, William, 269 f.
Robinson, Frederick, 117, 120, 124, 214
Robinson's Admiralty Reports, 68
Rodney, Caesar Augustus, 14, 51, 120
Ross, General Robert, 57 ff.
Royal Academy, 91
Rush, Anne, 15
Rush, Dr. Benjamin (father of Richard Rush), 5 f., 8 f., 17, 20 f., 30-43, 216 f., 251
Rush, Benjamin (son of Richard), 9, 18 f., 177, 227, 237, 270, 272
Rush, Catherine Murray, 8, 18 f., 30, 32, 33, 42, 81, 125, 177, 227, 272, 278, 279
Rush, James, 5, 67, 81, 224
Rush, John, 5
Rush, Julia Stockton, 5, 8, 19, 224, 249
Rush, Mary, *see* Cuthbert, Mary Rush
Rush, Richard, birth, 5; education, 6; law practice, 6 f.; Attorney General of Pennsylvania, 9 f.; Comptroller of the Treasury, 11 ff.; speech on war, 1812, 33 ff.; and John Adams, 43 f.; Attorney General of U.S., 47 ff.; during siege of Washington, 53 ff.; and

Rush, Richard (Continued)
common law indictments, 71 ff.;
Acting Secretary of State, 75 ff.;
convention with Bagot, 77 ff.;
Minister to England, 1817–1825,
79 ff.; student of English society,
82 ff.; and Commercial Convention of 1818, 104 ff.; and Arbuthnot-Ambrister affair, 126 ff.; and
American separatism, 130 ff.; and
Spanish treaty, 140 ff.; and Greek
independence, 150 ff.; conversations with Canning regarding
South America, 153 ff.; attempt
to negotiate a convention, 1823–
1824, 166 ff.; Secretary of the
Treasury, 177 ff.; representative
of "American System," 184 ff.;
protectionist, 199 ff.; and American Colonization Society, 203,
219, 274; candidate for Vice-President, 212 ff.; replies to Randolph, 216 ff.; retirement, 224 ff.;
and Chesapeake and Ohio canal,
227 ff.; and Anti-Masonic movement, 230 ff.; writes first series of
memoirs, 234 ff.; and "Toledo
War," 236; and estate of James
Smithson, 236 ff.; founding of the
Smithsonian Institution, 240 ff.;
Democratic party leader, 244 ff.;
and Oregon crisis, 245 ff.; more
memoirs, 245 f.; and Mexican
War, 247 ff.; Ministry to France,
249 ff.; Revolution of 1848, 257 ff.;
recognition of French Republic,
260 ff.; and Republicanism in
France, 264 ff.; recall, 269 ff.; retirement, 272 ff.; death, 279
Rush, Richard Henry, 177, 227
Rush-Bagot Convention, 1, 2, 77 f.
Russell, Jonathan, 78, 130
Russia, American relations with,
153 ff., 168 ff., 175 f.

St. Lawrence river, navigation of,
174
San Carlos, Duke of, 141, 143 ff.
Say, J. B., 184, 186, 192, 204
Sea power, 36
Sectionalism, in America, 203, 204,
220

Seminole war, 126-129
Sergeant, Jonathan, 211, 233
Shaler, William, 95, 103, 130, 134,
137, 144, 167
Sheldon, Daniel, 162
Silk, culture of, 199
"Simon Snyder," pen name used by
Rush, 219 ff.
Sinclair, Sir John, 97
Sketch of the Character of Mr. Canning, 214 f.
Slavery, national policy and, 203,
273 ff.
Slaves carried off by British, 106,
111 f., 116, 122
Slave trade, abolition of, 134, 154,
167, 171 ff.
Smith, Adam, 184, 186, 196, 213
Smith, Robert, 12-15
Smith, Senator Samuel, 12-15
Smithson, James, 3, 236 ff.
Smithsonian Institution, 3, 240 ff.,
249
Snyder, Simon, 4, 7, 9, 16, 25 f., 30 f.,
219
Sophie Mathilda, Princess, 94
Southard, Samuel L., 166, 180, 183,
216, 223
Spain, America and, 93, 126-129,
140 ff., 193; England and, 114 ff.,
126; revolt in, 1820, 145
Spoils system, 182 f.
State banks, 28
States' rights, 220
State House Yard, meeting in, 7
Stevens, Thaddeus, 233
Stewart, Commodore Charles, 82,
244
Stockton, Richard, 5
Story, Joseph, 19, 27, 50-52, 71-74
Stratford de Redcliffe, Stratford-Canning, Viscount, 167 ff., 175,
213
Stuart, Sir Charles, 162
Supreme Court, 50 ff., 67, 71 ff.
Sussex, Duke of, 93
Sweden, treaty with, 78
"Sydenham," 236, 245 ff., 272 ff., 279

Tariff, 53, 199 ff., 209 ff., 219 f.
Taylor, Zachary, 2, 247, 269 ff.
Temperance, 87, 202

"Temple," pen name used by Rush, 228
Texas, 247
Thiers, Louis Adolphe, 255, 257, 267
Thoreau, Henry David, 190
Thornton, Dr. William, 19
Thoughts on the Administration of Justice, 1809, 8
Tobacco, French monopoly in, 250 ff., 268
De Tocqueville, Alexis, 255, 264, 271
"Toledo War," 3, 236
Tonnage charges, 110, 148, 173
Transcontinental treaty, 128, 134, 140-145
Treason, law of, 52, 71 ff.
Trescott, William Henry, 275
Troppau, protocol of, 135, 146
Tuyll, Baron, 157, 166

Unity, international, 276
University, national, 189

Van Buren, Martin, 209 f., 234 f., 240 ff., 244
Vansittart, Nicholas, Lord Bexley, 88, 97
Vattel, Emerich de, *Law of Nations*, 68, 115
Vaughan, Sir Charles, 235

Venezuela, 144
Verona, Congress of, 135
Victoria, Queen, 239 f., 246
Vienna, Treaty of, 135, 138, 166

Wallace, Thomas, 112, 117
Walsh, Robert, 255, 258, 270 f.
War of 1812, 22 ff., 193
Washington, George, 2, 6, 43, 94, 254, 272, 277
Washington in Domestic Life, 277 f.
Washington, city of, 17-20, 179-180
Wealth, national, and national policy, 86 ff., 179 ff.
Webster, Daniel, 134, 210, 242
Webster-Ashburton treaty, 134
Wellington, Arthur Wellesley, Duke of, 67, 101 f., 228 f.
West, Sir Benjamin, 91, 145
West Indies trade, 93, 112-119, 123, 136, 148, 154, 172 f., 213 f., 219
Wheaton's Law of Captures, 68 f.
White, Dr. William, 30, 31
Wilberforce, William, 134
William IV, 239
Wilson, James, 71
Winder, General William H., 54-66, 217
Wirt, William, 49, 166, 180, 223

York, Duke of, 91, 94